No Return Flight

Haks Walburgh Schmidt

No Return Flight

13 Platoon at Arnhem 1944

Uitgeverij Aspekt

Picture choice:
Apart from the photos of the tanks on the Westerbouwing (page 165) there are no known pictures of the 13 Platoon/B Company action. Neither do pictures of Horsa 166 seem to exist. To still be able to give an impression of what it could have been like, some of the pictures on the cover and those on pages 140, 143 and 153 have been used.

A word of thanks for the use of the photos to:
ABM = Airborne Museum Hartenstein,
IWM = Imperial War Museum,
Gelders Archief,
and also for the many photos that the author received from the veterans and or their relatives and friends.

For the use of the photos it has been tried to ask permission from owners for as much as that was still reasonably possible. In some cases however it turned out to be impossible to locate or contact an owner. Should anyone have any questions on the use of the pictures, please contact the publisher.

No Return Flight
© Haks Walburgh Schmidt / Second revised edition 2019
© 2019 Uitgeverij ASPEKT / Aspekt Publishers
Amersfoortsestraat 27, 3769 AD Soesterberg, The Netherlands
info@uitgeverijaspekt.nl – http://www.uitgeverijaspekt.nl

Cover: Frans Kuijf
Inside: Thomas Wunderink

ISBN: 9789059118812
NUR: 680

All rights reserved. No reproduction copy or transmission of this publication may be made without written permission.

Contents

Monument in Writing pagina	9
Part 1: Morley 'Taffy' Williams	**17**
In Oosterbeek	19
Called up in The Royal Welch Fusiliers	21
Transfer to The Glider Pilot Regiment	22
Flight to Wolfheze	25
In German hands	29
Destination Stalag IVB	33
Life in Mühlberg	36
Hunger and Liberation	39
On the way home	43
Back home	49
Back to work	52
'Blackie'	60
An unannounced letter	63
Part 2: The Search	**69**
A New Millennium	72
An English letter	79
Step by step	91
Si, si, si, South American Joe	101
North Africa and Sicily	106
Italian intermezzo	110
Old friends	120
Waiter in a trench	126
The Lieutenant from Saskatchewan	128
Part 3: The battle of 13 Platoon	**135**
Day 1, Sunday 17 September 1944	139
Day 2, Monday 18 September	141
Day 3, Tuesday 19 September	147
Day 4, Wednesday 20 September	151
Day 5, Thursday 21 September, the morning	157
On the Veerweg	163

Day 5, Thursday 21 September, the afternoon and evening   170
Day 6, Friday 22 September   175
Day 7, Saturday 23 September up to Monday night, the evacuation   178
Savage and Gibson in the area of 'A ' Company   180
Evacuation across the Rhine   181
After the evacuation   184
Behind barbed wire   186
Stalag XIIA Limburg, near Koblenz   186
Stalag VIIIC Sagan, Poland   187
Pushing on to the west   189
Stalag XIB, Fallingbostel   192
Stalag IVC Wistritz   198
HEILAG IVD Annaburg   198
Stalag VII in Moosburg   200

Part 4: Civvy Street   205
John Glenn   207
David Patterson   209
Ted Clague   213
Cyril Crickett   217
Jim Isles   222
Eddie Flinn   225
Jack Kimber   226
'Pip' Hulse   232
'Gerry' Greasley   233
Joe Winstanley   233
Vincent Swarbrick   234
William 'Johnny' Walker   234
Edwin Ainsworth   239
Norman Savage   242
Frank Evans   246
Fred Terry   248
John Wellbelove   249
Tommy McDonald   253
Major Armstrong   256
Wilfred 'Gibbo' Gibson   256
'Click' Fidler   257
Eric Melling   257

Part 5: Epilogue	263
The Long Wait	267
Keeping an open mind	270
Wavy, not curly	271
Farewell too soon	273
Closer	277
Box in the attic	282
Appendix:	287
Individual overview	289
Poem '*What Manner of Men*'	293
'Some Thoughts' by Colonel John Waddy	294
Published Sources/ Unpublished Sources	299
Words of Gratitude	300
See Morley Williams on video	303
Morley Williams remembers the Battle of Arnhem and meets three of his passengers again after 60 years.	303
Glider Pilot Morley 'Taffy'	303
Williams remembered	303
1944- Newspaper clipping on Sergeant Kimber	304
Prisoner of War Next of Kin Parcels	305

Monument in writing

It was the discovery in 1998 of eight densely typed pages with notes from a British veteran of the Battle of Arnhem that set this story in motion. On these sheets, held together loosely with a rusty paperclip, Glider Pilot Morley Williams had recorded his experiences at Arnhem in September 1944. It continued with a vivid description of the months after the battle, when he was held in a German prisoner of war (PoW) camp.

I had found his notes when I volunteered to help prepare an exposition at the Airborne Museum Hartenstein in Oosterbeek. This presentation was to highlight the harsh fate of the more than 6000 British and Polish airbornes taken prisoner during that battle. Largely ignored in the Arnhem literature, because it seemed less heroic and because many felt ashamed of having been taken prisoner. Though they could hardly be blamed for it, we know now.

These PoW stories are in fact an inextricable aspect of 'Arnhem', as the men obviously didn't just evaporate after the fighting had stopped. These months of overcrowded, freezing and dirty camps with dwindling food and cigarette supplies, dependent on German guards and full of boredom and humiliation, put them in another battle. Now for their personal mental health and dignity. This part of the 'Arnhem' saga needed to be told as well. So the exposition "Liberators Behind Barbed Wire" was organised.

On a distinctly less epic level, I felt that by now I had read so many books on the Battle of Arnhem that I was looking for an opportunity to put my knowledge to some use. So, when the Airborne Museum asked for volunteers to help with the exposition, I joined the team.

It became my task to compile and edit the information magazine that went with the exhibition. As a journalist I was well cut out for the job. The other volunteers agreed and were clearly more interested in the other aspects. To me, the editorial task was an adventure, right from the start.

It was during this research that the archives of the Hartenstein Museum yielded the notes of this Sergeant Morley Williams. They contained precisely the kind of story we were looking for. I was happily surprised to find the address of this former Glider Pilot in the notes. Impressed by the opportunity to talk to somebody who had actually been there, I wrote him a letter. I asked for permission to use his notes for the publication and for a contemporary photograph of him, should it still exist. The answer came swiftly. Mr. Williams said he would be glad to be of help.

With his assistance I produced a brutally shortened version of his account for the exposition magazine. On publication in September 1998 it was well received by both the museum staff and many visitors. Although this was flattering, I felt a regret that too much of Williams' lively sketch had remained untold. Also, there were other aspects he had not written down that needed to be told as well.

With this in mind, I continued corresponding with Morley Williams and we gradually became friends. Being a proud Welshman, he was often addressed as 'Taffy'.

In the letters that followed, he told me how he came to join the Glider Pilot Regiment and how his relatives took that for an obscure branch of the Royal Army Service Corps (RASC), which is responsible for transport and administration. When Morley told them what he really did in the army, they were amazed to learn that these glider pilots were also fully trained combat soldiers. He told me how he as a child had dreamt of becoming a pilot, never expecting to actually realise that dream.

In our correspondence he elaborated further on his prisoner of war time experiences.

Untold and seemingly forgotten images flared up. In a deceptively casual manner he told of being locked in a cattle train in Apeldoorn with too many others for four infinite days and nights without food, drink or sanitation to a prisoner of war camp somewhere in Germany, near Frankfurt. And how they were left imprisoned in their stationary train at a railway yard, while airplanes passed by overhead. The men realised that these were probably Allied ground attack fighters looking for targets. Any terrifying second these pilots could decide that the train was a worthwhile target. But luckily, the planes flew on.

With resignation he told me about the wintry deprivations that he had to endure in his PoW camp near Dresden. Only after some insisting did he relate how he and every other war survivor had to fight again after the war ended in May 1945, trying to build a civilian existence. Silently trying to incorporate the ideals that he had developed as a reaction to the inhumanity and destruction that he had witnessed during the war. This time without allies, airplanes or armour.

I realised that his story simply had to be told, because it went so much deeper and wider than a one-dimensional battle report. And because it must have been quite characteristic of what so many people of a generation so close to us, had to go through in those days. While scarcely anything about it was written down in the Arnhem books. Each letter from and every telephone conversation with Morley Williams gave new building bricks that I added with care to his own original manuscript, 'Stalag Days'. In this way the story of Sergeant Morley Williams that forms the first part of this book, gradually materialised.

In the process it became clear that there was one thing that Morley Williams strongly wanted to find out about. In all those years he had heard absolutely nothing about the approximately 26 men he and his first pilot Ian Blackwood had landed on 18 September 1944 in an open field near Arnhem. As if they had marched into oblivion, like the fabled Roman Ninth Legion in the second century AD.

Morley, then well past 80 years of age, did not feel up to finding out himself anymore. In his working years the fate of his passengers was no more than a fleeting but unpleasant thought, like a pebble in his shoe. After his retirement in 1977, the question kept coming back progressively stronger. But without clues to start searching, he had been powerless to undertake any action.

Through Morley's reminiscences I realised that it would be likely that his passengers would have similar stories to tell. At the same time it alarmed me that not before long the passing of time would silence these stories for all time. If that was not happening already.

It turned out that Morley visited the Netherlands annually to take part in the commemorations for the Battle of Arnhem. He then had a busy programme and in between the various gatherings still frequently went for a walk in the streets of Oosterbeek, revisiting his own former battlefield. He wore his red beret, thought his thoughts and enjoyed the warm greetings of many local people. In Oosterbeek, a red beret is unconditionally met with respect and friendship.

In 1999 Morley and I met for the first time at the house of Mrs. Doedie Minderman, his hostess in Oosterbeek. He was very interested in me but also told me much about his glider pilot days, his painting and gardening. When I asked him if he could remember anything about his passengers, he slowly shook his head. He only had a vague memory of them, but confessed to taking a big interest in their fate, probably because as a pilot he still felt more or less responsible for them. He asked me if I, as a journalist, could perhaps find out something more. It sounded interesting to me and I sensed that he really wanted to find out, but because at that moment we could not do anything about that, the conversation went on to other subjects.

Mrs. Minderman showed me some impressively water-colour paintings by Morley Williams that were hanging on the wall in her living room. They were a present to her as thanks for her hospitality and friendship during his annual visits to the commemorations. Time flew and all too soon we ended our get together with his favourite Dutch meal, an "uitsmijter" (two slices of bread with ham and a fried egg on top) in the historic restaurant "Schoonoord". He insisted on paying and I accepted his offer, but only on the condition that next year he would be my guest. Intrigued by the matter of his passengers' fate, I imagined that it would not do any harm to ask around a little.

The quest for his passenger's stories is detailed in the second part of this book. Little did I know that the main part of search would take nine years, while the latest additions to the manuscript wouldn't enter the second English edition until 19 years had passed. In the beginning it even looked impossible to get started. Experts in the Arnhem battle community advised against it at all. Most veterans would be tired of yet again having to go over those ten days in September 1944, they knew for sure.

Therefore, in the first two years after the discovery of Morley's 'Stalag Days', no progress was made. Then two developments broke the deadlock.

The first one was the arrival of internet with its increased search and communication powers. The second was the publication in the year 2000 of the book *'Tugs and Gliders'* on the gliders at Arnhem. There I found the elusive key that launched my search.

From there I began focused investigations into as many published and unpublished sources as I could lay my hands on. These developed into interviews with various people that knew much about 'Arnhem'. At the same time, I went looking for the only real source of possible answers, the passengers of Morley's glider. Hundreds of letters and countless e-mails were sent and received and dozens of phone calls made. Various British newspapers articles appeared on my search that yielded new starting-points for follow ups.

Numerous trails were followed. In some cases it seemed as if the passenger was about to materialise from the mists of time only to dissolve again soundlessly into oblivion. But step by step a recognisable sketch was forming of a number of British young men who just like Morley Williams got involved in the dramatic events in September 1944. Some of them had hardly ever spoken about their experiences. Close relatives of Williams' passengers added personal details to the story, thus giving the soldier's stories an invaluable extra dimension. Although much was already irrevocably lost, I have been able to rescue some pieces of this puzzle of reminiscences. Every newly found bit of information was welcomed as a victory over time. And now on the eve of the second English edition in 2019, the amount of collected information has become bigger than I ever would have imagined possible. Virtually everyone's story has now been documented in more or less detail. But still, some essential facts and stories, have remained in the dark.

In the third part of this book the testimonies were pieced together, like a jigsaw puzzle. The compiled account follows the airbornes from the moment their large glider ascended from its RAF-station Broadwell in the middle of England, slowly rolling behind its' Dakota tug plane, to the fields near Wolfheze and the woods and trenches near Oosterbeek. This part of the book also speaks of that haunted, pitch black evacuation night when the pouring rain drenched the exhausted survivors to the skin and the Germans were firing mercilessly at the flimsy boats that ferried the airbornes of 'Arnhem' back to the safer south bank of the Rhine. The story now comes uncomfortably close because it no longer is about anonymous soldiers, but about men that you have become acquainted with, learned to like and often got to see their photograph.

The stories do not stop with the end of the fighting, but go on with the transport of the survivors to and their stay in overcrowded prisoner of war camps in Germany and Poland. There they endured new enemies like cold, malnutrition, vermin, lack of space and especially their severely restricted freedom and a feeling of humiliation.

Finally in the fourth part, the story follows a number of survivors of Morley's flight in their lives after the war. What did they encounter when they returned to civilian society and the interest in their adventures rapidly evaporated? In a time when war heroes lived around each street corner and when getting bread on the table for the family became the biggest priority? Arnhem seemed to disappear once and for all from their lives. Most of Morley's passengers did not talk about it anymore, but for many the memories came back as they got older. Some, unknown to Morley, returned to Oosterbeek, once or more often, to attend the annual commemorations. Family members often knew only a little of what their father, uncle, brother, cousin or husband had been through at or after Arnhem. Here, the roles changed and I started to answer questions instead of asking them. It also happened sometimes that my journalistic curiosity touched their family life in such a way that they developed interest in my own personal life. I was surprised by the friendly relations that arose with them. Many of them have encouraged me to continue with the research, for which I am very grateful. Over the years, I got to know several of them personally, because they came to Arnhem and I was able to show them the former battle fields. These were memorable occasions. For this reason I dedicate this book to all passengers of Horsa 166 and their families.

The epilogue was written for the first English edition, 5 years after the Dutch version had been published in 2004. It focuses on the men that are to this very day, still missing in action. A search that had become possible because I had found new information on them. Although no final answers have yet been found, I hope that this search contributes to solving their mysteries as soon as possible. A hope that with this second edition is renewed, but remains frustratingly unfulfilled.

And now, now the quest is completed, the question arises what in fact did all this research produce? For the survivors and for the relatives of those that did not return, new light has been shed on the fate of their friends, army friends, family and loved ones. For historians, the Westerbouwing account has given a clearer image of the struggle for this vital high ground.

For me as a writer and researcher the quest has produced the feeling that I have done everything I could to secure and take down in writing a small potsherd of human, personal history. Maybe even contributed a little to Morley's unspoken ideals. What had started as a seemingly simple question eventually even matured into a comprehensive project and even into a book in three editions. Many hundreds thousands of readers were given new knowledge and understanding of an event which put the Netherlands in 1944 in the focus point of world history. They hopefully gained new very personal insight in the lives and fates of a number of British and Canadian boys and men that came to our country to deliver it from a grim occupation.

Haks Walburgh Schmidt
August 2019

E-mail: haks@tekstburgh.nl

Part 1

'Taffy' Williams

In Oosterbeek

'Sergeant Williams, I want you to go to the forward trenches on the edge of the woods and tell the lads to deploy more to the right. If we stay so thinly dispersed Jerry will overrun us easily.' That is what Major Tony Murray said on Wednesday 20 September 1944 to Morley 'Taffy' Williams, Sergeant in the British Glider Pilot Regiment. It was almost ten o'clock in the morning and the 250 Glider Pilots of F Squadron were dug in in the Dennenkamp woods, east of the Stationsweg in Oosterbeek and south of the railroad track between Utrecht and Arnhem. Tensely, they waited for the Germans to attack.

Up until late afternoon on the previous day, everybody expected that the Glider Pilots could be kept in reserve. But then the already stubborn German resistance developed into powerful counterattacks. All available reinforcements had to be put into the line and so the Glider Pilots were deployed as infantry to assist the other airborne troops.

For Sergeant Morley Williams, the Battle of Arnhem began in earnest when he was sent to the forward trenches with the message from their commander, Major Murray. While walking the 200 metres through the forest towards his comrades, he suddenly saw a savage horde of German soldiers hurling themselves upon the British position in front of him, roaring and firing all their weapons. The position was quickly overwhelmed. Immediately, the Germans pushed on further, towards the Squadron Headquarters. Morley saw them coming in his direction and it did not take him a second to throw himself flat on the ground and take cover from the approaching Huns. Silently, he started to crawl back to Headquarters. It took him approximately ten minutes to get near enough to see it. But then he was horrified to discover that everyone had disappeared. He swore in silence but immediately pushed himself flat on the ground again. On his left and right attacking Germans noisily passed him by, but they did not seem to notice him. This encouraged Morley to act as if he had been killed. "Perhaps I can make it until nightfall and then sneak back to our own lines", he hoped. Morley assumed a convincing pose. "They said that there were no German front soldiers here," he thought incensed as he lay on his back in the forest ground and closed his eyes. At the same time the thought flashed through his mind that he was now utterly defenceless against any trigger-happy German soldier.

Morley's imitation of a dead man seemed convincing, because one German, who literally stumbled over him, left him untouched after some blood-curdling seconds of unspeakable anxiety.

But one hour later a heavy boot softly kicked him and he heard a voice saying in broken English "Come, Komm, Komm, Tommy, for you ze war is over." He sheepishly looked up and saw a German soldier in camouflage uniform towering over him with a rifle loosely under his arm. Morley's fears grew when he noticed that the German wore SS-insignia on his collar. The SS had the reputation to shoot without hesitation and take no prisoners. Morley got up slowly and brushed off the fallen leaves and sand from his airborne smock. Luckily, the SS-soldier only tossed a British cigarette at him and gestured him to walk in front of him to a nearby school building. Here Morley met some of his fellow Glider Pilots who had been taken prisoner earlier. Among them he saw Captain Robbie Robson and former roommate Johnny Wetherall. Johnny was wounded in the eye and his face was almost completely in bandages. Morley offered him a cigarette, but Robson warned Morley that he'd better be careful with his stock because there seemed little chance of resupply in the near future.

In the school there were two airborne chaplains, a Catholic and a Presbyterian. The latter asked Morley if he, being an unwounded non-commissioned officer (NCO), would be willing to accompany them to the Municipal Hospital in the north of Arnhem. Morley agreed and got transported to the hospital. There he was responsible for the temporary burial of 19 of his airborne comrades who had succumbed to their wounds in hospital. The bodies were wrapped in army blankets and had their identity tags or papers with them in small metal boxes. As they were laid to rest in shallow field graves in the hospital grounds, the Royal Army Medical Corps (RAMC) were tending to the many wounded inside the Dutch hospital. Between his sad burial tasks Morley felt expert enough to help with distributing bed pans to the patients. But not all of them appreciated his cheerful *"Here you are Joe; I've brought you a potty!"* One patient nearly threw a fit because of this friendly offer, which left poor Morley speechless. That is, until a grinning medic informed him that this patient happened to be a rather senior officer.

By the growing numbers of casualties Morley gathered that the fighting was heavy. Day and night both British and German wounded were brought to the Municipal Hospital. From time to time Morley met the hospital pharmacist with whom he occasionally got a chance to have a quick smoke and exchange rumours. The pharmacist claimed to be in contact with the local resistance and insisted that the Allied ground forces with their tanks were rapidly advancing to the Arnhem Bridge now. During one of those conversations Morley told the pharmacist how he got into the airborne forces and ended up in this Dutch hospital:

Called up in The Royal Welsh Fusiliers

My years of military service started with getting called up for the 7th Battalion of the Royal Welsh Fusiliers in December 1941 when I was 24 years old. I had been working as a skilled telephone fitter at the Post Office Telephones in Wrexham (Wales). Initially I was meant to become a pharmacist's apprentice, just like my elder brother. But by the time I was 17 and old enough, it turned out that there was not enough money at home to do that. So instead, I had to work in a hardware shop. But selling saucepans for one pound a week did not make me very happy. After a couple of years I started working for the Post and Telephone Office where I made £ 2.40 a week. I decided to become a skilled worker at the Post, which would increase my salary with 4 shillings.

Well, then came the war. I felt it my duty to join, as I did not want people to think that I used my reserved occupation as an excuse to stay home safely. This was no time to evade my responsibility. I wanted to be able to look everybody in the eye when they asked me "Well, what did YOU do in the war?" So that was why I resigned from my job. To my great satisfaction I got called up for the army only six weeks later.

After my basic training with the Royal Welsh Fusiliers and an additional course on the 3-inch mortar I heard that a sister battalion was to be retrained as parachutists. They were asking for volunteers. The extra pay, a shilling a day, persuaded a friend of mine to join, but the prospect of jumping out of an aircraft did not appeal to me very much. Shortly afterwards, a new circular appeared on the notice boards. This time they wanted volunteers for a new regiment that was to be equipped with glider planes. The prospect to become a pilot of sorts raised about a hundred applicants, including me.

I hoped that in such an army unit I would have the opportunity to use my knowledge and hopefully learn something more useful than I would do as an ordinary infantryman. Moreover, flying had been fascinating me since my childhood when I had flown a couple of circles over an airfield in a plane that was a circus attraction in Wrexham. But I never would have dreamt that a rich people's pastime like that would be possible for me. It did not seem dangerous, just exciting.

Of the 100 applications from my Regiment, 40 candidates were invited for further selection in London. There we underwent all kinds of written, oral and physical tests and once more 37 men were sent back. Of the remaining three, one was too old and another too tall. Only one, a certain, good looking, elegant, debonair, erudite candidate remained. Frankly, that happened to be me!

Transfer to the *Glider Pilot Regiment*

Early 1942 I was transferred to the depot of the new regiment on the Salisbury Plains in the south of England. I got my promotion to Corporal and was equipped with a red beret and Regimental cap badge. I confess that joining this newly founded and modern regiment made me feel quite proud. My family however was not noticeably impressed by my transfer to the Airborne Forces. My only brother had joined the much older and renowned *Royal Army Medical Corps* because he had been a pharmacist's apprentice. He did not think much of this novelty. At that time, he was already stationed in Trans Jordan. Although my mother did not show it, I realised later that she must have worried very much with both her sons now under arms. Especially because my father was killed in April 1918 in Flanders during the First World War while in the *Royal Marines*. My friends saw the *Glider Pilot Regiment* as an obscure form of transport. Not necessarily as a fighting force, but more a type of bus service for the transport of military staff from one airstrip to another. I myself was glad not to be

Morley Williams in 1942, still wearing Corporal stripes.

an infantryman anymore and hoped for a training which I later could put to good use in civil life.

In the beginning the training facilities on my base, the RAF airport Brize Norton, were still insufficient. As a result, our real flying training could not start until much later. In the meantime we acted as 'Tail End Charlies' in the rear gunner's turret at the tail end of Whitworth Whitly bombers that towed the Horsa gliders. Only if you were lucky could you occasionally get a ride in a Horsa. However, gradually more possibilities for instruction became available. My training started in Tiger Moths and Miles Magisters, which were single-engined airplanes. In these planes we learned to carry out all kinds of manoeuvres, such as slow roles, loops and things like that. As a result we got a feeling of how to handle airplanes. This was of great use when I first started flying training gliders, the Hotspurs, and also later in the big Horsa gliders. Finally, in June 1943 I was fortunate enough to complete the 110 hours on the training aircraft. Bizarre coincidence was that my first two instructors were killed in plane crashes. Luckily, when I was not on their plane.

Morley Williams in No 14 Course, 21 Elementary Flying Training School, RAF Station Booker, near Marlow, Buckinghamshire. Morley is the second from the right in the middle row, fifth from the right is Johnny Potts. (Photo through Bob Rose, third form the right, back row)

We had just been flying the Hotspur glider about ten hours when the first battalion of the Glider Pilots returned from North Africa and Sicily. That was in January 1943. I was taken on to the F Squadron as a co-pilot with the rank of Sergeant. Squadron Sergeant Ian Blackwood ('Blackie') was my first pilot. Harry Howard, one of my fellow pilots at the Squadron very well described him as 'not at all belonging to the typical Sergeant Major of Army folklore'. He was a banker by profession, serious and studious as a soldier, as befitted his rank and civil occupation. Nevertheless he could be 'one of the lads' when it came to mixing with his brother pilots at off-duty times. There were about 250 pilots and some ground staff in a squadron. Blackie and I were part of the Squadron Headquarters, but I did not have any specific tasks. I had to help wherever it was necessary, for example as a messenger. The Horsa gliders were nicknamed 'Matchboxes', because they were mainly built from plywood and did not offer any protection against hostile gun fire. We quickly got used to the movements and steep dives of the Horsa's, but only God knew how the soldiers travelling in the back must have felt at their first landings. Landing the big aircraft usually started with a very steep dive indeed, which made you feel you were about to crash.

One interesting experience was a night-flying exercise, when thirty Horsa's, after flying a triangular course over the Midlands, were to land in darkness on Netheravon, a grass drome on the Salisbury Plains. On casting off we could not identify anything on the ground. Eventually we bounced on the football field just outside the drome. With an infernal cracking noise the nose wheel was pushed in through the fuselage of the glider and next we sliced through an electric light pole (putting all the lights out in the drome). Finally we ended up in a sewerage farm with both the landing wheel on my side and the tail unit up in a tree. Luckily we had no special affection to any particular glider. Within a few seconds two more gliders, which had been following our wing lights, landed in the same spot. This episode resulted in nine gliders being scrapped. Yet the main casualty that night was one of our ground crew who got run over by a car in Marlborough when he was crossing the road to get some fish and chips.

When D-day arrived on 6 June 1944, only half of our squadron took part. The remainder of us were held back for any emergency operation. In September 1944 Blackie and I had flown 40 hours on the Horsa. From early June to 8th September we were continuously briefed for new operations which were cancelled at the last minute. This disappointed us enormously because we were constantly kept ready for action by rigorous training. We started to feel more and more that they were not going to use us in this damn war and we wondered if all our expensive training had been a waste of time, effort and money. And the next day we would hear again that a new operation was being prepared. That uncertainty was hugely frustrating. So when the plans for operation Market Garden were presented, we received them with all proper reserves, but as in previous occasions, the suspense kept increasing with every hour the plans were not cancelled. Would this be the one that would really go on? When September 17th came along and Operation Market Garden was still not cancelled, I started to get a little nervous and I was certainly not the only one.

Flight to Wolfheze

Blackie and I met our passengers on the RAF airfield Broadwell, which was our station. It was the first time we saw them. We Glider Pilots did not mix much with the other airbornes as they were stationed in different barracks in the Burford area. But when we did meet, we seemed to admire each other's grit. I told our passengers that I would not dare do their job, not for all the tea in China. To which they would answer that that was exactly how they felt about my job.

Around 08.00 hours we were all waiting together in the morning sun and smoking until the signal to start would be given. It took until just before half past nine before we could end the agonizing wait and got the signal to board the Horsa. Our destination was a Dutch city on the river Rhine, called Arnhem. Only a handful of staff of our regiment such as writers, cooks, batmen and drivers remained at the home base. While I was shuffling into the cockpit I looked at the hundreds of heavily packed soldiers who were just about to get in. Ground crews were running up and down the grass and the asphalt, cars were coming and going and the morning air seemed almost electrically charged. I noticed that my mouth was turning dry.

At 9.50 hours it was our turn to take off. The tow-cable on the ground in front of the glider unrolled slowly and with a gentle bump our plane set off. The engines of our Dakota tug of 575 Squadron were running full throttle and wobblingly the Horsa got airborne. As usual the Dakota took off a few seconds later. We were on our way!! The flight went smoothly, until after half an hour's flying we noticed that the tug pilot was having problems. He was rolling the plane's wings up and down. Blackie and I looked at each other and we understood that the Dakota was having engine trouble. As usual the communication between the tug and our 'matchbox' did not function, so the Dakota pilot could not tell us what was going on. Later we found out that his engines were overheating. We had no other option than to cast off and get ready for a premature landing. We warned our passengers to set their teeth and at 10.21 hours we landed at Essendon, east of Hatfield on a small airfield. Blackie and the Lieutenant commanding our passengers, left to arrange transport back to Broadwell. I stayed with the others and the glider. There we sat, rather unheroic, basking in the sun, in an English meadow, an illusion the poorer. Just when after so many cancelled operations, it finally happened to be our turn we got stranded! After a while Blackie and the Lieutenant returned and told us that a plane would come to pick us up and that we would leave the next day with the second lift. Thus in the early afternoon we were all on our way back to our base at Broadwell. The undamaged Horsa would be picked up later.

Monday 18 September

Our second attempt to get to Arnhem started under low clouds. As a result, the start was postponed four hours. It was not until nearly half past twelve that we could take off. We had been positioned at the end of the meticulously marshalled queue of waiting planes. Because of the weather we had to take position under the slipstream of our tug plane once we were flying. But when we got above the clouds, we could see for miles around and had a marvellous view of the deep blue sky. An endless stream of tug and glider combinations with the September sun sparkling on hundreds of cockpit windows offered a breathtaking spectacle and made us feel invincible!

Flying a Horsa was hard physical work that demanded full concentration and with the sun shining on our Perspex cockpit windows it did not take long before Blackie and I had stripped down to our string vests. To get an idea of flying a Horsa, imagine being in a car that is towed. Then you have to carefully keep in the tracks of the towing car at exactly the same speed to avoid sudden jerks that could rip off your bumper or break the towing cable. Flying a glider was a similar experience, but you had to anticipate your tugs' movement in three dimensions instead of in two. Blackie and I were taking over the controls for spells of ten minutes each, and when not flying we were map reading, especially over Holland, in case of any mishap. Should we be forced to land prematurely, we would at least be able to tell our passengers where we were. As a consequence we did not have much time to talk to them.

After crossing the Dutch coast, we carried on serenely as if we were still on exercise in the UK, although I understood later that we had been hit by a piece of shrapnel, with only very minor damage. Eventually we could see the Landing Zone (LZ) at Wolfheze. On the planned spot we cast off from the tug. To keep up enough speed we dived down under an angle of 45 degrees, while Blackie and I were looking for a good spot to land. As soon as we saw one, we started to fly less steep and thus decreased our speed. After a three and half-hours flight we made a normal landing. The moment we had stopped, our passengers leapt out through the doors on the left and the right. They lay prone in an outward facing circle ready to give covering fire, whilst there was a bit of shooting in the woods nearby, but no immediate danger. Meanwhile Blackie and I, exhausted after three and a half-hours flying, were emptying our thermos flasks of coffee in the cockpit four feet above the ground 'well protected' from any stray bows and arrows, spears or assegais or other enemy fire by the 'solid' three millimetre plywood skin and Perspex of the Horsa. Silly pair of buggers we were!

After a short while our passengers left us. They went to their Battalion Headquarters to join their own unit. We did the same and found Major Murray and our F Squadron Headquarters in a house in Wolfheze.

That same afternoon we set off in the direction of Arnhem by advancing on the north side of the Arnhem-Utrecht railway line. After a mile or so we were turned back by Divisional Airborne troops as there were some Germans blocking our route. So we had to work our way through the woods towards our meeting point at the Hartenstein Hotel area, the Divisional headquarters. Glider Pilots were meant to return to Great Britain as soon as possible. We were not supposed to participate in combat, although we were well trained to do so. We even had a safe-conduct signed by Monty, which allowed us to claim transport. However, as there was not yet a connection with the advancing ground forces, we *were kept in reserve at Hartenstein.*

It was late in the afternoon when we arrived there and we were instructed to pitch camp on the North West Side of the hotel near the Oranjeweg. At twilight we dug ourselves in in slit trenches, finished our haversack rations and went to a well earned sleep after putting up sentries. In the distance we could hear some shooting from time to time, but we had no idea what the situation was like.

September 19, 1944

Our day began quietly. In the course of the morning we saw Dakota's flying over us dropping resupplies. One container whose parachute failed to open hit the ground just a few yards from us. I am not certain but I think it contained boots and berets. Another Dakota came over with one engine on fire. It circled while dropping its resupplies after which its crew jumped out. Then, obviously with the pilot still on the controls, it crashed and burst into flames. It was a shocking sight and we all said that the pilot deserved the Victoria Cross. (About a year later I was to find out that I had actually known this incredibly brave pilot and that he did get the Victoria Cross).

The supply flights had only just finished when we received orders to break up. We packed our belongings and walked onto the Utrechtseweg, passed Hartenstein on our right and turned left at the crossroads at Hotel-Restaurant Schoonoord into the Stationsweg. Halfway along the Stationsweg we turned right into the Dennenkamp woods between the present Town Hall and the railway. Squadron Headquarters was set up in the middle of the woods and the Troops, Flights as we called them, formed a defensive line on the northern and eastern borders of the woods. Again slit trenches were dug, and then meals were prepared from the 24 hour packs. Obviously we were taking up battle positions. Although the shooting north of our position was increasing and seemed to come closer, we had not actually seen any Germans yet and again we spent a fairly quiet night in our trenches.

September 20, 1944

Up to Wednesday September 20 I felt like I was on exercise still in England, as we were ignorant of how things were outside our particular sector. But that was to change that day. It started in the morning, as we were bombed with mortars. The effect of the mortar bombing was

> *minimal - quite a bit of crunching noises but little damage because the trees took the brunt of the explosions and we were relatively safe in our trenches. For me everything started when I got captured by this Gerry later that morning, I guess somewhere between eleven and twelve o'clock.'*

Forcibly stubbing out his finished cigarette on the windowsill, Morley ended his story of how he wound up in this German occupied hospital. Before hurrying back to work, the pharmacist just might have caught a suppressed flicker of anger in Morley's eyes.

In German hands

On one of the last days of September it turned out that the hospital pharmacist was wrong about the progress of the British ground forces. Instead there was an unsettling rumour that the airbornes at Arnhem were pulling out. Later that day Morley was taken to the Elizabeth Hospital in Arnhem where he was sent to Apeldoorn under armed escort in an open truck with several other Glider Pilots. They brought him up to date about regimental casualties. Although he was proud of the achievements of his fellow pilots, the large number of wounded and fallen comrades horrified him. He did not hear any news about his first pilot Blackie. After arrival in Apeldoorn the Germans took their prisoners to a large railway shed. There was no food whatsoever available and that night they slept on the straw-covered floor and railway tracks in the shed, using their battle bowlers as potties.

The next morning their guards counted the prisoners and entrained them onto a long line of cattle wagons. There were about 30 men in each wagon and Morley counted 20 wagons. Therefore he took that there must be about 600 prisoners of war on that train, all captured at Arnhem. Morley ended up in a wagon with only glider pilots. Because there were so many people in each wagon, there was not enough room for all of them to lie down on the floor, so they had to take turns for a rest.

> *'If it wasn't your turn you could only sit on your haunches or simply stand up. There was but a small space of about 6 by 24 inches through which we could view the world outside,'* as Morley explained.

Then the train departed and four endless days in the wagon followed. The prisoners of war were not let out of the wagon and they did not receive any food during this period. Morley and Danny Sales, also from the F-squadron, shared an Oxo cube and a small piece of dried vegetable they had found under the straw. At one of the many stops another glider pilot, Charles Thackery paid a pound for a cup of water.

Peeping through the 'window' the prisoners of war (PoW's) gathered that the train was going south travelling down the Rhine. As time went by it was changing track further east, but eventually it continued to go south. As the train kept changing direction, they had no idea where they were going. For one of their regular long stops they were halted in the marshalling yard in Cologne. This area was a regular target of air raids by American and British bombers and while they were parked there, there was another air raid warning. Morley and his comrades could only hope that their own air force wouldn't bomb them. When the man who was watching through the 'window' saw that the aircraft flying overhead were American P-38 Lightning fighter planes they heaved a huge sigh of relief, because fighters did not throw bombs.

When the air raid alarm was over, the ghostlike journey resumed. When the train arrived at Frankfort-on-Main, Morley was standing in front of the peephole. He could see that some of the German civilians who were waiting on the opposite platform gave them a rather hostile greeting. One of them got extremely excited. Morley remembered him in particular because he was a long-necked, streaky looking fellow with a Hitler moustache, wearing a collarless shirt with a black greasy edging where his collar should have been. He was showing his displeasure at their presence by venomously booing and hissing. It seemed to Morley as if he wanted to get in the wagon. The man reminded him of rubber-necked Nat Jackley, a well-known comedian of the time. Morley responded with a gracious reversed Churchill salute.

Later that day they passed by a completely bombed-out car factory. Morley was strongly affected by the indescribable destruction. Shortly afterwards the Arnhem POWs reached their destination, the town of Limburg an der Lahn, about 30 kilometres east of Koblenz and north from Frankfurt. The wagons were emptied at the station and the POWs were marched through the cobbled street to their destination, Stalag XIIA, just outside the town.

Dazed, hungry and dirty after the exhausting journey, PoW army number 4208939 Morley Williams and his comrades entered the camp. Here they had their first meal in four days. Their joy over the coming food disappeared quickly when they had a good look at the 'banquet' before them. It consisted of boiled beet tops and was dished out of a dustbin with a ladle made out of a tin from a Red Cross parcel. Most of the men who were taken prisoner at Arnhem had lost their mess tins and eating tools during the battle and therefore had to borrow such equipment from the old *Kriegies*, as the prisoners of war were called.

The first taste of German rations resulted in most of the new prisoners having the runs, Morley amongst them. So they spent a lot of time in the camp lavatory, a brick-built building with a concrete floor out of which sprouted several earthenware pipes acting as toilets. Underneath was a vast tank, which was emptied each day by a squad of *Jerries* under the command of a *Hauptmann*. In both doorways were manholes in the floor that were opened by the Jerries when they arrived on the scene with loud shouts of *'Raus, raus!'* (Out, out!) to make clear that everybody should leave the lavatory. Unfortunately one poor soul had the runs so badly that he was late clearing the deck and in his panic to escape he fell through the manhole in the cesspit. For the next few days he could be seen wandering about the Stalag wearing a sort of kilt, improvised of his sole army blanket, while his clothes were drying very slowly in the damp October weather.

According to the Geneva Convention the food they received from the Germans was supposed to be equal to that issued to their fighting troops. But the newly arrived airbornes could not believe that fairy tale. How could any soldier possibly fight on that pigswill?

For the first weeks at Stalag XIIA Morley was given the responsibility of supervising the issue of the food to a hundred men, mostly paratroopers and Air Landing Brigade wallahs that had been captured at Arnhem. In the Stalag there was also a French paratroop sergeant, a little Algerian, and a Tahitian called Pita Tahoni. Morley had to be very strict to see that there was no fiddling with the rations. Normal issue was a few half-cooked potatoes, some skilly (boiled beet root tops, or bottoms, Sauerkraut), a piece of black bread, dab of margarine, a dollop of jam, Ersatz coffee or mint tea. At the end of the first week Red Cross parcels were dished out, one parcel between two men, three men, or even four men, depending on the supply situation. For ten cigarettes from that first Red Cross parcel Morley managed to get hold of a Parker fountain pen. Unfortunately there was no writing paper to be found and soon he decided to change it for a pair of scissors. With these scissors and a loose gate hinge he found somewhere lying about, he made his own cup, knife, fork and other utensils.

The parcels came from the U.S., some from the U.K., from India and even once or twice from Argentina. The contents also varied. Sometimes Del Monte tinned fruit, Klim (American powdered milk), dry egg powder, oats, tea, coffee, dried fruit, tinned meat (Spam) or salmon, and cigarettes (Phillip Morris, Camels, Chesterfield, Players or Craven A). They shared the food as fairly as possible, but there was never enough to satisfy their hunger. Non-smokers used the cigarettes for barter purposes.

Smokers invariably cut their cigarettes into three. Each third part was opened out and together with the dog end of the other two included in a new, hand rolled cigarette. They used cigarette papers, which were somehow on the market at one cigarette for a packet of papers. Unfortunately these papers were gumless, but by using some of their jam ration as substitute glue they managed to make it stick. Morley shared his rations of food and smokes with a fellow Glider Pilot, Johnny Bowen, an estate agent from Halesowen, Birmingham. He remembered that they never fell out once throughout their Stalag days. "After the war I called at Johnny's house, but he was not at home. I didn't announce my name to his daughter but left her a third of a cigarette as a visiting card. Some time later when I eventually caught him at home, he told me that he had identified his unknown caller immediately", Morley still remembered years later.

At first Morley's group in Stalag Limburg was billeted in a brick building with three tiered bunks. In an adjacent compound there were a number of Sikhs living in Bell tents, whose toilets were buckets outside the tents. The Glider Pilots had often watched them doing their ablutions sitting on their buckets, picking their noses, or wiping their bottoms in full view of all. There were no rolls of toilet paper at hand and so they used 4 x 4 inch squares of paper from pads which were purchased for a cigarette each from inside the camp. The Russians who were in control of the bread market, also used these papers to present their merchandise. But the slices of bread were a bit bigger than the pieces of paper. The bread-sellers had often only just finished cleaning the lavatories and had not washed their hands yet. Therefore the bread was not always really clean.

After a few weeks there was some unpleasantness in the Glider Pilots' building. One of the lads had become a bit light-fingered and had pinched someone else's rations. He was caught in the act and a council of war was installed. As NCO's (non-commissioned officers) and gentlemen they decided to report the thief to the Stalag Man of Confidence. That was a senior officer who acted as a go-between between the Stalag Commandant and the Kriegies. After that, the poor devil spent the next fortnight in the 'cooler'.

Shortly after this incident, somewhere in November 1944, the Arnhem prisoners of war were moved to a marquee, bedding down on a mere layer of straw. Those who did not have any greatcoats were issued them from a common pool. Morley's was a Belgian army greatcoat, much thinner and lighter than the traditional type, but beggars could not be choosers, so he had to make do with this wretched garment. They were also issued one blanket and used both items to try and keep warm at night in addition to keeping all their clothes on. Apart from the cold there were other nightly disturbances in the rather crowded new tent. A Tyneside chap suffered from nightmares and kept waking everybody up with his strident voice. This got on their nerves more and more. By that time, without having had a bath since leaving Blighty and without any change of clothes, they started to suffer from lice and a popular activity was to chase the little blighters with their lit cigarettes. Morley had two pairs of socks and wore both at all times, alternating their positions every so often, giving the outer pair a shake to get rid of any debris.

Destination Stalag IVB

After about ten days in this accommodation Morley and some others of the Arnhem prisoners were marched back to the railway station. Once again he was sent off on a railway journey. This time of a three-day duration and of a more luxurious nature than the earlier one. Yet in the same type of cattle wagon. With the same number of men in each wagon and also with straw on the floor, but this time they were fed each day and they were let out for their ablutions.

When they learned that the thief was travelling with them, they agreed not to have him in their wagon. After three days on the train they arrived at the permanent Stalag IVB (Mühlberg on the Elbe) and they were allocated to various huts. No one wanted to have the thief in their hut and he was sent to one of the other huts which was mainly occupied by Americans.

Stalag IVB was truly a multinational camp. It included Russians, both European and Asian, Yugoslavs, Americans, British, as well as French-speaking Canadians, Dutchmen, Belgians, Poles, and on different occasions, Danish policemen and even some women who had been involved in a Warsaw uprising. The Stalag language was English because of the large number of Anglo-Saxon inmates. There were at least 10,000 men in the Stalag that covered an area of about 5 or 6 acres. A double line of barbed wire between which stood the sentry towers surrounded the compound.

Main entrance to Stalag IVB, where Sergeant Morley Williams was kept as prisoner of war. (Photo Dick van Maarseveen, Rijksmuseum NG 1983-9)

The hut had three-tier bunks, eighty in all, but there were 160 men to be accommodated, so the men had to double up in each bunk. Morley shared his bunk with Johnny Hartmann, a Jewish parachutist. As a journalist he had spent some time in Helsinki in Finland. Johnny was fluent in German and was soon able to get hold of up-to-date editions of the *'National Zeitung'* and also made contact with the owners of a secretly held radio in the camp. Between these two sources he was able to give fairly accurate accounts of the military position on the Western European Front to the huts in their compound.

Almost as soon as they arrived at the Stalag, Morley and the other Glider Pilots were visited by Willy Atkinson. This well-known Squadron Sergeant Major of the Glider Pilot Regiment looked remarkably spic and span except for his regimental cap badge that he had lost after having been captured in Normandy. He had replaced it with a cardboard replica. He looked so fit that Morley thought he must have built himself a reserve supply of food in the past few months. With his parade-like appearance Atkinson stimulated the other Glider Pilots to behave as disciplined and smartly as possible and thus to preserve some of their self-respect despite their humiliating circumstances.

There must have been a list with the names and home addresses of the new intake, because in a very short while Morley was visited by his old school friend Trevor Roberts (Royal Air Force) and Billy Miller, whose father he worked with in civvy street and who was also from his old school. Thirdly, a cousin to a neighbour from his home town Wrexham whom he knew by sight only, came to say hello.

The bunks in the huts originally had thirteen bed boards and where the boards had been whittled away to provide fuel for the various improvised cooking gadgets, the gaps had been covered with cardboard from the Red Cross parcels flattened out. As long as not too many boards were taken away, the bunks remained solid enough. The boxes themselves doubled up as pillows. The palliasses (straw matrasses) were made of rather open meshed sacking and contained what had gradually become chopped straw and of course they leaked straw. Johnny and Morley now shared their two blankets and two greatcoats to keep warm at night, quite necessary in the approaching central German winter. Even more so, as there was no glass in the windows and their huts were fairly open to the harsh winter winds blazing in from the East.

Most of the lads in the top bunks, rather than climbing down off the top bunks, hung tins on the rafters as substitute potties to avoid having to go to the latrines in the middle of the freezing night. One night, one of the chaps above Morley and Johnny stood up to relieve himself and inadvertently put his foot in the gap between two boards and down came a deluge of pee and straw. After only a mild protest Morley and Johnny rolled to their other side and went back to sleep dreaming sweet dreams of freedom and food. That was, until the following morning.

The huts were double-ended with a communal washing trough in between. In the centre of each hut was a brick-built stove. The stovepipe went horizontally through the centre of the room and then straight up the end wall and finally out through the roof. The horizontal part was used for drying clothes, but its main function was a support for some laths of wood on which some flattened out Red Cross cartons had been fitted to act as a table. Benches had been kindly provided by the Master Race, so the men were able to play cards (two or three-handed Patience was Morley's favourite game), Whist or Chess on a pocket sized board. On this table they also cut up their rations of German black bread. There was a library in the Mühlberg Stalag where the most popular books seemed to be those on food. There was also an officially recognised market where non-smokers could swap their spare cigarettes for tins of food or bread. Although the Stalag commander officially disapproved, the Germans occasionally participated in this activity as well. They were especially interested in coffee as their issue was of the Ersatz variety and bloody awful. The Russian Government did not recognise the Geneva Convention and so 'Ivan' never received any parcels, but as they did the dirty jobs, emptying the night soil with oxen-drawn tanks and dumping it in some local field, they were able to do some outside bartering with the farmers. Morley remembered watching one Russian PoW returning to the compound, unyoking his ox and stabling it, then unscrewing the top of his dung tank and pulling at a piece of string to which a loaf of bread wrapped in a dirty piece of brown paper was attached. He then cut it up in smaller pieces and traded it in the market. Morley decided on the spot never ever to trade bread from a Russian again, although they controlled the complete bread market.

Life in Mühlberg
The Stalag counted two real organisations. The first one was the Stalag IVB pigeon-fanciers and the other one, the IVB Motoring Club. The motoring club, alas without any mode of transport, was very active in the production of a wall newspaper that was circulated through each hut once a month. There was also a hut on one side of the Stalag that was used as a Stalag theatre. Admission in the usual currency, for instance one cigarette. Morley only went once. He looked at some sort of variety show with a resident comedian and a display of hypnotism by a Dutch Kriegie. The former was a well-known sight round the camp as he had a pet dog which he was able to afford on his earning on the stage, but, later, when things became tough,

the dog disappeared and rumour had it that he had eaten it. Morley was amazed one day to witness the unexpected sight of a woman coming out of the theatre. She started to urinate against the wire in a most unfemale manner. Having mentally recovered from this unusual scene, Morley realised that he had been looking at a male actor taking part in a French theatrical play.

However, boredom and passivity were daily enemies. Morley tried to keep occupied and entertain himself as well as he could. With the pair of scissors from Stalag XIIA and a pair of clippers he had bought later, he set himself up as a barber. Not very successfully though, as the scissors, having been used for various jobs, were quite uncomfortable for his clients. His old 'mucker' Reg (Nobby) Clark, an engineer in civilian life, made himself a blower out of a bed board, some old milk tins, a couple of bootlaces, the innards of a cigarette rolling machine, some buttons, and a few cut bits of tin to act as the blades fan. By turning a handle he was able to waft air vigorously onto a few pieces of inflammable rubbish on which he could do some cooking. That was, if he had anything to cook. He and his odd machine were soon banished to the washing room next door, as it made a lot of noise and stunk to high heaven.

Impression of daily life in Stalag IVB (sketch by Morley Williams)

Another of Morley's comrades, Lofty Jenks, launched himself as dealer in the market. He bought and sold whatever he could to make some profit to buy food with. They also played cards together. Geoff Higgins and Jock Wilson played chess on their pocket-sized chessboard, while Johnny Hartman gave regular updates on the latest news about the situation outside the camp to whoever wanted to listen. They borrowed a gramophone and kept on playing Bing Crosby's "I'm dreaming of a white Christmas". Morley and his comrades firmly believed that it would only be a matter of time before the Allies would win the war and that quite soon their captivity would be a thing of the past. This thought was sustaining them, especially with Christmas 1944 coming up, along with snowy, cold and dark weather. Morley's thoughts were also with the people in Oosterbeek and Arnhem for whom it would be so much more difficult to share the faith of the prisoners of war in a happy end after the failed operation in their home towns. Yet Morley felt isolated from the outside world in Stalag IVB and there was always the lingering anxiety of what might happen if the cornered Germans were pushed too far and might take revenge on the Allied PoW's. The German Stalag guards ran things and there was no choice but to obey and to wait. Plans for the future only went as far as his next meal.

Morley was always hungry and tried to find information in the library about growing potatoes or vegetables. He was more interested in trying to get hold of a simple raw potato than in reading the recipes in cooking books of which it was clear he would never be able to make. But with Christmas 1944 coming up he decided to treat himself to a Christmas pudding out of a week's supply of bread crumbs, milk powder, a few prunes and raisins, two powdered up saccharines, two grated chocolate squares and some oatmeal. He quite enjoyed it but was really sick shortly afterwards. Probably one of the ingredients had gone bad. Red-haired Charlie Waterhouse, who was also in Morley's hut, dedicated a lot of time to growing a magnificent red moustache and sideburns.

The British Prisoners of War did not make much contact with their German guards, other than with Feldwebel Weitz, who counted them in 'Fünfs' each morning whilst on parade outside, and once a month escorted them to the showers in another compound. And then of course, old 'Pop' who visited their hut for his ten o'clock coffee every morning. He suddenly disappeared one day and the supposition was that he was sent to the Russian Front because he had become too friendly with the enemy. There were occasional visits of German guards who cleared the prisoners from the hut to make a search in it for items that could be used for escaping. Morley angrily referred to them as bandits or Goons, because they were unscrupulous. There was a story that in one hut they discovered a piece of wire sticking out of an inside wall. They immediately and savagely stripped the wall to the end of the shed and all the way back only to find a piece of paper saying 'Jerry, you've been had'. The captured airbornes did not care whether the story was true or not. They just enjoyed this well-deserved put-down of their warders.

As pastime Morley liked to go for a walk along the barbed-wire fence around the camp. He often met other prisoners who sometimes joined him on his walk. They talked about the latest news, discussed the progress of the Allies or whatever came to their minds at that moment. One day as he was taking his walk with Johnny Hartman, they saw, on nearing their hut again, what appeared to be a lynch mob outside the neighbouring hut. In the middle of it was the thief from the earlier Stalag again, being beaten with bed boards. Obviously he had laid his hands on somebody else's food again and got beaten up for it. Johnny and Morley continued their stroll, shaking their heads. Stealing from your own comrades was about the lowest thing you could do, they agreed without a trace of compassion.

Hunger and Liberation

By February 1945 the food situation was getting very worrisome. Parcels that before were being shared between two men now had to be shared by three, four and once even seven men. Then the time came that there was no issue at all. Due to the constant air raids the Germans suffered severe transportation problems and seemed unable to get supplies to their prisoners of war. Indeed supplies were sometimes brought in by Canadian Red Cross trucks from the Baltic port of Lübeck in order to help the prisoners. Once a wagonload arrived at the local Mühlberg railway station, but it brought only jock straps and ping pong balls, which obviously could not be eaten. The desperate yet powerless anger of the prisoners lasted for days. Everybody became very pernickety in his food preparations. One quartet of non-smokers, including a future Lord Mayor of Leeds, Kenneth Travis-Davidson, used a very complicated ritual in their daily share out. After very carefully slicing their daily ration of bread they adjusted each pile until they were absolutely satisfied that each pile was exactly the same, then they drew lots to decide who would have first pick and even then there would be further careful examination. Food on the market was rumbled with and one day, this same group bought a tin of salmon from a Russian in the market. Now, all the tins in the Red Cross store were pierced on arrival by the Jerries to prevent their being used in escape attempts. Then the recipients quickly seal them with a dab of issue margarine to keep the salmon from going bad. When the quartet eventually opened the tin, they found that the tin was full of earth, with only a flimsy piece of salmon under the seal. Obviously, this Russian first ate the salmon himself, filled the tin with earth and the last slice of salmon to cover his deceit and then sold it as if it were new. Not surprisingly, the Russian salesman was nowhere to be seen over the next few days. Morley also saw a paratrooper who usually shared his rations with a Polish American, cutting up their joint ration. After they ate their food, his mate went to his bunk for a bit of shut-eye. The Para, after making quite sure that the other one was asleep, picked up a crumb that must have fallen on the floor when they sliced their ration and put it surreptitiously in his mouth.

On February 13th, thick smoke clouds and even flames were visible at the eastern horizon. From what they could see, they gathered that it must be an enormous fire. 'Dresden!' said one of the prisoners who had been put to work there once or twice. The town was some 70 kilometres to the south from Stalag IVB and there were several other ranks from the Mühlberg Stalag working there at the time of the bombardment. A few days later, on their return, some of them explained that the town had suffered big fire bomb raids. But soon after, the daily hunt for food required all their attention again. Prior to the shortage, Morley and his friends used to peel the half cooked potatoes issued to them by the Germans and give the peelings to Russians who were begging at the door. However, now that the food supply was so uncertain the British used the peels themselves and made them into crisps. Once a Russian appeared at their door and did a bit of begging. He was met by one of Morley's comrades, nicknamed Spandau (after the fast-firing German machine gun). He was a regular soldier and old time Stalag inmate, who had, in his tours of duty in India, picked up a smattering of Urdu and Hindustani, some Arabic whilst serving in North Africa, some Italian on transit through Italy as well as a few choice expressions in German at Stalag IVB. In his native cockney accent and with his flair for all these 'lingos', he told the Russian to "Sod off". There were also Russians who made things they could trade with. Morley remembered one who arrived at their hut with a metal box with very artistic indentations that he had made from scrap metal. Lastly there were some Mongolian Russians who served in the German Army as camp guards, but they were cold-shouldered by everybody.

In March and especially in April 1945 the inmates saw the local population fleeing westwards for fear of the Russian's Red Army. According to newsman Johnny Hartmann the Russians were now within fifty miles of Mühlberg. The prisoners of war from other, more eastern Stalags were being marched over long distances in a westerly direction and were arriving at Stalag IVB. Obviously these camps had been evacuated by the Germans who took their prisoners further west. Among the incoming prisoners Morley recognised Glider Pilot Paddy Caves, looking very weak and wan. He also saw Johnny Southy who used to share his hut in Broadwell and was very proud of his lovely blonde hair. Johnny explained that he had escaped from the march, but had been recaptured after a few days of freedom and was then brought to Mühlberg. To Morley's surprise his hair was grand as ever. After a few days Paddy Caves was taken away from his comrades in Mühlberg. They were never to see him again. It was not until many years later that Morley found out that he died shortly afterwards and was buried near Berlin according to the Regimental History.

During the first weeks of April the Germans were still ruling IVB when suddenly an English-speaking woman appeared in the camp. She was from the Leipzig area and turned out to be widowed in the First World War and to have remarried a Luftwaffe officer. She was allowed to take refuge in the Stalag where, by a bizarre twist of fate, her British son, a RAF-aircrew member, was kept PoW.

On the twenty-first of April, Johnny Hartmann told them that the Huns were expected to pull out during the night. But on waking up the following day the Huns were still around, although Hungarians had taken over the guard duties. From the camp, masses of German military equipment and vehicles could be seen fleeing on the roads nearby in a northerly direction while American and British aircrafts were continuously strafing traffic on the railway, using rockets. The planes raised great cheers from the inmates when they hit their target, especially a hit on an ammunition train got a standing ovation. The guards just stood there and watched sullenly. That night, the Jerries finally did pull out, accompanied by their Hungarians. An emergency group of the inmates under a Lieutenant Jessop had been organised to maintain some form of discipline and to guard the meagre food supplies left by the Germans. To avoid possible problems, the group had been internationally composed.

The next morning a roll call was made at the usual time, but before a count could be made there was a shout: 'The Russians are here!!' and everybody rushed to the wire. There they saw Red Army soldiers approach, in their thousands. Mostly on foot, with one or two cars and a few horse-drawn Samovars to make tea. They soon took over the Stalag from the previous Allied emergency organisation. The sentry boxes between the wires though, remained empty as to make clear that Stalag IVB was no longer a prison. The date was 23rd April 1945.

Now that the people in the camp were free to move around, the men forced a passage under the wires and spread over the countryside, which had been largely deserted by its civilian population. From the houses, they brought back jars of fruit and meats sealed with wax. Morley found a Flemish Giant at a farmhouse, but just after he had taken it with the idea of giving it a chop, the farmer suddenly appeared. Being a gentleman, Morley was about to replace the big rabbit back in its hutch, when the farmer indicated that Morley could take it if he wanted to. They conversed for a short while in broken German and English. The German farmer explained that he had been a prisoner of war in the First World War and had been detained in Park Hall, Oswestry in Wales. In addition to the rabbit, Morley had also got hold of a basket, a metal tray and a tablecloth, with the intention of living in a more refined style.

On creeping back under the wires to the camp, he could hear a thumping noise to find that he had not accomplished the job of killing the rabbit. When he got into the hut he found Bruno Pichak, a Pole, feasting on his own, on a suckling pig. The Russians had captured Bruno in the early days of the war. Then on his release, he had made his way via the Mediterranean to join the Free Polish Army in the United Kingdom and married a girl from Dunfermline. During the Arnhem operation the Germans captured Bruno again.

In the first week after the liberation, Morley and his comrades were content raiding the countryside far and wide. Ration-wise they started to live a more comfortable life. But they were impatiently waiting to see what was being organised for their return to the UK. However, all they heard was that the Russians were organising some sort of celebration on May Day, the communist holiday. But not being too ardent supporters of Communism or left-wing Socialism, a lot of the PoW's said "sod it" and started drifting away from Mühlberg on their own in all sorts of direction. Morley saw Geoff Allen, Billy Mack and Reggy Freem leaving in an easterly direction towards the Polish border, but he and many others decided on a course to the Northwest.

On the way home
On one of the last days of April 1945 Morley collected his kit and any spare food and said farewell to his friends who were still in camp. That morning he crept out under the wire for the last time and set out towards Torgau where the Americans and Russians had met. This was about 25 kilometres away from Stalag IVB. Morley hoped that the Americans would be able to get him back to the United Kingdom. After five or six kilometres, he stopped on the roadside to roast some small potatoes, when he heard somebody shouting his name. He saw Fred Butchery from his hut in Mühlberg coming towards him. Fred joined Morley and together they had their potatoes. Without any hurry they dawdled along in the warming early May sun and leisurely inspected the wrecks of some aircraft near the road. They identified a Dornier 217, a Heinkel 111 and an American Thunderbolt P-47. Shortly afterwards, as they were approaching a hamlet, suddenly an enormous Russian soldier appeared, and 'invited' them by slowly waving his machine-gun, to the farmhouse in the hamlet. Fred tried to explain that they were 'Angelski' (British) and Morley wanted him to know that he was 'Welshki'. However, the Russian kept insisting. When they got in the farmyard, the man in charge of the Russian contingent, possibly a Sergeant of sorts, asked them to sit at a table in the yard, jovially and loudly greeted them as allies. The table was decked out with a nice clean tablecloth and after a short while they were regaled with a sumptuous feast, at least by their recent standards. During the meal two blindfolded Germans were escorted from one outbuilding to another. Morley gave Fred a quick look, but they had no idea about the eventual fate of these prisoners. After the meal the sergeant took them into the farmhouse buttery, got hold of

a cup and dipped it into the milk churn. Morley thought greedily "Aah, pure liquid milk at long last!" But on knocking back his ration in glorious anticipation, he found out that it was not milk at all, but Schnapps. He was rolling around as if he was drunk, causing his good friend the Red Army Sergeant to roar with laughter. After some coughing and drying the tears that ran over his cheeks, they were out in the yard once more. There they found the soldiery building a party, singing and dancing with a couple of 'Fräuleins' from the neighbourhood to music, provided by a squeezebox. Morley and Fred were invited to join the party, but after excusing themselves and shaking hands with everyone they set off to continue their journey. Some distance later, they came to a farmhouse where milking was in progress, and scrounged two mugs full of fresh, warm and real milk from the farmer. They left and continued to yet another hamlet but here encountered drunken Russian soldiers staggering about, firing their rifles into the air. In one of the farmyards there was a pump and after they had a thorough wash and scrub, the farmer offered them a bed. As the Russian N.C.O. and his troops were so paralytically drunk, they decided discretion was the better part of valour and returned to the farm where they got the fresh milk. Bedding down in the stable, Morley told Fred that this was their first night in liberty again, but Fred muttered half asleep that it was still a long way home back to England and Wales.

The next morning they woke up early and after a good wash and another cup of milk they set off once more towards Torgau. Soon a young German by the name of Alfred joined them. It started to drizzle and Alfred kept on chattering in his native German. They understood that Alfred's' mother had stayed on at their farm while his father was with the Wehrmacht in Italy. He kept on about 'Hitler nix gut' and 'Nazis nix gut' and that if the USA, Britain and Germany would combine forces, they could destroy the Russian menace. Alfred did not appear to approve of the French either. They had apparently taken over the duties of the enlisted farmers in more ways than one, because there were more Tricolores waving in the breeze in the villages than white flags of surrender. The German boy did not stop talking, although Morley and Fred had no clue any more what he was on about.

Eventually the three of them arrived at Torgau. In that small German town they came across some Americans who advised them to find a place to sleep in the now empty Wehrmacht barracks. An hour later a

South African told them there were no barracks there at all. So, they would have to look for another place to bed down.

The local bridge over the Elbe was destroyed but a temporary Bailey bridge had been erected. However they were barred from crossing it at that time because of a huge number of refugees returning eastwards. The river was not wide but fast-flowing and therefore could not be crossed by swimming either. The town itself was on the west bank of the river and from their side the silhouette looked very impressive, almost fairy-like. On the east bank a steadily growing drab crowd of displaced people was gathering. Everybody was trying to find a place to wait until the bridge opened up again for westwards traffic. Morley, Fred and Alfred scouted around a bit and actually did find the barracks the Americans had been talking about and with some relief set up camp there. On settling in to one of the many rooms, they dined on bread and cheese. Alfred moved out, as he was frightened of the Russians in the barracks. Fred and Morley appreciated the silence now that they did not have to listen to his unceasing chatting any longer. Then they set out to get together a store of food, tinned or otherwise, and other essentials such as sheets, blankets, change of underwear, delousing tablets, mirrors, plates, a stove and cooking utensils. As it was not clear when they would be able to cross the bridge they wanted to be prepared for a longer stay in the barracks. When Fred went scouting he met a French family and from them he got some pork, which they fried for tea.

The third of May there were still hordes of people crossing the river from the other side. Fred went for a walk but never returned. So Morley presumed that he had got across and forgot about this travel companion. There was a rumour that transportation had been organised back at the Mühlberg Stalag, but Morley decided to stay because he thought his chances to get westwards from here were better.

He got himself a pushbike and then moved his kit to a downstairs room. When he went for a walk, hoping for an opportunity to cross the river, he met a Yank looking for war-souvenirs, but at this stage of his travels Morley decided he was going to keep anything he had. Then he met a Ruskie who took him down into the cellar of the barracks into a long corridor and presented him with a bag of what looked like dog biscuits. Actually they turned out to be iron rations. When Morley managed to get hold of a hat box of white honey shortly after, he could have a meal. He broke the biscuits, soaked them in water and when they split open, he fried them. With a coating of honey they were delicious.

On the fourth of May he had a cup of good thick soup from other people nearby early in the day in preparation to moving out. Despite the rumours that the bridge would be opening soon, there was still a hold-up, due to the vast numbers relentlessly crossing the bridge in the opposite direction. Then a Russian battalion of hundreds of men, a few horse-drawn Samovars and one car started moving straight through the waiting crowd causing a lot of extra chaos. During the hold-up Morley met Fred Parker and Powell from his hut in Mühlberg. Fred gave him a couple of cigarettes but Morley forgot to thank him for this nice gesture. There must have been up to a thousand people waiting to cross, British, American, French, Dutch, Italians and even some Germans. After one false start, the crossing started about midday. Over the bridge there were one or two press photographers, because the Reds were taking Torgau over from the Americans. The latter were lining up for chow as the crowds from the eastern bank passed through their lines. With restrained relief Morley finally reached the west bank.

He also passed by the Americans waiting for their food but he did not get a chance to have some himself. Morley was not too worried because he was pleased to be on the other side of the river and he decided to continue walking for a while. He had lost sight of his friends again. After a few miles he felt a bit peckish and was fortunate in meeting some Russians at a crossroads who invited him to dine with them, which he gratefully accepted. The menu contained chicken, potatoes and onions, all cooked in a bucket. After the meal, he bade them farewell and carried on for a fair distance. Morley was getting impatient and wanted to get home soon.

Later in the afternoon, he met a group of Polish ex-prisoners of war in a small town, who had found shelter in an abandoned mayor's house. Together with these new friends he had a meal again. Apparently the mayor had vamoosed because the Poles discovered that 'alles weck'. Morley did not stay long, since he wanted to get as far as he could before dark.

Soon after his farewell to the Poles an American truck that was on the look-out for returning Allied prisoners of war picked him up. He was given a white bread roll, a packet of cigarettes and his very own box of matches, such luxury. He celebrated his contact with the western Allies by taking a mouthful of the bread roll, only to spit it out right away because it tasted like plastic. Morley threw the rest of the roll away; he had become so used to the taste of German black bread, that he did not like the American rolls. Then he put a cigarette in his mouth, tried to strike a match, failed and threw the box of matches away too. Eventually he scrounged a light from one of his fellow travellers. The American truck took them to the airport in Leipzig that was used as a transit and meeting point. On their way to Leipzig they passed through the town of Eilenberg, which had been pulverised in raids by the Allied air forces. Morley estimated it had must have been at least three quarters destroyed. The airport of Leipzig turned out to be overcrowded with Allied ex-prisoners of war waiting for a flight home. Therefore Morley and many other stray servicemen were moved to the city of Halle, to the former Luftwaffe camp there, some 40 kilometres to the west of Leipzig. They arrived in Halle in the small hours of the night and were fed on white bread, peanut butter, marmalade, tinned hamburgers and hot sweet tea. They made themselves as comfortable as possible in the old administration building and slept.

On the 5th of May, they were brought up to date regarding the military situation. The German surrender was expected at any moment. Morley was told that it was not known when and how he would be able to leave Halle. He started to properly organise himself; fixing up new quarters, getting deloused, gathering together some new, proper storage space for his clothes, and, from a common kitty, fresh, clean clothes. Here he met some fellow glider pilots from Stalag IVB who had left the day before him. There were George Collette, Bradbere and Joe Arthur Binns. In the afternoon they went to a movie show in a hangar, an Abbott and Costello film, but Morley did not stay to the end as he was suffering from a bit of eye-strain. A new incoming group included Jimmy Hutton, who like George Collette and his pals had left IVB on the day previous to Morley's departure.

The following day, the 6th of May, Morley had a scout around and took a look at the wrecks of aircraft in the scrap yard near the Luftwaffe camp. There were Focke Wulf 190's, Messerschmitt 109's, Stuka's, three-engined Ju-52's and Heinkel 111's. It was a good thing these things did not fly anymore, he thought. When he returned to his sleeping accommodation he found out that he had to take over the duties for the day, dishing food and cigarettes out, because the group leader was missing on this day. The food was very well cooked by a New Zealand Catering Sergeant nicknamed Kiwi. He managed to get some extra rations from the local mayor, this included Ersatz-coffee, bread, eggs, jam and saccharine tablets or powder. The coffee was okay if it was made sweet and strong enough.

By now Morley had acquired a more varied wardrobe, including one pair of German, and one pair of American socks, one pair of German underpants, a Yankee sweater and combat jacket, and a pair of British ammunition boots. Morley strolled about a bit and took a couple of walks into the local village with Joe Binns and others but saw the shops were shut. They found the villagers not too badly off, but very smarmy and not in need of any sympathy from the Glider Pilots. There were no young and healthy men around, only those unfit for military service. The youngsters persisted in asking for chocolate and 'gum chum'.

May 8th- Peace was officially declared. They heard speeches by the King and Prime Minister Churchill on the radio, but were more interested in getting home. The waiting was getting more and more frustrating. Even more than the wait for the Arnhem operation. That night however, there was continuous firing of Very lights, probably to celebrate the end of the war. Still, the uncontrolled festivities had a bit of sinister ring about them. By that time Morley had written to his mother by airmail to ask her to air his civil clothes because he was on his way home.

May 9th - Morley carried on pottering around and waiting for things that did not seem to come, like so many adrift all over Europe. One of the other PoW's tried to make a radio from bits and pieces from the aeroplane wrecks, but he couldn't get the damn thing to work.

May 10th - A large party set off to the flying area. Morley watched them leave and selected a cycle and a fairly good rucksack from the kit they had left behind. The bike was in better condition than the one had owned in Broadwell. For a second he wondered who had been using it while he was away. However a large section of that party returned again as their places had been taken by some French and Indian liberated

PoW's who had been flown to France instead. Luckily, Morley did not have to give his new belongings back. Obviously the former owners had managed to get away. Tea-time arrived and they were told that they were due to go the following morning at 8.30 a.m.

May 11th - At half past eight Morley heard that departure had been postponed again. His group was asked to supply cooks and cookhouse fatigues. A few hours later he was informed that his party could leave that day after all. So, Morley said goodbye to his bike and went to the runway where the Dakota transport planes were already waiting. Morley was flown to Epinal in France. From there, they travelled by passenger train to Le Havre and his hopes that everything would go smoothly now were rising.

Nevertheless, the journey still took two days partly because the train apparently got lost in Paris, as they passed the Eiffel Tower twice and Morley was pretty sure they only had one. At long last they arrived in Le Havre on the French coast where they were given a high standard meal, provided by the U.S. Catering Corps.

There Morley met someone from RAF station Broadwell, his base. This man turned out to know Bob Griffiths, a RAF-Navigator and a friend of Morley. It offered Morley a chance to send a message to his mother to let her know that he was working his way back home. Without any further delay they were flown to Horsham in West Sussex, Great Britain. On disembarking Morley got on his knees and kissed the ground, so pleased was he to be home again. After a short while, he was moved to Aldershot where the Airborne forces were encamped. Here he was given a final and effective de-lousing and new kit. In his 'General Questionnaire for US/British ex-Prisoners of War' Morley wrote "*Bad living conditions in Stalag 12A, overcrowded tents and barrack huts, bad and unsatisfactory food, sanitation practically non-existent, no apparent arrangements by Russian for release of Allied PoW's at Stalag IV B.* Some days later he was sent home by train for a three-month repatriation leave.

Back home
Travelling through the green British landscape after all those long months in Germany felt strange and familiar at the same time. And when the hills and mountains of his own Wales, crowned with white clouds, appeared

on the horizon, he quickly lit a cigarette and inhaled as deep as he could. He could hardly control his impatience to see his family and home again. The train arrived at Wrexham Station and Morley suddenly got the feeling that everybody was watching him. Actually, hardly anyone in the bustling station paid attention to the fairly thin soldier in a rather new and spotless uniform. There were so many about. Morley flung his bag over his shoulder and walked home. His mother, who had been on the lookout for some days already, was standing at the front door. He saw a glimpse of relief in her eyes for having him safe and sound back home. However, she only said that he looked very thin. His brother was not at home because he was still in Transjordan with the R.A.M.C. (the medical troops). That same night they wrote him a letter to tell him about Morley's safe return. For the first few nights, Morley had to sleep on the sofa because his aunt and her daughter were staying with his mother. His uncle, who was a vicar, had recently died and therefore his family had to leave the vicarage. After some time they found a house for themselves and Morley was able to sleep in his own bed again. His mother explained that the wife of another glider pilot by the name of Bill Bailey, had been visiting her over the past months. Morley explained that Bill and he had become friends during their glider pilot training. A sister of Sergeant Reg Bruce, who died at Arnhem, had also been to see her. Bruce, like Morley, had been assigned to the Squadron Headquarters. One day after coming home Morley went into town to his cousin Gaynor's chemists and weighed himself. The scale indicated he was just eight stone (50.8 kg) and that was twenty days after he had started stuffing himself. When he left the chemist's and continued his walk, he, as if by magic and in no time at all, found himself in the company of six or seven former prisoners from Stalag IVB, who spontaneously started a reunion of sorts. Morley's mother had a lot of farming relatives in the neighbourhood and thanks to their good old home cooking, he steadily got back to his normal weight. Some weeks later Morley received an invitation from the Mayor of Wrexham to take part in an official reception in honour for the prisoners of war who had returned home. His mother, a total abstainer, accompanied him. When he accepted the glass of beer offered as a toast by the town council, she did not say anything, but Morley knew that she must have been shocked. He smiled in silence.

In that summer of 1945, Morley spent a lot of time outside in the country. He went for long walks and visited all the old well-known places. He also visited the 74-meter high waterfall in Pistyll Rhaeadr in the Berwyn Mountains and stood there for a long time, staring at the endless stream of wildly tumbling water. When he was small, he used to go there on his school holidays while staying with his dad's father who lived in that area. Little Morley was accompanied by another 23 cousins at those gatherings.

But the summer months of the repatriation leave passed by all too quickly and in the beginning of September 1945 he had to report for duty again to the Glider Pilot Regiment. He found himself in a mixture of former prisoners of war and very green recruits. As a veteran he was treated with respect, even by his instructors. He had put on weight considerably, due to the good old Welsh home cooking and weighed in at thirteen stone (82.5 kg). He needed the harsh military training to bring him back to his normal weight of 11 stone (about 70 kg). In the first months Morley picked up his flying lessons on the Tiger Moths again, which were followed by a few weeks' training on Hotspur gliders. However, before he was able to take the conversion course onto the Horsa's he was told that he would be demobilised at the end of the year. Japan had surrendered in August and the British armed forces were returning to peacetime strength.

After his demobilisation early 1946, 29-year old Morley did not really know what he wanted to do. In Mühlberg he had been so busy with daily survival that he hadn't thought much about a new future profession only that he did not want to go back being a civil servant at the Public Telephone Company. As a temporary solution he decided to work as a gardener, because he longed to be outdoors as much as he could.

In 1946 while still on Demobilisation leave, his name was drawn out of a hat and he was asked to be present at the first reunion at Arnhem in the Netherlands. He still had his uniform and he joined a group of Glider Pilots that formed the guard of honour at the rebuilt bridge when Dutch queen Wilhelmina, in the presence of Airborne commander General Urquhart, officially reopened the bridge. These days were very special, full of memories and stories. During the ceremony, Morley wondered what had happened to the passengers of his glider. Where would his first pilot Blackie be and what would the others be doing? Who had returned from Arnhem and Oosterbeek and who hadn't? After the ceremony, Morley had a good look around but he did not spot anybody he had flown to Wolfheze with. When he returned to Wrexham, he packed away his uniform. He would not need it anymore. Back home he did find out that the Dakota pilot who they had seen crashing on the 19th of September 1944 actually was awarded the Victoria Cross and he learned who the pilot was. It was David Lord, who had been apprenticed as a chemist with Morley's brother and had been to their home in Wrexham, where he had met him. He also discovered in a bookshop a book with the whole production of wall newspapers of the motoring club from Stalag IVB. The producers of this wall newspaper, once released, managed to get their publications back and had it published in a book under the title Flywheel by Webb and Bower. He bought a copy and marvelled again at the quality of the illustrations, considering the primitive conditions under which the original was produced. In the following years Morley gradually lost touch with the Regimental Association. Every now and then he still visited some army reunions, but that was it.

Back to work
Building up a civil existence forced the events of the war slowly to the background. While Morley was working as a gardener, he found out that Group Captain Leonard Cheshire, the multiply decorated war hero, had set up a kibbutz-like residence in England. The 'Vade in Pacem' group ('Go in peace') offered demobilised soldiers and their families help in their transition from military life to their renewed civil existence.

"The idea was for 'a classless colony in which training, prosperity and fulfilment would result from united effort and mutual support'. It was a quite rigidly structured community. It was an 'ardent democracy with a military tinge', quite rigidly structured", explained Jill Roberts, Archivist of the Leonard Cheshire Foundation in 2003.

War hero Cheshire was the best known Bomber Command pilot in Britain. He survived more than 100 flights over Germany and was the youngest Group Captain in the Royal Air Force. During the war he had specialised in marking targets from low altitudes, mostly in a Mosquito fighter-bomber. To do that he had to fly at a very low and dangerous 200 feet above the ground. He reached a much greater precision at target marking than was possible from higher altitudes. In 1945, he had been an observer for the British government in the nuclear air raid on Nagasaki. Possibly, these war experiences made Cheshire develop an idealism in which aid to his fellow men was paramount. Morley sent him a letter and became a member of the community in Le Court in Hampshire. The residence community wanted to be as self–supporting as possible and therefore grew its own vegetables. There were even some sheep and chickens on the large, but slightly run down estate.

The house of the Cheshire colony in le Court, Hampshire in 1947. Morley Williams' Room was near the bay window on the far right. Photo Leonard Cheshire Archive)

Morley enjoyed his life at the community residence during the first two years, but then the group ran into financial problems. 'Chesh' was not there due to an illness which made him spend time in a health resort. He even left temporarily for Canada for further recovery. During his absence, Morley left the community because of an argument over money. The members of the group wanted to borrow money from a young man who suffered mental problems and therefore was not able to take a good decision. Morley considered this unfairly taking advantage of the man and resigned from the community.

He then took a job as a workman at a landscape gardening company in the area of Windsor, because he still was happiest when he could be out in the open countryside. After six months he decided that there was no future in this business and registered himself with the Labour

Exchange, the employment agency. In 1948, he happened to pass Le Court again where the Vade in Pacem community used to be. The large mansion now seemed abandoned. He hesitatingly pushed open the monumental front door and walked into the hall and the silent corridor. Then a door opened and to his surprise there stood Chesh himself, who greeted Morley by asking where on earth he had been all that time: "We have been looking for you everywhere, Morley!"

Then Morley heard that Arthur Dykes, one of the older members of the former community, was incurably ill and had asked Chesh for help. Chesh, who had recovered, decided to take Arthur to Le Court, his own house, to look after him. Arthur had been asking often for Morley, so Morley decided to move in the large residence for six to eight weeks and help with the nursing. Chesh's return to Le Court turned out to be the beginning of Cheshire homes, a welfare organisation taking care of people with a handicap. Over the years the organisation opened fifty residences in different countries all over the world. Chesh offered Morley a job in the project, but Morley did not consider a future in nursing and shortly after the death of their friend Arthur, he left Le Court again. However, he always kept in touch with Chesh. Soon after he found a job as a temporary civil servant in Chelsea. From time to time he met another glider pilot there and so he heard of a reunion. He went to the reunion and met Major Murray, his old commander of the F- Squadron. Morley told him what happened to him after he had gone forward with the Major's order to redeploy. The Major shook his hand and complimented him on his vigorous behaviour at the time. When Morley finished his job in Chelsea, he found employment at the Ordnance Survey, the public map making department. He received his training on the job and was often stationed in the Midlands, North Wales and Cheshire.

Morley continued living in Wrexham where he looked after his aging mother, although it was not easy to combine. So he changed to the Board of Inland Revenue Income Tax Office. This required him to pass a difficult entrance examination which he did successfully. During the next ten years Morley worked as a tax civil servant. Then, after his mother's death, his desire to be back in the open air got the better of him again. He was tired of bureaucracy and inquisitive bosses and applied for a job at the Ordnance Survey once more and remained there for the rest of his working life. He became a cartographic draughtsman (map-maker) at the scales of 1/1250 and 1/2500. When he was stationed in Merseyside, surveying near a school, he met his good friend and fellow Glider Pilot Bill Bailey again. Bill was a science teacher at a college in Liverpool. During the following years they kept in touch regularly. Daughter Jan Cooper remembered:

"At the Battle of Arnhem, Morley was taken prisoner but my Dad escaped through the woods down to the Rhine where he was wounded. Luckily, he returned to England and, after being in hospital, returned to his unit. At the camp, he used to ride Morley's old bike around the base. Apparently it was very old and rickety but at least it was better than walking. Dad was sent home to Liverpool on leave and he and my Mum went to visit Morley's elderly mother in Wrexham because he was still a prisoner.

The first time Morley and Dad met up again after the war was an amazing coincidence. Mum, Dad and my elder sister Carole were on holiday in North Wales when they literally bumped into Morley, his mum and his auntie. Neither of them could believe their luck in meeting up again in such a way and they remained close friends.

Morley had returned to work as a surveyor and would visit us in Liverpool. We never had any warning; he would just turn up and always received a warm welcome. Carole and I loved to see 'Uncle Morley' and he would show us card tricks, do sketches and taught us how to play Solitaire.

He lived in a bungalow in Ruthin, in North Wales. There he had an Alsatian dog who, he claimed, would do the weeding for him by scratching up the weeds with her claws. He also kept bees and would bring us jars of home-made honey. Mum can remember him giving her a cutting from a broom tree in his garden which grew into a beautiful tree covered in yellow flowers. Morley also came to us here in Gamlingay and came to help us celebrate my parents' 50th wedding anniversary in 1993.

When they were together in Oosterbeek my dad or mum would send him upstairs for a clean shirt or send him to the hairdresser for an urgently needed haircut, so their hostess Doedie told me. There were only very few people that he would listen to. After my dad died in 1996, Morley phoned mum very regularly to see how she was and told that he would 'keep an eye on her'! And she would watch over him a little."

To this, former Ordnance Survey colleague Peter Bingham and friend added in 2017:

> When I worked at the Ordnance Survey many of my colleagues were ex-servicemen. Which was not very strange as it originated as a military organisation. Several even from the same Regiment as Morley's. So, when I saw the book Arnhem on the Horizon on Glider Pilot Johnny Wetherall's experiences at the Battle of Arnhem, it naturally attracted my attention. In it, he of course, mentioned many of his fellow Glider Pilots.
>
> It was only as I progressed through the book that I realised that I knew one of them personally. This fellow Glider Pilot, nicknamed 'Taffy' was in fact 'my' Bill Williams. I had closely worked with him in the late sixties. I then discovered Bill's book No Return Flight which I've found a pleasure to read. Here he uses the name Morley instead of Bill. And I would be happy to add a little more on this remarkable friend.
>
> I met Bill when he was posted to the small town of Market Drayton around 1968/69 to revise the 1/2500 scale, severely outdated maps. Our office covered an area of approximately 100 square kilometres of rural farms and small hamlets. It was situated in a bungalow in the back garden of a house on a quiet road in the middle of the town. The team consisted of a Team Leader and three to four surveyors.
>
> Both Bill and I had been posted here to carry out the revision and survey of the rural countryside around this small market town. Bill lodged at a small village about six miles away in a Public house called the Bull, which kept a menagerie of animals and birds in the field behind the pub. This fitted well into Bill's character of liquid refreshment and something of the unusual in accommodation.
>
> Bill did talk of his wartime activities at times and especially of his capture, in a slight variance on the published. He did say that as the second German soldier came and kept staring at him, Bill eventually could not keep his face straight and burst out smiling which was luckily taken in the same way by the capturing soldier.

In the Ordnance Survey in those days the starting time each day was strictly adhered to. All surveyors had to sign in in a book on their arrival. Once 08.00 AM had been reached, a red line was drawn under the last name. Anyone arriving later was deemed as being late and was warned about late timekeeping. On one occasion we were visited by a manager who was at least four grades higher than ourselves. This was a morning that Bill, typically, overslept and arrived for work two hours late. We all wondered what was going to happen. Remember these were the 1960's and discipline was still rather strict. We thought that Bill was going to be in real trouble. The few minutes after Bill's arrival were a bit tense and stony-faced until after a little while the conversation came around to where people had served in the war. It transpired that the manager had been an RAF pilot and with Bill's flying and war time experience, the little matter of lateness was soon completely forgotten.

Another wartime instance remembered by Bill was that he kept getting into trouble whilst training. To earn his wings he needed to master such aircraft as the Tiger Moth. Unfortunately though, Bill kept landing on airfields that had been installed with arrester wires for aircraft landing practice. Bill kept forgetting this and on more than one occasion ripped the tail skid off his plane.

Typical of Bill, when I was just married in 1968 he gave my wife and I spare household items as we were just starting out on married life. An old push mowing machine, pans, cups, saucers, plates, some of which we still have in our cupboard nearly fifty years later.

Bill left Market Drayton for the wilds of Wales but I kept meeting him at various Ordnance Survey meetings. At one time I believe he lived in a corrugated tin house, part way up a mountain in a very remote part of Wales.

The last time I heard of Bill was following the lead from the reconstructed Horsa glider. Through some colleagues I tracked him down to an old people's complex just outside Oswestry, a town a little larger than Market Drayton on the Welsh borders. Eventually I managed to speak with the trained person who looks after these types of complexes which allows older people to live independently but have someone watching over them. The lady I spoke to said that Bill had definitely been living there for a while but unfortunately had been asked to leave because he was unsettling the older ladies. She would not go further in detail, but I just thought that would be Bill, always having fun.

Peter Bingham

Enjoying these stories about Morley, I passed them on to Morley's godson Tim Rogers. He replied enthusiastically:

Dear Haks,
Thank you so much for this fascinating account. That's the Morley I remember. The 'corrugated tin house' he lived in was called, 'Y Caban' or 'Caban' alongside a country lane outside the village of Llanelidan near Ruthin. I visited him there when I was a boy. To me, at that time, it seemed a fab place to live. Like a 'den' for grown-ups. He had a beautiful German shepherd dog that he adored, and she adored him. She was called Carla. He would say, "This is a very clever dog. She speaks Deutsch!"
  "Really?"
  "Yes. Watch this. "Carla, Lizenzee down!"
  And of course she did lie down which I thought was marvellous. He adored that dog so much that he had her likeness painted by an artist on silk. I wonder what happened to the picture.
  Morley could do all sorts of tricks that were guaranteed to amuse a small boy. The sort that Tom Sawyer would have been proud of. In fact that's who Morley was to me. A sort of grown up Tom Sawyer. My parents loved him - as did so many of his friends - because he was a lovely man but incorrigible. Hopelessly untidy. His home - wherever it was - always smelled of stale socks and cigarettes. But he lived as he wanted to live. A bachelor to the end.
  I remember at the 'Caban' (which as you can probably guess is Welsh for 'Cabin') that he showed me how to avoid washing up mugs or cups because he would make a new one out of an old tin can. He would cut the can in half - around the middle - bend over the edge to make it safe. And voila! A new mug. I think it was a trick he had probably learned in the PoW camp when they had to make do with whatever they had. But he didn't tell young Tim that. In fact he never talked about his war experiences to me or my family. I think my father probably had some

idea. Dad was in the RAF Aircrew. He was a Sergeant - gunner and wireless operator. Flying in Coastal Command initially, then Beaufort Bombers in North Africa. He was lucky to survive as most of the men who signed up alongside him at the beginning of the war did not.

Tim Rogers

In these ways and every now and then Arnhem kept coming back to Morley. Even on television, through a documentary called *Jane's War* in which he recognised the story of the English woman who in the last days of the war, was brought to the Mühlberg Stalag to save her from the advancing Red Army soldiers. In one of these wild coincidences of war it was the same Stalag where her son, a captured RAF pilot, was held.

Morley retired form work in January 1977. He moved to the town of Oswestry in Wales, approximately twenty kilometres southwest of Wrexham. He enjoyed gardening and beekeeping and devoted a lot of time and attention to painting with pen, ink and watercolour. When he was settling in Oswestry, he suddenly remembered the story of the German farmer whose rabbit he had wanted to take, thirty-two years ago. The man told him at that time that during the First World War he had been kept in a British prisoner of war camp in Oswestry. A mere two kilometres from his new house, Morley realised.

One day, while visiting Bill Bailey, Morley learned that a Glider Pilot Association had been founded where veteran Glider Pilots came together. The British Army had stopped using gliders in 1957 and Morley's former unit had amalgamated with other units to become the Army Air Corps. It was just before 1984, the year in which the fortieth commemoration of the Battle of Arnhem got a lot of attention. Morley and Bill Bailey both decided to become a member of the Glider Pilot Association and to go visit their former battle grounds.

When he went to Oosterbeek in 1984, Morley enjoyed meeting a number of his fellow Glider Pilots there. It was the first time that he was back in the Netherlands. In a long-standing tradition, many of the veterans stay with the inhabitants of Oosterbeek. Through the help of the organisation 'Lest We Forget', Morley was accommodated at Mrs. Doedie Minderman's house, together with Anne and Bill Bailey.

Mrs. Minderman said: "When they arrived, Bill Bailey was very upset, clutching his handkerchief. Later I discovered that he had been one of the soldiers who had passed in front of my house, guided by the white ribbon as they retreated towards and over the Rhine. It was a coincidence that he was staying here, just where he had had such terrible experiences."

She, as a 16 year old, had been living in Oosterbeek during the battle. Her house had burned down and she and her family had to take refuge in cellars and to pass through the front line on their way to the west to safety. Connected by their mutual experiences, Mrs. Minderman and her airborne guests got on so well that they reunited again at her place every year, thus building a pleasant friendship together.

Getting off the bus on a trip to the former battle zones in Oosterbeek, Morley suddenly saw one of the other passengers looking at him, grinning in mischievous recognition and making gestures as if he were cutting somebody's hair. Morley was pleasantly surprised when he recognised Geoff Higgins as the mime artist. Geoff was one of the victims of his amateur hairdresser's career in the Mühlberg Stalag. To Morley's relief he saw that Geoff's hair had not suffered permanent damage from his experimental haircuts.

Back home in Oswestry, Morley began to commit his revived memories of the Battle of Arnhem to paper. It was a report that eventually turned into eight densely typed sheets of paper. He never imagined that it would one day grow into a book, many years later.

'Blackie'

At one of his first meetings of the Glider Pilots in England, Morley met his first pilot, Squadron Sergeant Major Ian 'Blackie' Blackwood. Morley immediately recognised him as he walked into the room. Morley felt that the former Sergeant Major had not changed at all, but he seemed to be slightly limping. Blackie did not see Morley at first, because he was standing with his back to the door, talking to someone else. Morley walked up to him, tapped him on the shoulder and asked casually: "What actually did happen to B For Boozer Two?" He knew that 'B For Boozer One' was the code name of the glider which Blackie had flown to Sicily in 1943. Blackie turned around in disbelief, saw Morley, his former second pilot at the Operation Arnhem and exclaimed: "Morley!! How wonderful to see you again!" He warmly shook Morley's hand and introduced him to his wife Nancy. Morley knew that Blackie had got married in the beginning of 1944, but he had never met Blackie's wife before. After excusing himself politely to the other veteran, Blackie and Morley started a lively conversation about what had happened to them during all those years. Blackie still remembered that Wednesday 20 September of 1944 very well:

> *"After you were sent forward by our Major with a message for our forward section, we saw that they were overrun and our position turned into a dangerous chaos. Therefore we were ordered to withdraw to our Headquarters in Hotel Hartenstein. First we crossed the Stationsweg in a western direction and after that we went south towards the Hartenstein area. The Germans eliminated a lot of our lads, among them you. We did not know how many were killed or captured. Luckily, several were able to join us again later. It turned out that our F Squadron had suffered heavy casualties. The next day we received orders to go to the Oranjeweg and entrench ourselves at the North West Side of the area defended by our remaining troops. We stayed there until the evacuation but there as well we had a hard time."*

Morley found out that of the six man-strong Squadron Headquarters Captain Thomas Plowman, Lieutenant Stanley Culverwell and Sergeant Reg Bruce had perished. "Half the group", he said and Blackie nodded in silence.

Blackie continued his story and said that a bullet, which went straight through his left thighbone, hit him on Sunday 24 September. On a stretcher on the bonnet of a jeep, he was taken to a first aid post. Blackie was adamant that he was helped by a Medical Officer with an RAVC-insignia on his sleeve, although he found it difficult to believe that a veterinary surgeon would have come along in an airborne operation.

Squadron Sergeant-Major Ian 'Blackie' Blackwood, First Pilot of Horsa 166

After having waited on his stretcher for several agonising days without much further medical aid, he was eventually transported by ambulance to Apeldoorn. There he was operated on by a German surgeon in the local hospital. Blackie explained that he got only a couple of days to recover and that already on 9 October he arrived at the Stalag XIB Pow camp in Fallingbostel (near Hannover, Germany). His injury confined him to sick bay until Christmas 1944. His leg healed slowly because there was a lack of everything and therefore he was in a lot of pain. At Christmas he was finally declared healthy and got discharged from the hospital barracks. He was then brought to the adjacent Stalag 357. The Stalag was terribly overcrowded and the already poor food supply got worse and worse. Blackie and his comrades developed the habit of saving their ration of treacle for Sundays. On one of these Sundays they found to their dismay a dead mouse in their treacle tin. It probably had, driven by hunger, fallen in somewhere in the past week and got the worst of it. It turned out to be really hard to scrape the treacle off of the dead animal and put it back in the tin in order to be able to start their Sunday feast after all.

Liberation arrived for Blackie on 16 April 1945. He was then 28 years old. He returned by plane to an air field near High Wycombe. There he had to report his experiences by word of mouth and he was sent on repatriation leave. After some time he had to appear before a commission in charge of the administration of the prisoners of war. As a result of his leg injury Blackie was declared medically unfit and rejected for further service in the Glider Pilot Regiment. Nearly a year after he was wounded, Blackie was dismissed from service on 21 September 1945. Looking back, he missed the companionship enormously and kept an interest in news of his regiment and the fate of so many of his comrades, as he had already been in the Territorial Army since the Thirties. He went back to work in one of the banks in the City of London. In the job that he had left six years before. He devoted much attention to his young family. Blackie told Morley that he had a son at Christmas 1944. With a mixture of pride, pain and pity he recalled that at that very moment he had been so far away in captivity. In the following years, Blackie and his wife Nancy whom he met in 1942 as WAAF (Women's Auxiliary Air Force) on the Netheravon air base, had a daughter and another son.

Initially Blackie received a small disability pension until the Department of Pensions informed him on 10 September 1946 that his allowance had been raised by a payment 'belonging to the granting of your Military Medal'. He was rather surprised by this information, as he had never heard anything about a decoration in the two years that had past since Arnhem. On his request for clarification, the Ministry reacted with a rather formal reference to the London Gazette of December 1945 in which was officially announced that Squadron Sergeant Major Ian Blackwood was decorated with the Military Medal. He received the decoration rather unceremoniously by mail. Blackie felt that at least his own Regiment should have told him what he got the decoration for, although he suspected that they were also in the dark about it. He didn't learn much more from a further verbal inquiry at the War Department either. He only was told that only the higher decorations were entitled for personal and individual citation. That did not help much to communicate the appreciation of the Empire that usually is symbolised by the awarding of military decorations. Thus Blackie walked around with a military decoration for some remarkable action during the Battle of Arnhem without exactly knowing what it was that had earned him the medal. It was only after 36 years in 1982 when Blackie set eyes upon the text in which he was mentioned in dispatches. He read:

This Warrant Officer has been a member of the (Glider Pilot) Regiment for over 3 years and as a Squadron Sergeant Major has shown excellent organizing ability. He took part in the invasion of Sicily and piloted a glider to Arnhem. Throughout the Battle of Arnhem he displayed exemplary bravery, devotion to duty and disregard for his own safety. During every enemy attack Squadron Sergeant Major Blackwood was to be seen cheering on his men, and his personality and contempt for danger was mainly responsible for his section remaining intact. He was wounded in the face and hands but refused to leave his squadron and was wounded a third time and taken prisoner. He has now been repatriated."

Blackie was proud to be mentioned although he considered it a tribute to his fellow pilots as well, as they stood firm with him. The memory of having been with this selected group of independent and versatile spirits was his real reward, better than his medal.

An unannounced letter
Every year since 1984 he stayed with Mrs Doedie Minderman in Oosterbeek. Her parental house was one of the first to be destroyed. Her older brother and sister helped the British Medical Troops with the care for the many wounded British, Germans and civilians who were accommodated in hotel restaurant Schoonoord in the centre of Oosterbeek. The hotel had been used as a Red Cross Hospital during the battle. Doedie's brother and

sister were taken away as prisoners of war to Apeldoorn, but they managed to escape. After the withdrawal of the British troops, Doedie, like everyone else in Oosterbeek and Arnhem, was ordered by the Germans to evacuate the area. She spent the last months of the war with her family as evacuees in Bilthoven which lies some 60 km to the northwest of Oosterbeek.

Over the years a more or less steady group was formed of Glider Pilots, their family and people from Oosterbeek. Occasionally, they visited each other in England as well. Morley met Blackie regularly at the meetings of the Glider Pilot Association, but was not able to persuade him to return to Arnhem. It was at the end of February 1998, when, out of the blue and quite unannounced, a letter from an unknown Dutch journalist dropped onto the doormat in Morley's home in Oswestry. With growing stupefaction Morley started to read it.

Dear Mr. Williams,

Some time ago you handed a report of your experiences during and after the Battle of Arnhem to the Airborne Museum Hartenstein in Oosterbeek. This lively and fascinating account would be a fitting contribution to the exposition that the Airborne Museum intends to organise on the fate of the British prisoners of war of the battle. The exposition 'Liberators behind barbed wire' would open in April 1998 and run until November of the same year.

Part of the exposition would be a special magazine that in a number of short articles is to give an impression of what happened to them. We have used your account to write such an article which is included in this letter. We would like your permission to publish it. We would also kindly request you to read our article to see if it is factually correct. Should you have a contemporary photograph of yourself we would like to publish that along with the article. Of course we would return that photograph immediately after use. The magazine would appear both in Dutch and in English.

With respect and friendly regards,

Haks Walburgh Schmidt
Editor of the Exposition Magazine

Morley lit another cigarette and wondered how the Airborne Museum got his report. He was certain that he himself had never left it there. The only thing he could figure was that one of the versions he had shown to his Dutch friends eventually must have ended up in the museum archives. Obviously they now wanted to use it for some sort of magazine for an exposition.

He wondered what the museum people could use from his story, but he also felt strongly that younger generations should know what it was like to be captured in a Nazi German camp for prisoners of war, so he decided to co-operate. Morley stubbed out his cigarette and started to read the article carefully. In the next few days he began looking for the photograph of 1943, which showed him with Corporal stripes. When he found it he sent it together with his corrections to the mentioned address. While he was walking back from the postbox he was curious to know what would happen next. Would there really be a magazine with his story in it?

In the meantime in the Netherlands I, the journalist who decided to approach the Arnhem-veteran, tried to weigh the chances that this Mr Williams would meet my request. When would he receive the letter; what would he think of it and, most importantly, would he answer it? How long did it take a letter to get from the Netherlands to Wales anyway?

Less than two weeks later I found his answer on my doormat, hiding between the leaflets for saucepans and other household utensils of any normal weekday. I sat down, had a coffee and started to read the letter. Mr. Williams replied that he had read the article and to my pleasure I found him satisfied with it but for some small details. His authentic story, together with the enclosed photograph was a valuable contribution to the exposition. The magazine was nearing completion and in mid-April the English (5000 copies) and Dutch (15.000 copies) edition of the magazine were printed at the Arnhemse Courant. I of course sent Mr. Williams the English copy I had promised him.

The exposition was a success, the magazine was greeted with interest and everyone concerned was pleased with the result. Truly a reason to relax and look back at my feat with satisfaction and go back to the saucepans and leaflets of every day.

But after the fuss of the official opening of the exposition, I read

Mr. Williams' Stalag Days notes once more and that was when it dawned on me that there were still many things that were in need of further clarification. I found it fascinating to hear first-hand what had happened to someone who had really been there. I for example hoped he would be able to tell me more about what it was like to fly into battle, about the days before he was captured and many other subjects which he had not yet mentioned, but that still would be interesting to put to paper. Would he remember who he flew to the battlefield and what happened to these people? Would he have met any of them after the war?

On the other hand, it was quite possible that he was fed up with all this questioning fifty years after the events, so maybe I should not bother him. As time went by I kept turning the matter over in my mind. For months.

Then in September 1998 the annual commemorations of the Battle of Arnhem arrived again. I finally cut my Gordian knot and decided simply to go to Oosterbeek in the hope to meet Williams. Perhaps seeing him in person might break my deadlock. I expected that it wouldn't be necessary to make an appointment, but this proved to be a big mistake. Many people from the Oosterbeek area and countless visitors from outside the region and even abroad participated in the commemorations. At the Airborne Museum they were only able to tell me that Mr Williams had already visited the exhibition a few days before and that he was full of praise over it. Disappointed about my shy and unsuccessful visit I slunk off home. I would have to write to Mr Williams in order to find out more. Remarkably enough, this unsuccessful meeting seemed to be exactly the push I needed to finally write him a letter in November 1998. I apologised for having missed him in September and I explained that I was curious to find out if he had had any reactions on the article. At the same time I told him about the many questions that had come to my mind and that I hadn't been able to put those out of my head ever since. I also mentioned my hesitations to bother him with these questions.

Williams received my letter on 11 November, Armistice Day, when the British commemorate their victims of both World Wars. To my surprise he answered very quickly. He had absolutely no objections to discuss my questions. He even encouraged me not to be shy.

This then, was how my correspondence with Morley Williams started and each letter he told me just a little bit more about his time at the Glider Pilot Regiment. He described how he used to dream about being a pilot when he was only a boy. And how he had to struggle after the war, just like so many other survivors of the Second World War, to build a civil life again.

In September 1999 he came to the Netherlands once more for the annual commemorations and this time we agreed on meeting each other at Mrs Minderman's house in Oosterbeek. I arrived perfectly on time at the given address, but I had to wait a little for Mr Williams, because he had just left for an afternoon stroll. After about a quarter of an hour, I heard the front door open and an elderly, fairly short man entered the house in Oosterbeek. Slightly bent and with a walking stick, but with a firm step and a red beret with the regimental emblem elegantly on his head. Mr. Williams was pleasantly surprised to see me and I found in him an extraordinary modest and friendly man with an almost timid but keen sense of humour. Although somewhat hard of hearing, he was still very interested in the world around him and full of stories about the past. He turned out to be a painter and draughtsman (and not without merit) and he knew a lot about beekeeping and gardening. He was not war-minded at all. However, he was still a heavy smoker. "Filthy habit," he would say, only to light a new cigarette straight away. Many of his comrades who also visited the Netherlands every year called him 'Taffy', because of his Welsh origin. He invited me to call him Taffy as well which in conversation I did. Mrs. Minderman, his Dutch hostess, joined us and soon the conversation flowed and was very entertaining. I told them that my interest in the Battle of Arnhem dated back to the seventies when I was 15 years old and had just read Cornelius Ryan's book 'A Bridge Too Far'. Then, I felt fascinated that world history could come so close. Some 15 years later I had to visit Oosterbeek for my work and afterwards, acting on impulse, I walked into the nearby Airborne Museum.

This visit rekindled my interest in these historic events and resulted in my participation in the organisation of the exhibition ' Liberators behind barbed wire' in 1998.

September 2002: Morley Williams on Landing Zone 'S', the spot where he landed Horsa 166 on 18 September 1944. (Photo Tim Rogers)

I asked Morley if he still remembered the airborne infantry unit he flew to Arnhem. He thought that it was a platoon of the Dorset Regiment. Although he felt a strong bond with them, he explained that he had only seen them during the three-hour flight to The Netherlands. Still, the thought of what might have become of them had stayed on his mind all these years. He knew all too well that a search for answers to their fate would be quite complicated. He told me that he had often been on the verge of beginning to look for them himself, but as he had no clues, he had never managed to make any progress. Could I, as a journalist, possibly find out who were in his glider to Arnhem? Well, if it was not too difficult and time-consuming, of course. Fascinated by Morley's striking eyewitness accounts, I promised him that I would give it a try. And when I said goodbye, about an hour later, Mrs. Minderman accompanied me to the door and whispered: 'You would do my old friend an enormous favour if you could look into it, but just see what you can do. If you do not succeed, it would just be bad luck and we'll just have to live with it. But please, do give it a try.'

Part 2

The Search

Driving home again I wondered what on earth I had got myself into. How was I to find out what had happened to some 23 British Arnhem veterans, more than half a century after the events? While having to do my research from my own country, the Netherlands. If they had been in their twenties, just like Morley, they would now be well over seventy or even in their eighties. And how many of them would still be alive after all these years? How could I possibly go looking for them amongst the roughly 60 million people currently living in the United Kingdom? And how likely was it that they were willing to talk about these events to a total stranger? In other words, how could I possibly live up to my promise to Morley?

First of all, I needed to get a clear picture of what I would actually like to know from them. Of course, firstly about what happened to them after they said goodbye to Morley and Blackie. Were they sent to the bridge in Arnhem or did they stay with the main force in Oosterbeek?

Secondly, I was curious to know what happened to them in the aftermath of the battle. Did they all come back across the Rhine on that dark evacuation night of 26 September? Were any of them captured, just like Morley and Blackie? Were some of them wounded or did some even become fatal casualties? It would be a challenge to

puzzle those pieces together into a coherent story. After all those years it was not likely that all the pieces could be found.

Furthermore, I hoped that they would be willing to tell me more about their lives before and after the war as well. So, we could get to know the person behind the soldier too. As if they were your neighbour, your soccer teammate or your colleague at work. With a sinking feeling I realised that those were many questions to many people indeed.

Having collected these personal stories I could present meaningful findings to Morley. I decided to first tell him about the search, the initial contacts and about the stories of the childhood days of the men he had flown into Arnhem. The experiences of his passengers during the battle would then follow quite naturally in a separate chapter. The report, I felt, could be best concluded with an impression of their lives after the war.

About mid-October 1999 I had a clear picture of what I wanted to do. The time had come to really start the search. The first thing to do was to look in the books on the Battle of Arnhem and look for the Dorset Regiment that Morley had mentioned. I would ask the Airborne Museum Hartenstein in Oosterbeek for information. Feeling optimistic and energised, I congratulated myself with my sound plan and good start.

Immediately, I was disappointed. No Dorset Regiment units whatsoever came to Arnhem by glider. The only Dorset battalions involved were part of the ground forces that were meant to relieve the airbornes at Arnhem and Oosterbeek and take over their positions. All books on Arnhem agreed on that. This meant that Morley must have been mistaken and that the first trail had come to a dead end straight away.

Undaunted, I now put my hope in the Airborne Museum Hartenstein. Mr Aad Groeneweg OBE, vice chairman of the Airborne Museum foundation, also confirmed that no Dorsets came to Arnhem by glider. But he did offer a new perspective when he said that of many of those gliders it was still known what cargo they had carried. There were enthusiasts in the Netherlands who still had these lists. If Morley remembered the chalk number of his Horsa, then it should be fairly easy to find out whom he and Blackie had flown to Arnhem.

But this door remained closed as well. After 55 years Morley had no idea anymore what that number was. Over the telephone he told me: "Those chalk numbers were scribbled on the side of the glider to know which cargo had to go to which plane. They were not very important to us. I am very sorry, but I cannot recall the number of our plane." When I told him that the lead of the Dorset Regiment had also turned up nothing, he realised there were no clues left to continue the search. "What a pity", he answered softly after a short silence. "I would have been happy to know what had become of those lads and whether some of them are still alive". After putting down the phone I could feel the disappointment behind those seemingly unemotional words. It was the end of November 1999 and the plan seemed to have come to a grinding halt already. Still, I wanted, if only for Morley's sake, to come up with at least some answers.

A New Millennium
It would take until the new millennium for a breakthrough to emerge. In June 2000 a new book about gliders was published in Arnhem, written by one of the people who studied chalk numbers and load manifests. In this book 'Tugs and Gliders', on page 108, I found the following excerpt:

> ...*Chalk number 166 with pilots Sergeant-Major Blackwood and Sergeant Williams. The cargo consisted of 28 soldiers of 13 Platoon, B-Company, 1st Battalion The Border Regiment under the command of Lieutenant Wellbelove, as well as a handcart for luggage.......*

Excited, I immediately wanted to tell Morley the good news, but then I realised that with a little extra effort I could probably tell him even more. I knew there was a book describing the history of the First Battalion of The Border Regiment during the Second World War. Now that I had discovered which platoon of this unit had been in Morley's glider, I could check if that platoon was mentioned. So with some strength I resisted the temptation to call Morley directly with my news. Instead I picked up the book 'When Dragons Flew' and leafed through it, full of electrified expectation. The deadlock seemed to be broken.

A meticulous search for 13 Platoon followed in the history of the much bigger First Battalion, The Border Regiment. On the platoon itself little could be found, but extracts on the far bigger Battalion painted a clear background. Then I made a new discovery. In one of the appendixes of the book 'When Dragons Flew', the 'Battalion Roll, Arnhem' was published. This was a list with the names of the 788 men who served in the Battalion during the Battle of Arnhem. Alongside some of these names I found their platoon numbers and the name of a town or village in Britain. I moved on the edge of my seat and looked for the entry '13 Platoon'. Going through the list line by line in alphabetical order the following names appeared:

Private Edwin Ainsworth	Blackburn, Lancashire
Private Albert Ashbridge	Workington, Cumberland
Corporal Cyril Crickett	Wigan, Lancashire
Sergeant Victor de Muynck	Edinburgh, Scotland
Private Telford Fidler	Workington, Cumberland
Private Edward Flinn	Cleator Moor, Cumberland
Private John Glenn	Collyhurst, Manchester
Private Charles Earnest Greasley	Grantham, Lincolnshire
Private Philip A. Hulse	Wallasey, Cheshire
Private Francis James 'Jim' Isles	Thornton, Lancashire
Corporal Robert John Ivison	Workington, Cumberland
Private Francis Edward Jarvis	Sunderland
Lance Sergeant John 'Jack' Kimber	North Shields, Northumberland
Private Thomas McDonald	-

Corporal David Turnbull Patterson	Ilford, Essex
Private N. Savage	-
Private Vincent Swarbrick	Preston, Lancashire
Sergeant Frederick Terry	-
Private Joseph Winstanley	St Helens, Lancashire
Lieutenant John Arthur Wellbelove	Canada

Before my very eyes abstract history transformed into real names of real people. It was as if a long closed door creaked open and a ray of light shone upon the secret that was hidden behind it. Slowly I read each name and tried to picture the man behind it. They were in their twenties, early thirties then. Maybe they had just left school or maybe they already had a job when they were drafted into military service and volunteered for the Airborne Forces. Did they have sweethearts or were some of them married or, had any already become a father? Would they have minded going to war or did they feel excited about joining up like the generation before them in the First World War? Would they remember Morley or their flight to Wolfheze? These questions tumbled over me like an avalanche and at that moment my last doubts disappeared. I would not stop to recover and write down their stories from before, during and after Arnhem. Little did I know that it would take me some 19 years to get there. And even then questions would remain unanswered. First of all, of course, for Morley, and then for younger generations and everyone who values knowing the fate of a chance collection of people in that disastrous miscalculation of the Battle of Arnhem. Also I intended to bring the people I might find into contact with each other. That is, if they would be interested, of course.

I called Morley on the phone and told him that I now had a trail and that I would report back to him as soon as I had the complete story. He was delighted and very eager to know the outcome of the search. I knew he'd be lighting a cigarette after he had put down the phone.

I tried to calculate the chance that I could find those people or their stories. It seemed to me that it would be quite an experience for Morley, after all those years, to hear what his passengers had been through at the Battle of Arnhem. I decided to collect all the details I could find and try to fit them together. By interweaving them with the extracts I found in various books about the First Battalion, The Border Regiment, I hoped to be able to send Morley as complete and structured a story as possible.

The Border Regiment, Carlisle

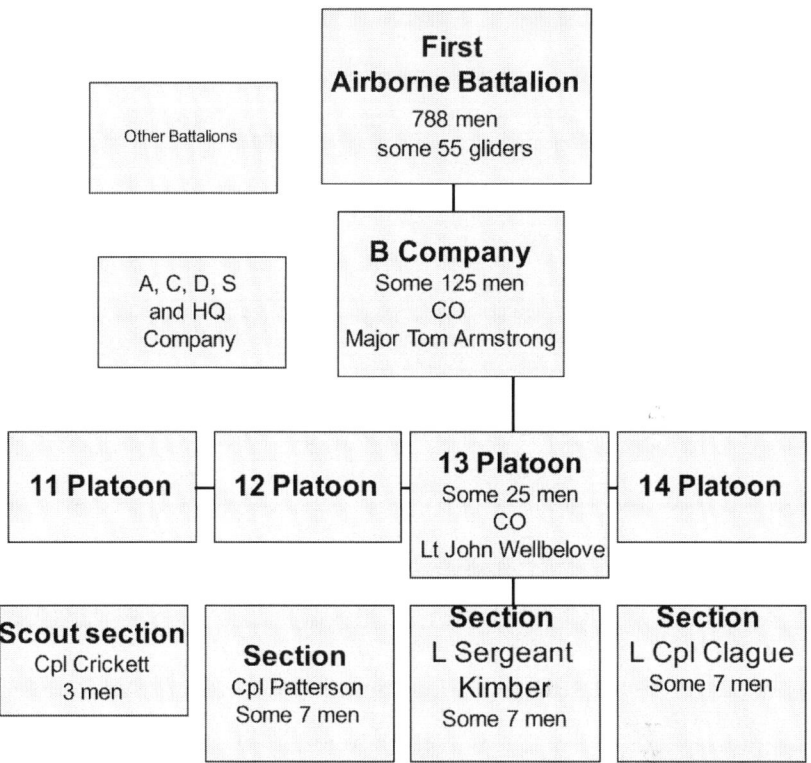

Organisation Regiment into Batalion and Platoon

But what did I have to do to reach this goal? I now had 20 names, but according to the book 'Tugs and Gliders' there should be 28, and according to Morley there should be 23. Other sources mentioned that a Horsa could carry 25 people into battle. What was the right number, were there names missing and were the names I now had, correct? What in fact was a platoon or a Border Regiment? Maybe I should start with those questions. After all, that was just a matter of looking it up.

The Border Regiment turned out to be a sort of permanent military administrative centre in the British army that brings together and trains able-bodied men of the region into fighting units in order to transfer them to the regular army. The recruits from The Border Regiment came mainly from the English counties of Cumbria and Lancashire around Carlisle. From 1873 on, the Regiment was established in the almost 1000 year old Border fortress Carlisle Castle. The Border Regiment, just like similar Regiments from other parts of Great Britain, cherished a great tradition. With its own commemorations, parades, and other ceremonies a culture was built that gave the new recruit a sense of pride as soon as he had proved himself to be a worthy member of the Regiment. In peacetime the Regiments had one or more battalions of about 800 men in the regular army.

One battalion was divided into companies of about 100 to 120 men. A company was in turn divided into platoons of about 28 men.

In august 2001 I asked the Regimental Museum in Carlisle Castle what a platoon like 13 Platoon consisted of and how it was structured during the Battle of Arnhem in 1944. The curator of the museum replied:

Dear Mr. Walburgh Schmidt,

A platoon in the First Battalion, The Border Regiment, or short 1 Border, comprised 28 all ranks. (This was exactly the number of men that could be transported in a Horsa glider). What you have to remember is that the organisation and equipment was not sorted according to absolutely rigid rules and regulations and that there was a shortage of personnel in that phase of the war. There were no surviving documents which give accurate details of what every platoon was equipped with, but I could give you a general idea.

The general arrangement seems to have been three sections of seven men commanded by a Corporal or Lance-Corporal (one step less in rank). The scout section which each platoon seems to have had was of four men commanded by a Corporal and one of the men was sniper-trained. There would be the Platoon Commander, usually a Lieutenant with his batman/runner and possibly a signaller.

In each section would also be one Bren-gunner (light machine gun) with his No.2-man who would carry spares and ammo and be equipped with a Sten gun Mk 5 or a Lee Enfield rifle. The officer and perhaps the signaller carried a .38 pistol; some officers may have had Browning 9mm pistols or even a Colt .45 (this is only general supposition). Men were trained to handle all these weapons.

We have a general list of the weapons held in the battalion and in addition to what I have mentioned above, the platoon had a PIAT (Projector, Infantry, Anti Tank weapon) carried in one of the sections. There would be another sniper rifle, and one 2 inch mortar. It would seem rifles were distributed on the basis of five rifles to two Sten Guns. The Sten gun was more for defensive purposes while the rifle was a more offensive weapon. The platoon had two hand-carts which carried a reserve of ammunition, and presumably grenades, PIAT rounds and 2 inch mortar rounds. It would also have carried things like their tents, extra rations and spare clothing. Each platoon probably also had one signaller attached from the Signal Platoon and a couple of 2-inch mortar men. From what I have been able to understand from talking to veterans, they took as much ammunition and grenades as they were able to carry, but within the weight limit for the glider (the weight of every man with equipment in a glider was calculated -for obvious reasons). You should also remember that soldiers often adapted their equipment to suit a particular personal preference. There are no 13 Platoon photographs in our archives. I would like to advise you not to expect too much from your search. Most of the veterans, although willing to help, have been interviewed at length over their experiences. Most of what they recall has been published in 'When Dragons Flew' and they do not feel that they could provide anymore information. What you also have to remember is that the Arnhem battle was only nine days out of the whole of World War Two and many of these men served for three or four years and in some case for the whole of the War. On the other hand, don't let these words discourage you. I welcome your research and would be most interested to hear about your results.

I hope that this has been of some help.

Yours sincerely

Stuart Eastwood
Curator

The curator brought valuable information, but his letter also had a sobering effect. On the positive side, many of the people I was looking for had never been interviewed before. I hoped their stories, combined with existing knowledge, would produce much new knowledge from another point of view. Taking the curator's warning to heart, I decided that if the results remained disappointing for too long, I would cancel the search.

Again, I went through 'The Battalion Roll, Arnhem', the appendix of the Battalion book 'When Dragons Flew'. I now concentrated on the towns and villages listed next to the personal names. It turned out that they showed which place the soldier came from when he entered The Border Regiment. Would it be possible that a number of those men still lived in the same place today?

Of course, these entries were more than 50 years old, but there was a chance that they were still living there or had returned there after retirement. Maybe relatives who lived in the same town could help me out. I expected that many of the counties mentioned in the list, were not very urban and had many medium-sized and smaller provincial towns, where people might tend to stay put more than in the big cities. I also realised that there were not many other options to start investigating open to me. Anyway, the books showed that 13 Platoon had never before been investigated and nothing was ever published on the adventures of a single glider. Fair enough for starters.

The next thing for me to do was to find an English telephone directory in which I could look up the places and addresses mentioned in the Battalion Roll. The fastest way to find that would probably be the internet. One would expect that sooner or later I should find something.

On one of the last warm and sunny evenings of October 2001 I took the list from the 'Battalion Roll' and set out to work. The English telephone directory was quickly found. Anxiously I typed in 'Albert Ashbridge' and the town name 'Workington' as a random first combination. It gave five addresses. The combination 'Edwin Ainsworth' and 'Blackburn' gave eight hits. When looking up Sergeant De Muynck, I accidentally saw a photograph of him in the book 'When Dragons Flew'. This told me that he was in 12 Platoon and therefore no longer part of my search. A stark reminder to remain critical about my information. Another blind spot in my search was that not every name had a platoon number in the Battalion Roll. This meant that I would possibly not recognise some names as belonging to 13 Platoon. Still, the only thing I could do was to trust my selection from 'The Battalion Roll, Arnhem.' As soon as I traced someone, he could hopefully verify my information and add to it where possible from memory. After a few evenings of searching the internet I had possible addresses from most of the mentioned 13 Platoon members. There were hundreds of them.

An English letter

Then, late November 2001 I wrote my first search letter. When looking for the name/place combinations, I found some names that had only one hit. I theorised that these could be either promising, or just as likely, be an indication that I would never find that man.

Of course, I took the optimistic view and started writing to a person that matched the description of Corporal David Turnbull Patterson in Ilford, Essex. I introduced myself as a Dutch journalist doing research on the Battle of Arnhem and specifically on the fortunes of 13 Platoon, The Border Regiment. I apologised at length in case I was addressing someone who happened to have the same name, but was not the person I was looking for. But should the addressee be the right person then I hoped that he would answer my letter. Also, I expressed the hope that my question would not disturb him as some of the memories stirred up might not all be pleasant. I enclosed a return envelope with my address to make replying as easy as possible.

Whilst trying to convince myself that this was only an experiment to see whether my search had any chance of succeeding, I found myself impatiently waiting for the mail after a few days.

Bleak autumn days went by, Sinterklaas, the Dutch version of Santa Claus, was celebrated on 5 December, but still nothing happened. Until on Wednesday 12 December 2001 a letter arrived from England. Back from its trip to England, my prepaid envelope contained a single A-6 sheet with the following handwritten message:

Dear Sir,

Yes, I am David Patterson, ex 1st Battalion, The Border Regiment, the man you are looking for. I am now 82 years old and my memory is not as good as it used to be. But, if you like you can telephone me. This is my telephone number (....) Thank you for your interest. I shall be happy to help you.

Kind regards,

D. Patterson
13 Platoon

After more than 50 years it looked as if the silence was finally broken with the tearing open of an envelope, I thought to myself, with the letter of former Corporal Patterson in my hands. I sat there and let the breakthrough sink in. The letter contained nothing specific about 13 Platoon yet, but he was asking me to phone him. The following evening I tried to pluck up the courage for the telephone call and kept rehearsing what I was to say. I found myself stuck with a feeling of stage fright. What could he possibly still tell me after all those years and how should I phrase my questions to him? I took a deep breath and decided to just wait and see how the conversation went. Luckily the time in England was one hour earlier than in the Netherlands, so when I phoned him at half past nine Dutch time, for him it was only half past eight. Still a reasonable time to call. The telephone rang for a long time and just when I decided nobody was home, the phone was picked up. 'Hello' I heard and in the background there was the nervous bark of a small dog.

"One moment please. I've just returned from walking my dog and I have to take off his leash!'" Then I heard the dog calm down and Mr Patterson returned to the phone. When he discovered it was the Dutch journalist who had asked him about his Arnhem adventures, he was immediately interested. He said he was very surprised and that he had never expected to talk about that time again. Carefully I asked him some questions and urged him to tell me if he did not want to elaborate on matters that were too painful. But that did not seem to be necessary and David Patterson told me a lot. He promised to put his memories of Arnhem on paper for me, and enthusiastically told me how he, prior to joining the army, was on the verge of a professional soccer career with Bedford Town. He was already playing in the professional youth league. Mr. Patterson wasn't boasting, as his Soldier's Service and Pay Book confirmed. It said that on entering his military service on 30 May 1939, he was a professional soccer player. As a promising sportsman he already had a more than excellent physical condition, even before army training. That, together with his large stature and his Scottish background was reason to recruit him in the Scots Guards. The Guards Regiment has the ceremonial duty to protect the British Royal Family and heavy demands are made on the recruits fitness, presentation and military correct behaviour.

Time flew past and after half an hour I heard his dog becoming restless again. "Oh, he wants his supper" said Patterson and that seemed to me a good point to wind up our conversation. He asked me to continue our contact by telephone, because arthritis was making it hard for him to write much. Naturally, I promised to take this into consideration as much as possible and thanked him again. I hoped to call or write to him again as soon as possible. He said he was looking forward to it. I put down the receiver and was very excited about this first solid result.

I used the next day to let the news sink in and then started on my notes. Reading over them new

Corporal David Patterson was a professional soccer player with Bedford Town

questions appeared. What did he remember about the landing and following events? Would he be able to make a sketch of the positions of his platoon and did he have photographs from that period? As soon as I could without being impolite, I phoned again and had another pleasant and informative conversation. "I still have a picture of me in the uniform of The Border Regiment, where I am wearing the sleeve emblems of a sport instructor" he said and he promised to send me the picture. Also he wanted to try to make a sketch of the situation as he remembered it. In the following telephone calls more and more details surfaced. He spoke highly of the new Canadian lieutenant who took over command of the platoon in the summer of 1944, before the unit set off for Arnhem. He remembered an amusing event during one of those silly and exhausting speed marches the platoons had to undergo in order to stay in top condition prior to the Arnhem operation. While 13 Platoon, together with the rest of B Company was running hard and sweating under the August sun, they passed another unit that was resting on the roadside. And of course there were men who thought it necessary to make funny remarks. David Patterson was running beside his lieutenant, John Wellbelove, who looked at Patterson and grinned: "Shall we stop and teach those guys some manners?" David quickly told him not to bother, although he did not believe the Canadian was serious. But it was typical of him. "Wellbelove shared the hardship with us without hiding behind officers' privileges. He didn't feel better than the rest of us and that was something I had seldom seen in an officer. This attitude earned him a lot of respect from us", Patterson added.

Having received his notes on Arnhem 1944 through the mail, I put them in a separate file marked 'The Battle of 13 Platoon'. I also added the notes I made during our telephone calls. I guarded them like a treasure but it was clear I would have to find a lot more information before a complete picture of the fate of 13 Platoon emerged. When he asked whether I had found anything about the other members of his platoon I had to admit that he was the first one I had contacted. I then asked him if he remembered any other names from his platoon. It didn't take him long to mention his Lance Sergeant 'Jack' Kimber whom he described as: 'A good man to have as a Sergeant. He could get along with everyone.' Lance Corporal Eric Melling, he remembered, was his best army buddy and just like him an excellent athlete and sport instructor. Corporal Edward 'Ted' Clague was just like Patterson, Section Commander, and of Private Jim Isles he recalled that he was in the same section and that he had only joined the platoon shortly before Arnhem. The last name he mentioned was that of Private Frank Evans, but he only remembered that Frank was relatively new to the platoon.

Thrilled about the expanding story of David Patterson I checked the names in my list. Patterson's information confirmed that Kimber and Isles were in 13 Platoon. New were the names Melling, Clague and Evans. Those names did show in the Battalion Roll, Arnhem, but stated no specific platoon number. As Patterson had mentioned details about them I felt safe to assume that they were indeed in the same platoon as he was.

Having only just started, I was very content with the unexpectedly good results. My next step was to concentrate on the names mentioned by Patterson, because they already seemed more familiar. Searching for Lieutenant Wellbelove in the vastness of Canada was to be postponed to a later stage when I would be more experienced in the art of searching.

Before Christmas 2001 I started writing to all the Kimbers, Mellings, Clagues and Evans from my printed list of addresses. For Kimber, Melling and Clague I limited myself to sending only ten letters, because there were so many hits that it was impossible to contact them all. The combination Eric Melling from Wigan for example delivered more than 200 hits. For Jim Isles and Thornton I had three hits so all three of them got a letter. Frank Evans and Chester delivered a single address to which I would also send a letter.

In January 2002, even before having sent the last letter of this batch, I received a reply to one of the Isles-letters. John Isles, the only son of Jim Isles from 13 Platoon, replied that he got my letter through somebody in his town with the same name and that he and his father had spoken a lot about Arnhem. He would be happy to tell me more about his father and about his adventures during the airborne operation. The exchange of letters continued through e-mail and gradually the following picture of Jim was formed.

'Jim' was borne on 24 December 1924. In his childhood he was fascinated by the big steam engines that ploughed the fields in the neighbourhood and the heavy steamrollers that were used for road works. He wanted nothing better than to become a car mechanic, but because of lack of money this was not possible. In the years between his schooldays and the call for military service he worked as a gardener. He loved to go fishing, to watch cricket and was also a great fan of Blackpool Football Club. He was called into the Kings Own Lancashire Regiment, where he attended a recruitment session of an officer who was looking for volunteers for the new Airborne Forces early in 1944. Jim found this so challenging that he enlisted. Home on his next leave he proudly told his parents and his wife-to-be about his joining the Airbornes. Her parents who had both witnessed the First World War, were to Jim's amazement not at all pleased about the transfer of their future son-in-law. Their shocked reaction was: 'Oh no, Jim!' Apparently they were afraid that by doing this Jim actually went looking for the danger. Jim's own parents were not very happy either with the transfer. But there was no way back anymore. Jim joined the First Airborne Battalion of The Border Regiment. During his training he got to know Robert 'Bob' Barnes and Eddie Flinn from the Northern mining town of Cleator Moor. In the evenings the three of them liked to have a pint in the local pub.

Before joining, Bob was a miner and Eddie was a carpenter by profession and like Jim they came from the Kings Own Lancashire Regiment.

His son John also talked a lot about Jim Isles' Arnhem experiences. Often in short fragments, but everything I heard about the Arnhem episode I saved in the file 'The battle of 13 Platoon'. Already, it seemed clear that Jim Isles remembered different things than David Patterson. Therefore, the decision to firstly gather all personal memories and then try to fit them together later on, seemed to be a good idea in order to form a comprehensive picture.

Pte Jim Isles was working as a gardener until he was called up (picture taken in 1945)

Pte Robert 'Bob' Barnes was a miner and would have preferred to join the Navy

While waiting for reactions to the letters to Kimber, Melling and Clague I started looking for the story of Bob Barnes. My letter to an F. Barnes in Cleator Moor reached his aunt. She appreciated it enormously that even so many years after the events there were still people who were interested in the story of her nephew and his contemporaries. Through her I got the address of Bob Barnes' sister who told me that her brother was a quiet boy who, at that time, was working in the local iron ore mines. Actually, he did not want to join the Army at all, but he had enlisted with the Royal Navy. He had already filled in the Navy forms and had given the letter to his mother for her to mail it. With the Navy he hoped to see something of the world and have the red dust from the mines swept from his hair and lungs.

Strangely, no reaction came to his application and Bob grudgingly decided to enlist with the Army eventually. His sister remembered how relieved his mother was that her son was not going to sea. She had been so terribly worried that he could drown at sea if something happened to the ship he would be on. No, she thought, her son would be in a much safer position with the airborne troops. In the following letters I heard much more about Bob Barnes' fortunes during the Battle of Arnhem. His sister told me not to hesitate to contact her, should I have more questions. I gladly promised her that I would write or phone should the need arise.

Eddie Flinn, the third of the friends, also originated from the small industrial town of Cleator Moor of some 10,000 people, known for its iron works industry. I did not understand why the two Flinns mentioned in the telephone directory did not answer my letters. In a small town like that you would think that they would be related, but not even a scribbled reply to say that they did not want to have anything to do with my research was sent. Even a reminder, sent in January 2002, remained unanswered. Since the other three open searches took a lot of work and attention, I decided to let the Flinn search rest for the time being.

I continued to look for Kimber, Melling, Clague and Evans, the four other names that David Patterson had mentioned. In the meantime the correspondence with John Isles and the sister of Bob Barnes continued. Together with sending new search letters the correspondence started taking up more and more time.

Little was happening in the search for Lance Sergeant Kimber from North Shields, in the first weeks of 2002. A pity, because I had secretly hoped that as a Sergeant he could possibly have known just a bit more than the other three, who were Privates. The weeks went by, but not until February 2002 did a stray letter return from the widow of a certain Mr Kimber. You can be sure, she wrote, he was certainly not the man you are looking for. For an instant I wondered what she meant by that, but because her letter did not make me any wiser, I decided to stay focused and leave it at that. That letter though, seemed to seal the fate of the search for John Kimber. Nor did David Patterson have any clues in what other way we could continue either.

The Melling letters only produced one reply. It was a polite and interested answer, but unfortunately it did not bring me any closer to the story of Eric Melling. When talking to David Patterson again, he was not at all discouraged with this disappointing result. Which was the typically airborne state of mind, I learned. He remembered that his friend Eric was married and that his wife's name was Annie. It could very well be that she could tell you more, he thought aloud. Encouraged by this suggestion, in March 2002 I wrote to ten Mellings from Wigan, addressed to as many as I could find with the initial A.

Again I had to wait. The contact with the families of Isles and Barnes and of course, the regular contact with David Patterson continued and now and then they gave me new scraps of information. These I passed on to the others in the hope that it would lead to new memories.

In April 2002 it turned out that the Clague letters had brought nothing more than the suggestion that the name comes from the Isle of Man. The problem with the Clague search was that there was no town of origin mentioned in the Battalion Roll, Arnhem. The unfocused attempts to write to people with the name E. Clague in Liverpool, Plymouth or even in an intriguing little town called Musselburgh in Scotland, had proved useless. In the time between December 2001 and April 2002 I had written some thirty letters to people named Clague, but without any results. Just for a short while a glimmer of hope shone when in May 2002 a Mrs Clague from Workington wrote back that her father-in-law was named Clague and that he had been at Arnhem with the First Battalion Borders. But that Mr Clague was named Joe and had passed away sometime ago. No one knew a Ted Clague in her family. When checking the story in the Battalion Roll, Arnhem it turned out that the name was indeed mentioned twice. A pity that they were not even related, I sighed. Apparently, Ted Clague could originate from anywhere in England. That also fitted with the change that the First Battalion, The Border Regiment, underwent when it was transferred to the Airborne Forces. From that moment on soldiers from all over the United Kingdom could join the battalion.

When I vented my frustration to David Patterson, late May 2002, he suddenly recalled that he thought he saw Ted Clague in a television program covering the Armistice Day, 1999. David said: "On that day we in Great Britain commemorate the truce of the First World War and I thought that it was at one of the street interviews with veterans that I saw him. I believe that Ted said that he was living with the Chelsea Pensioners. But I am not completely sure of that, because it was only a short interview and my memory is not as good as it used to be."

I decided to check the story and sent a fax to the Chelsea Pensioners Home in London. Unfortunately, in this famous home for veterans no one knew a Ted Clague of The Border Regiment. In a flash I remembered that the BBC could probably tell me more if this Mr. Clague really was on television. The BBC referred me to the veterans' organisation The Royal British Legion and the Market Garden Veterans, but neither of them had any clues on Ted Clague. It seemed as if he had vanished from the face of the earth. Maybe he had emigrated immediately after the war and was therefore out of reach? Still, he could just as well be living in England, but had never been in contact with his old mates. That might explain why the veteran organisations had never heard of him.

Luckily, David Patterson's tip in the Melling search did produce some progress. As it turned out, there was indeed an Annie Melling living in the town of Wigan, Lancashire. She answered my letter in June 2002. But, alas, she did not know an Eric Melling and the name Eric was not recognised in her family. While I disappointedly wanted to put her letter aside I noticed that she advised me to contact the Registry Office in Wigan. Although it would surprise me if they would give me the information just like that, I still gave it a try, but sadly to no avail. They could only tell me someone by the name of Annie Melling had passed away in 1986.

Towards the summer of 2002 the trail of the story of Eric Melling also seemed to have evaporated. I now seriously doubted whether I would ever be able to find the remaining passengers, because after the trail-blazing contacts with David Patterson, the son of Jim Isles, and the sister of Bob Barnes, it had become ominously quiet indeed.

More encouraging was that my studying the literature on the Battle of Arnhem was beginning to show some results. Slowly, I was getting a better picture of the role the First Battalion, The Border Regiment, had played and where, in the vicinity of Oosterbeek, they had been positioned.

It was a fascinating notion that it takes so little effort to visit the locations where sixty years ago trenches were dug and battles were fought, while nowadays one can walk there undisturbed as if in a park. Now and then 13 Platoon was mentioned in a book, but never more than a few words. The only names that were mentioned were those of the Canadian Lieutenant Wellbelove and of Cyril Crickett, another corporal. But there was no mention of Patterson, Clague, Kimber, Melling, Isles, Evans, Barnes and Flinn. I did, however, find a picture of Vincent 'Johnnie' Swarbrick in an Arnhem book. I was utterly surprised to find out that the book was written by a certain Jim Longson, who prior to Arnhem was in 13 Platoon. My attempts to trace Swarbrick through him did not succeed, because neither his publisher nor widow had any idea where the picture came from. In my search I came into contact with somebody with that name, who had done a lot of family research on the Swarbrick family. Therefore I was confident I would have no trouble finding him. The namesake sent me a vast computer database, containing several hundred Swarbricks, some even dating 200 years back. Alas, the Vincent Swarbrick I was looking for was not among them. In fact in those two hundred not one Vincent appeared in the family history at all. As my inquiry with the publisher of the book that held his picture produced no results either, the kind face in the photograph remained without a story to accompany it. It wasn't until much later that a letter to the Preston edition of the Lancashire Evening News established contact with his daughter, Pamela Wilson. She wrote:

> *'Vincent or 'Vinnie' was born in Preston in 1924. His army Record of Service states his birth date as June 23 in 1923. I think he may have given that date to get into the army a little earlier. So at 17, nearly 18 years of age he enlisted on the 12th of February 1942 in the Royal Lancashire Regiment. (Height 5 ft., 3 ¼ inch, weight 9st, 8 lbs, fresh complexion, blue eyes and brown hair.) This was a Territorial Army unit. At the time he had a job as shop assistant in Preston. About half*

a year later he was transferred to the King's Regiment and then in April 1943 he joined the airborne Border Regiment. Strangely he had already qualified for his glider badge in March 1943. He had also done a War Course Rifle 2nd Class and Light Machine Gun Course 2nd class in March 1943. He must have been in the Sicily airborne operation, as his Record of Leave mentioned an embarkation leave from April 30 till May 4, 1943 and a Christmas leave from December 19, 1943 till January 2, 1944.'

Vincent 'Vinnie' Swarbrick in North Africa

When I compared the photographs I received from her I found that the Longson picture of Swarbrick did not seem to portray the same man. Checking his army number I found that Pamela Wilson's photograph had to be the real 13 Platoon Vincent Swarbrick. The identity of the other Border man remained a mystery.

In the meantime, the summer of 2002 was about to begin and that did not seem to be a good time to bother people with this sort of difficult questions. For weeks I did not receive a single reply.

In June a contact arose with the editor of the 'Family History Monthly', an English magazine on family research. The editors were very interested and even wanted to do a complete story on my search for 13 Platoon. I realised what an exceptional opportunity this was and wrote an extensive article. A story like that would of course draw much more attention then a short appeal. Apart from that it was a useful reference for my project. I wrote the article in the summer and on receiving the article the editors told me that they would print the article in the September issue to coincide with the Arnhem commemorations.

In the meantime, the Airborne Museum Hartenstein sent me an enormous pile of Regimental magazines of The Border Regiment from the sixties and seventies to read. These did not only contain articles on the post war Border Regiment, but also offered retrospectives on the Battle of Arnhem and other famous Regimental battles. It seemed to be a good place to search for the names of 13 Platoon, but I did not find any, not one. Not even in articles on Arnhem or in the obituaries. Again I asked myself how far I should go in looking for information before deciding to abandon the search. Where did you draw the line?

Just when I decided that the magazines had not brought me any useful information, I saw in one of them a notification of the British War Pensions Funds. A new straw to

clutch on to. Maybe the Fund, as a supplier of war pensions, could help me, or they could show me new ways to get back on track. I put my questions before them and quite quickly they replied. Although they sympathised with the cause of my search, they regretted to inform me that since 1998 it was their policy not to answer these requests anymore. Researching them proved to be a too heavy burden on the financial resources of the Fund, while the veterans that needed its support hardly profited from these efforts. Fearing that my search for John Kimber, Eric Melling and Ted Clague would fail here, I opened all registers and tried to persuade them with glowing arguments to nevertheless help me. I understood that they were not allowed to give me private addresses for privacy reasons, but would it be possible to forward my letters if the addressee was in their files. This way the privacy of the veteran in question remained protected and he could freely decide for himself whether or not he would answer my questions. I thought that this would be possible without involving any trouble or extra costs. After two weeks I received the Fund's answer. They had looked at my request again, but their former reply remained unchanged. When phoning them to get more information the Fund suggested that I should inquire with local historians. With Kimber and Melling this was indeed a possibility, because besides their names I also had a place name, but with Clague this information was missing. By this time it was early September and people were coming back from their summer holidays.

Step by step

Again I searched the North Shields phone directory for the name Kimber on the internet. Through the local library I came into contact with a local historical workgroup. Would the members be able to tell me any more about John Kimber? Did he live or had he lived in North Shields? Would they be able to trace family? With typical British helpfulness Eric Hollerton of the historical work group dived in their archives. The results of their search left me with a problem. They discovered that somebody with almost exactly that name died in 1987. Could that be the John Kimber I was looking for? It seemed unlikely, because obituaries of course have to be very accurate. Was it then my information that was incorrect? In conclusion they told me that the city of Newcastle was close to North Shields. Maybe relatives of John Kimber were living there or had moved there. It was through their contagious enthusiasm that I instinctively felt that the trail was warming.

With the help of the internet telephone directory I indeed found several J. Kimbers in Newcastle. With a sudden flash of inspiration I also mentioned my email address in my letters. I had not always done this before, because I expected that the people I was looking for probably would not be very familiar with this form of communication. Luckily, there were only four addresses and in a last but determined attempt to trace Lance Sergeant Kimber, I wrote to all four. It was then early October 2002. I just did not want to accept that after all those months of research I would end up with nothing at all. I wanted to speed up the delivery of those letters to Newcastle and tried to imagine how someone would react to such an unusual letter. Although the other correspondence required a lot of time and attention, my mind was often drawn to the Kimber search. Finally, after three weeks and just when I was starting to lose hope, I received an email with a photo attached of Lance Sergeant John 'Jack' Kimber in uniform! A second cousin from Newcastle, also named John Kimber, wrote me that his great-uncle Lance Sergeant John 'Jack' Kimber had indeed been with the airborne forces in Arnhem. He explained to his slightly baffled Dutch correspondent that people with the name John in England are often called Jack. 'Jack' Kimber had two brothers, Oswald and James, who were also in the armed forces during the Second World War.

John 'Jack' Kimber (on the right) together with his brothers James (left) and Oswald(centre) who were also called up for the armed forces

The three brothers were also on the picture second cousin John sent. He turned out to be Oswald's grandson. It was unbelievable, after all these months I had finally got results. Although the information was not very detailed, I was especially happy with the picture. Finally a solid lead. Although further questions to the second cousin did not give me any additional details, I now went full speed ahead and tried to get more information through the local papers that very month, October 2002. The Newcastle Chronicle placed a call in the section 'searching for' and a niece of Lance Sergeant John Kimber responded. The deadlock was now finally broken. She sent me several pictures of him and his brothers. After checking the details with Hollerton, the local historian, I began to put together the story of John Mathewson Kimber prior to the war years.

John Kimber was born on 22 April 1913 in North Shields. His father was killed in the First World War, so John never knew him. His elder brothers also had only vague memories of their father. The loss of her husband meant that their mother had to raise their sons on her own with little more than his war pension. John attended the primary school at the Newcastle Royal Jubilee Schools, which was founded by Quakers as a welfare institute for the education of poor children of all denominations. Until 1971 the building stood on the corner of Preston Lane and Albion Road across from the parish church in North Shields. The primary school had left the site years before and was replaced by a small park. Before John Kimber joined the army in 1940, he worked as a bartender in the Royal Arms, a pub in Nile Street on the corner of Russel Street in North Shields. He shared rooms with his brother James. In that same year, Nazi Germany started the Blitzkrieg in Western Europe which led, in June, to the evacuation of the British Expedition Forces at Dunkirk. The First Battalion of The Border Regiment was amongst the evacuated troops, but was not yet part of the airborne forces which, at that time, had not been founded. John was called up for duty and was assigned to the Black Watch Regiment. The battalions of this regiment had suffered great losses in 1940 on the European continent. For recovery and personal completion a battalion of the Black Watch was stationed in Llanelli, in Wales. John was assigned to this unit and left for Llanelli. In the local dancehall 'The Drill Hall' he would meet his wife-to-be, nurse Nancy Morgan.

Unfortunately, the niece and second cousin could give few details about Lance Sergeant John Kimber´s fortunes during the Battle of Arnhem. But the information they did give I added with great care, together with the photos, to the stories of David Patterson, Jim Isles and Bob Barnes that I already had in my folder 'The Battle of 13 Platoon'. If I received more material, I could perhaps combine it with what I had already found and clarify details. The folder was still very thin, but unmistakably putting on weight. I wondered whether more stories about Eric Melling, Frank Evans and Ted Clague could be added. Longing for more quick results, I decided late October 2002 to write to the Army Personnel Centre of the British Department of Defence. I had toyed with the thought of doing this before. They surely should have something about 13 Platoon in their archives. So far I had assumed that they could not give me this kind of information due to privacy reasons. But the slow progress of my search made me change my mind. I would try it anyway, if only to make sure I had tried every imaginable source and to leave no stone unturned. With this in mind, I wrote to the Army Personnel Centre.

Again I produced a passionate letter with, what I believe were compelling arguments to give me the details that I was looking for, or to pass on my letters to the men involved. But, unfortunately, my careful considerations meant little to them. The clerk of the Army Personnel Centre turned me down. The army archives did not contain anything that would enable him to meet my request and pass on my letters to the persons I mentioned. The files in question had not been updated for more than 40 years, which made it very unlikely that they could be of any use, he wrote. He referred me to The Border Regiment Museum in Carlisle Castle and the Imperial War Museum in London. My reply that he seemed to be a bit too pessimistic, did not persuade him. Slowly I started to see a pattern. The way through the official authorities and archives so far always resulted in a dead end. Just as the curator of The Border Regiment Museum had predicted. Apparently they did not have The requested information or were unable to release it. The only search methods that were proving successful were the address searches, tips from the found friends from 13 platoon itself, help of local historians and the appeals in papers.

With renewed energy I started to work on the Clague search again, when the article in 'Family History Monthly' magazine started to pay off. A lady from Manchester sent me a list with possibly interesting names and addresses for the Clague search as well as for many other names that were mentioned in the article. She had taken the names from the Electoral Roll, a list that contains the names of all voters in the United Kingdom. It was an impressive list. Surprised about the amount of work she needed to have done to produce the list, I asked her what her interest was in my search. It turned out that she herself was searching, already for years, for her family history. The personal stories from her parents during the Second World War had given her insight into the way normal people tried to survive during the war. She recognised that aspect in my search and that was why she had responded to my article.

   Apart from the list she also suggested that I ask the Manchester Evening News to publish an appeal in their very popular column 'In touch' where people could place appeals for friends or relations they had lost touch with. The paper covered more or less the area where the people I was looking for might live. Also, it was one of the largest evening papers with a circulation of 180.000. I succeeded in placing a search appeal for Ted Clague in the Manchester Evening News. I also seized the opportunity to ask for information on the 11 other names of 13 Platoon, but that did not bring results.

The Clague search appeal, however, was successful. On 6 October 2002 the letter I had been looking forward to for such a long time finally arrived.

Dear Sir,

I am E.D. Clague, 1st Battalion, The Border Regiment. Was at Arnhem in September 1944. What does this all mean? I heard from an acquaintance that something was in the Manchester Evening News.

E.D. Clague

I quickly wrote back to him and told him why I was looking for him. It was no doubt helpful to be able to tell him that I had already found a few of the others of his platoon. Also, I sent him the English article I had written for 'Family History Monthly'. This turned out to be a good start for further contacts and I phoned him regularly. Unfortunately Mr. Clague's memory wasn't so good anymore, but together with his son Doug he was able to bring back some memories. Ted Clague started to tell his story:

Being the oldest son of a large family in the austere 1930's my mother used to turn a 'blind eye' to my dodging school and sneaking off to work on the local farms whilst my Dad was at work at Camell Laird shipyard in Birkenhead. I regularly worked as a beater for the gamekeeper on Lord Leverhulme's country estate and was always around animals, even at home where, like many people at the time, we had the family chickens and ducks.

There was an occasion once when I got some work with a visiting circus and was responsible for letting a lion escape. Of course, on this particular day my father did find out about me missing school because he read the story in the newspaper on his way home from work.

On several occasions my Dad took me to the Isle of Man where our family came from to see if any of my uncles would help me to a job of sorts. But nobody wanted to run risks with this little tearaway that I was in those pre-war years. My Dad had served in the Sherwood Foresters Regiment in the First World War and had been decorated for valour, being severely wounded whilst capturing a German machine gun nest. I still keep a piece of shrapnel that the doctors removed from his chest when he got to the field hospital.

His son Doug added:

Dad was a supporter of the rugby club Tranmere Rovers and often went to see the matches together with his brother Norris. When he went out to go camping in the Cheshire countryside, Norris used to go with him. When they were a little older, their interest in bicycles developed into the love of motorbikes and the two brothers and their father competed in scrambling, which included racing off the road, in fields and in woods. This scrambling later developed into modern sports like motor cross and trials. My Dad drove James and AJS motor bikes and my granddad's shed was still full of motor parts when I came to visit him as a little boy. When my Dad was fourteen he, now officially as well, left school. He became an apprentice carpenter and that he stayed until he joined the army, shortly before his eighteenth birthday.

Edward 'Ted' Clague (left) in Italy and Tommy McDonald whose presence in the left picture would only become clear when in 2012 his wedding picture was discovered.

From his army days before Arnhem Ted still remembered:

> *"In our billets in Burford, early 1944, my bed was next the bed of 'Pip' Hulse, a good friend of mine. We used to call him the bookworm because he liked to go reading on his bed when we came back from a training. Pip was a fairly big man, but a pleasant bloke to have around. He was the Bren gunner of the scout section from 'Joe' Crickett. I also remember David Patterson and Eric Melling because during the training they amazed every one with their incredible fitness. I think they were both asked to become Physical Instructors. But if I remember well, they didn't fancy that very much.*

Every detail they told me, I stored safely in my folder 'The Battle of 13 Platoon'. When Ted Clague mentioned the names Hulse and Melling, I hoped that he could help me trace them as well. But, unfortunately, Ted had no new clues about them. So as far as Hulse was concerned there was still no progress.

To pick up the trail of Eric Melling from Wigan, in November 2002 I wrote to the local weekly paper, the Wigan Courier. A question to a local or regional newspaper usually proved to be much more effective than contacting authorities or writing letters. Also it saved a lot of time and prevented wasting energy. Still, it would take till January 2003 before the Wigan Courier would print my request in the form of a little article. After that everything went fast. Somebody by the name of John Kelly responded with utter surprise.

Wigan, 29 January 2003

Dear Mr. Schmidt,

> *First let me thank you for your information concerning my uncle, Lance Corporal Eric Melling at the Battle of Arnhem. I must tell you that it was a great shock to me to find this article in The Courier because it is a free paper which had never before been delivered to the area where I live. Yet the first time we receive it, there was an article on the front page asking for information about my long dead uncle. As you can imagine, it was difficult after such a long time to get information about him as all his siblings are now dead and all I had to rely on were my own memories from childhood and stories I recall from my parents and other uncles*

and aunts, of whom there was only one survivor, the wife of his younger brother Harry, who he met whilst they were both serving in the forces. As she was from a totally different part of the country she didn't know much of the family history before then. It's a great pity that we couldn't have got into contact just over twelve months ago as Harry died just last January and he could have provided any information you required.

I can tell you that he was twenty one when he was killed, so that would put his birth date about 1923, but I can't tell you the actual date. I think that he worked for a haulier. He was next to the youngest of eight children, five boys and three girls, of whom my mother was one. He was always very fit and athletic and was always an outstanding athlete at school. I did know that in the army he was so accomplished at physical training that his superiors wanted him to stay on as a P. T. instructor at the barracks in England, but he declined because he wished to stay with his comrades. He was also a married man, having got married to his sweetheart Anne whilst he was home on leave. I recall the wedding and the reception, although I don't recall the actual church as I was only about five years old. I am pleased to send you a copy of his wedding photograph.

I hope that this information will be of help to you in your research into 13 Platoon and I will do my best to see if I could discover anything else that will be of interest to you. I would also be very interested to know the reasons for your research of 13 platoon in particular, and also if you plan to write more about their part in the battle and also if you intend to publish anything. I would also be obliged if you could recommend any further reading on the subject as all there was in my local library was a tour guide to the Battle of Arnhem. Hoping to hear from you again soon. I remain,

*Yours Faithfully
John Kelly*

I was just as surprised as he was by the coincidence that Mr. Kelly received just that one paper in which my appeal was published, while my letter had already been lying with the editor for weeks.

Eric Melling (standing, third from the left) and Annie Winstanley (sitting in the centre) on their wedding day on 28 april 1943

Things did not stop at this windfall. In February 2003 seemingly out of the blue I received an email from a certain Mr. Flinn. He had happened to read my article in the 'Family History Monthly' and was convinced that the Edward 'Eddy' Flinn I was looking for was a relative of his. When Mr. Flinn asked his elderly relatives, they confirmed his assumptions. I was astonished that a sleeping search had spontaneously sprung back into life again and remembered how, more than a year ago, I had tried in vain to get into contact with two people carrying the same name in Cleator Moor. Now it turned out that Eddy Flinn didn't live in Cleator Moor but in a little village close by. Apparently it was not in the same telephone district as Cleator Moor, because the address had never shown up before. I first wrote Eddy Flinn a letter because I did not want to surprise him with questions that he probably did not expect. It did not take long before his son-in-law sent me an email in which he replied that Eddy Flinn approved of my contacting him by phone. When I phoned he and his wife were just watching the telly. I explained that I was the Dutch journalist that had written to him about the Battle of Arnhem and asked him if he had time to take my call. He agreed and asked his wife to turn the volume on the television down. I introduced my story and the background to my questions, told him about the people I had already found and asked him what he could tell me. In general terms he told me what he remembered, but added that he did not like to talk about his memories. It was easier for him to talk about the time prior to Arnhem. He was 14 when he, like many others, left school to learn a trade. Eddy Flinn became a carpenter until he was called up for the Army. He knew Bob Barnes because both came from Cleator Moor and had played around the same church when they were still at school. It turned out that Bob Barnes, Jim Isles and Eddy Flinn went to the First Battalion, The Border Regiment together, because their whole unit was transferred from the Kings Own Lancashire Regiment in order to cover the losses the airborne battalion had suffered at the landing at Sicily in 1943. Apparently this had little to do with volunteering. In 1944 all three of them turned 19 and they were looking up in awe to the older platoon members who already had fought the Germans.

Edward 'Eddie' Flinn earned his living as a joiner before he was called up in the Kings Own Lancashire Regiment

Although Eddy Flinn at first said little about Arnhem, in following telephone conversations over the next few months he told me more and more. Also, the sparse information about the time after Arnhem I carefully stored in the file 'The Battle of 13 Platoon'. When I asked him for photos from that time, he answered that he no longer had any. But because he said this without any hesitation whatsoever, I doubted whether this was true. Could he maybe ask his wife, I suggested. That he did and indeed a photo was found. Now I had a photo in uniform of everyone I found, which put a face to the names and stories.

This seemed to be a good moment to take a mid-term review. After more than a year of searching, dozens of letters, lots of emails and various newspaper search appeals, I now had discovered more about four of the six names that David Patterson mentioned. Only the letters and the paper search appeal for Frank Evans was still unsuccessful. And I had not yet started the search for the Canadian lieutenant. Again I went through my notes and separated the post-war information from the stories about the war. The post-war material went in a different folder. In the end, this folder would produce the last part of the stories of Morley's passengers. Apparently it was good to persist and hope for some good fortune to make progress. That was all the stimulation I needed to continue.

Si, Si, Si South American Joe
Besides searching for the people David Patterson still remembered, I had also written letters to other people on the list of members of 13 Platoon. Among them was Corporal Cyril Crickett, who was the only 13 Platoon member quoted in the book 'When Dragons Flew'. In this book he told that, as the glider commenced landing at Wolfheze, he was horrified to discover a large haystack that seemed to linger on the exact same spot the pilot intended to use for the touch down. He saw the haystack approaching fast and realised that for all of them the air landing would be over instantly should the lightly built glider strike it during touchdown. Startled, Cyril Crickett wondered whether the pilots might have overlooked the haystack. When I told this story to Morley, he pretended to be offended in his pilot's honour: "Out of the question, he couldn't possibly have seen that. He was in the back, buckled up in his seat belts. In a Horsa, passengers sat with their backs against the side walls, facing the centre of the plane. At the very most he might have spotted that haystack during a turn when we were approaching the landing strip. However, I myself can't remember seeing any haystacks in our landing path", Morley said. It should be fascinating to bring Mr. Cricket into contact with his glider pilot Morley and have them settle the matter among the two of them once and for all.

Fortunately, finding his home address through the internet took little time and in October 2002 I tentatively posed my question about the haystack in a letter to him. Keeping in mind what the curator of The Border Regiment Museum told me about contacting Arnhem veterans, this is how my letter to Mr. Crickett read:

One haystack in September 1944

Dear Mr. Crickett,

At the Arnhem Commemorations last September Morley 'Taffy' Williams said to me that he wondered what haystack you were worried about when you landed near Wolfheze on 18 September 1944. His interest is understandable because he was one of your glider pilots that flew you to Oosterbeek. Morley, today a youngster of a mere 84 years, made his comments after having read the summary that I made for him to shed some light on the fate of the platoon that he flew to Wolfheze. He remembers you and the others from 13 Platoon jumping out of the glider while he and his first pilot reached for a well earned cup of coffee after an uneventful flight. Then you each went your separate ways and that was the only thing he knew. But he has always been interested in learning what happened to you in the days and months following the glider landing.

And that's where I came in. In 1998 I helped the Museum to organise its exhibition 'Liberators behind barbed wire' by editing the exposition magazine. That is how I came into contact with Morley Williams. I have met him three times now and in our interesting talks he mentioned his desire to find out what had happened to his passengers. I have been doing some research and actually came up with some things that he didn't know. This interested Morley strongly and as you are mentioned in these quotes several times he was interested in getting into contact with you to find out how you have been in all these years. I therefore send you and Morley Williams each others addresses. I expect that he will write you one of these days and hope that you are interested in talking to him. I hope that you will enjoy renewing your acquaintance with him. If you like I could send you the information I have gathered so far. Possibly you could check it and may be even add some new details.

I hope that you have found my letter interesting reading. Please, don't dispute the haystack too long as it was only a detail.

With respect and friendly regards,

Haks Walburgh Schmidt

On November 21, Mr Crickett's reply reached me. He was grateful for receiving the address of his former glider pilot. They had already had a very pleasant conversation, he said. Once we got to talk about our experiences during the war, we forgot all about the matter of the haystack, he wrote. Cyril asked me whether I had already noticed that the sum of the figures of the Chalk Number 166 of his Horsa was 13, being his platoon's number. He hoped that my quest for 13 Platoon would bring him answers to questions that no one had been able to solve yet. I rejoiced at his willingness to help me. This letter turned out to be the start of an extensive and rewarding correspondence, which proved to be as fascinating as the exchange of letters I had with Morley. Cyril Crickett told me that he left school at the age of 14 to become an apprentice with a building contractor. At this firm he learned all about the practical aspects of the construction and maintenance of houses and other buildings. He stayed with this company until the war broke out. In his spare time he used to play soccer a lot, and he enjoyed a game of cricket. His family name was in no way related to the sport, he added dryly. He also loved gymnastics. As he got older, he started cycling, camping and rowing, and he joined a rifle club. He loved to go on long cycling tours with a friend. Sometimes they rode over 60 miles a day, for example to the hills in Northern England or in Wales. At the end of the day they would set up their tent at a beautiful spot, spend the night and return home on their bicycles the next day. In those days, there were no such things as derailleurs, mountain gears for bicycles or lightweight tents. The year 1939 brought many changes for Cyril. In May he volunteered for the Territorial Army, and on September 1 of that same year he was mobilised into the regular army. In 1941 he joined the airborne forces. The period preceding their Arnhem mission was eventful for Cyril and 13 Platoon too. "Would it be interesting to tell you something about our platoon's history as well?" he asked me. That would be great, as I was also curious to learn about the events previous to Arnhem. I returned his letter, and within a few weeks Cyril sent me an elaborate report. He narrated:

> *"In the autumn of 1941, when I was still serving in the Manchester Regiment, I saw a notice on the board, calling for volunteers for the new airborne forces. I was still only 20 years of age, which was one year too young to join the parachutists. I could only join the glider borne troops, because there this minimum age didn't apply. I volunteered and got*

called up for the selection procedure. There was a medical check, an eye test and a kind of interview in Catterick. The demands in those days were still very high. You already needed to be in an excellent physical condition, be a good marksman and be right handed. The good physical condition was needed because after landing airborne troops don't have much means of transport. As resupply behind enemy lines is often difficult, one has to use his ammunition as effectively and economically as possible, in other words be a good marksman. Being right handed was necessary because the bolt of a rifle is best operated by the right hand. Left handed people need more time, which is not always available to an airborne soldier.

After the test I was sent back to my unit with the message that in due time I would be told the results of my application. It would last until the end of May next year (1942) before I was told to report to the First Battalion, The Border Regiment in Barton Stacey near Southampton in the South of England. Having arrived there, I found a well equipped camp with good food and even hot showers. Especially the hot showers were a virtually unknown luxury.

To begin with we received a basic training of six weeks. When the instructors felt you weren't up to it, they could send you back to your old unit. But you could also quit yourself if you found it too demanding.

And it was hard and demanding! Unending marches over fields, muddy paths and through stinking drains. There also was an exercise whereby we wore full kit, the steel helmet and carried our rifle. We were on a road with telegraph poles on the side. When Lt 'Tracker' Cleasby, the chief instructor, blew his whistle we ran a distance of two telegraph poles, walked two telegraph poles then ran for two poles again. This was kept up four miles until you thought you were going to die. The instructors were also in full kit, so they must have been very fit as well. I also remember the 'Otter Run' where we had to cross the Test, a small river, seven times and at the end had to struggle up a haystack. We practised river crossing by rope, going hand over hand and often falling in. Another method was to strip naked apart from your helmet, wrap all your clothes and equipment in your gas cape and float this with your rifle on top in front of you. To see a platoon of men wearing nothing but tin helmets is a sight not to be forgotten easily. In the last two weeks of our basic training we did everything on the double, from the moment we got up to the time we went to bed again. After the first six weeks you were *judged to see if you could stay on. And I could stay.*

In September 1942 we, the new recruits, were transferred to Ilfracombe near Plymouth on the southwest coast. Training was stepped up a notch there. We did many exercises where we were taken out on a truck, abandoned and told to get back as best we could. Sometimes we did landings from sea after which we were taken off by sea again. When we came back from such exercises with blackened faces, it sometimes happened that people on holidays in the area gave us chocolate or cigarettes. They thought we were returning from some secret operation. Our not too tenacious denials were unable to stop this generosity.

Generally we were trained to develop improvisation skills and to further improve our physical condition. An especially feared exercise was the so-called Ghilli Crawl. That was a way of running with bent knees, but the rest of your body as upright as possible. This way of running enabled you to move behind a low cover and still keep an eye of what was going on around you. That could be life saving but was exhausting to do.

Towards the end of our stay we went to Woolacombe for our baptism of fire. We had to walk in line abreast along the shore, whilst machine gun and rifle fire was aimed from the front, above and behind us. On reaching two lines in the sand about eight feet apart we had to lie down between the lines. There was a further session of firing with bullets flying over you and some hitting the sand close to your head. We then rose to our feet, continued to advance with more firing, and on reaching the end were told that was it. Just as we all relaxed an explosion 20-30 yards away showered us with sand and scared the living daylights out of us! Whether that was an initiation joke from our instructors or a lesson to always remain alert, I don't remember. In T (Training) Company we wore a slip-on company shoulder designation in black on both epaulettes. B Company, of which 13 Platoon was a part, wore first white, then purple bands on their epaulettes. The change of colour came about because the white could be confused with officer cadet shoulder stripe designations. These bands helped to foster company esprit de corps within the unit. After Ilfracombe we from B Company went for two weeks to Kiddlington for our glider training. That was very exciting. Especially when the glider cast off. The engineless wooden plane immediately went into a very steep dive which gave the unsettling feeling of an impending crash. However, we also found time to help out on the local farms and were rewarded with *lovely home-made bread, cheese and scrumpy. This was a tasteful supplement to our army rations.*

By the end of 1942 we received our red berets. In the beginning we didn't really like them, but as the reputation of the airbornes grew, we began to take more pride in them. Especially when the civilian respect for us increased.

North Africa and Sicily

During the last quarter of 1942 and the first months of 1943 training of the airborne battalion continued unabatedly. In those days Cyril got his nickname Joe, which was derived from a popular song called "*Si, Si, Si, South American Joe*". "Si, Si, sounds like the initials of my name" Cyril clarified. He didn't recall to whom he owes this nickname. In March 1943 the PIAT (Projector Infantry Anti-Tank) weapon was introduced, which offered the infantry the possibility to combat tanks, without being dependent on anti-tank guns. In spring 1943 rumour had it that the First Battalion, The Border Regiment would be going to North-Africa. After the American invasion on November 8, 1942, the Allied Forces had obtained a firm footing in the western part of North-Africa. From the east General Montgomery and his 8th Army were advancing, thus enhancing the chances for the Allied Forces to dislodge the German and Italian armies from North Africa.

Already before joining the Army, Cyril Crickett was a versatile sports man. He worked in house construction

Sure enough: on May 16, 1943 the First Battalion sailed in strict secrecy for the Algerian city of Oran. On embarking, they were not allowed to wear their red berets or shoulder flashes, as possible spies could easily identify them as airborne troops boarding for an attack. As space was very limited aboard the *SS (Steamer) Cheshire*, many were pleased to find that training aboard was impossible. A drawback of this lack of space however was the fact, that conditions were rather primitive. On May 26 the convoy arrived at Oran, where temperatures were already reasonably high. From Oran, the convoy continued its journey to Tunisia. The change from early spring in England to the sand, heat and drought of North-Africa was substantial, yet their excellent form allowed the men of The Border Battalion to get accustomed to the new conditions rapidly. In Tunisia, 13 Platoon participated in exercises involving gliders, which "was not quite satisfactory for us, as we landed on the wrong spot and were forced to walk for many hours in the blazing sun in order to reach our assembly point", Cyril recalled. By then, North-Africa had been cleared from the Axis armies, and the generals were preparing the invasion of Sicily, still in secrecy, of course. The moment for 13 Platoon to fly into real action for the first time, was slowly approaching. The relocation to Algeria was a significant omen. On July 9, 1943 the hour had come! As part of the British-American invasion army, 13 Platoon boarded two American Waco gliders at 19.00 hours, when it was still light. Their destination was Sicily. The aircraft Cyril was on, had been nicknamed 'Bad Penny' by its passengers to let fate smile upon them. However, neither of the two aircrafts ever reached Sicily, as they were cast off from their tug plane too soon, and had to land on sea in the dark of night. Cyril related:

> *"At about nine o'clock, half past nine in the evening, the glider pilot warned us that we were going to make a landing on sea, since we had been cast off too early. The anti-aircraft defence of the Allied invasion fleet beneath us had opened fire on us, as they feared us to be German bombers. Subsequent to the firing many tug planes had quickly cast off the towing cable. Our glider lost height rapidly, and splashed down forcefully on the water. This caused the nose of the glider, which could swing upwards, to open, and the seawater to gush in. The first thing I remember after the splashdown was being under water, quickly releasing my safety belts and groping my way out of the aircraft. My hands found a hole in the roof and I tried to fight my way through. But I was horrified to find myself caught by my kit. I tried to remain calm and sank back to get rid of my gear. This wasn't an easy thing to do, as I had to remove an extra ammo belt I was carrying around my shoulder first. Only after I disposed of this belt, was I able to take off my other things and get out of the glider. I heaved a sigh*

of relief and noticed that I had been the last one to leave the plane. We checked if everyone was there, but one of the pilots turned out to be missing. We were not able to find him and consequently gave up the search after a while. The other pilot was injured. We therefore laid him on the wing of the glider, which remained afloat as it was made out of wood and canvas. We inflated our lifejackets, threw away superfluous equipment and clang to the plane in the fairly choppy sea. There was nothing else we could do but wait for daylight to come and to hope that we would be picked up. By turns someone could climb from the water onto the wing for a short rest. We could not all be on the wing, as this made the wreck start to sink. There was a tremendous lot of jellyfish in the water, but I don't think anyone of us was stung. In the distance we saw another glider in the water, but it was too far away to go over to. I have no idea whether it was the other plane that carried members of 13 Platoon. After a while three lads decided to swim to shore, despite the risk of exhaustion. I only recall that 'Click' Fidler, who would later be in Arnhem as well, was amongst them. We agreed that the ones who stayed behind with the plane would regularly shout and whistle, in order to enable them to return to the wreck if they wanted to. One of them actually returned. The other two, as we found out later, were picked up after a while by a Greek destroyer. The lad who was with Fidler was admitted into sickbay as he showed signs of exhaustion. We were shocked to learn that he was later killed on that ship, when it took a direct hit in the sickbay.

When morning came, the group that had stayed behind with the floating remains of the glider was picked up at eight o'clock by a landing craft from the SS Winchester Castle, a troopship of the invasion fleet. When we boarded the ship, we were filmed for the newsreel. Not long after our embarkation we were ordered to go to bed. After we slept soundly for a few hours and had a decent meal under our belt, we felt a lot better that evening. The Bad Penny has never been the subject of puns again. Evidently, the troopship had already accomplished its task at the invasion, as it did no longer head for the Sicilian coast, but sailed for Malta. From Malta, we went straight to Egypt via the eastern Mediterranean. We felt like we were on a luxury cruise with dolphins at the bow and sunshine galore. When we were told that many gliders had landed in the sea, which caused the death of many of our comrades, we realised how lucky we had yet been in spite of everything that had happened.

Our only task aboard the troopship was to keep our quarters tidy, and to collect our daily ration of Canadian Ice Cap beer. I was even fortunate enough to run into an old classmate on the ship. Again and again we were amazed by the coincidence that brought us together on the ship, and whenever he was off duty, we would spend many hours smoking and leaning over the railing, talking about lots of things."

Via the Suez Canal, *Winchester Castle* sailed to an army camp near the Bitter Lakes in Egypt, where the rescued airbornes went ashore. They still had not heard what had happened to the other glider of their platoon. After three weeks the rescuees were flown back to their base in Tunisia. On arrival they found out that the nine occupants of the other Waco glider of 13 Platoon had been in the water for hours as well. Jack Kimber told them that they were brought down by their own invasion fleet, after nervous anti-aircraft gunners caused the American tug pilots to panic and to cast off the towing cable while the gliders were still too far from the shore to land safely. Possibly Edwin Ainsworth, Gerry Greasley and Pip Hulse had been aboard that plane as well. In the course of the morning of July 10 they were picked up from the sea by the destroyer '*HMS Beaufort*' (L14) of the British *Royal Navy*. During the days the men of 13 Platoon were aboard the *HMS Beaufort*, the ship was serving as a decoy for a large German gun on the Sicilian coast. This gun created a lot of problems to shipping traffic and the troops that were coming to shore. *HMS Beaufort* was ordered to sail back and forth in the field of fire of this heavy gun in order to entice the German fire. This scheme succeeded frighteningly well, as could be deduced from the shells that landed very close to the ship. Fortunately however, neither the ship nor the members of 13 Platoon were hit. Allied planes and the British monitor *HMS Lord Roberts* with its two huge 15 inch guns managed to locate and silence the German gun. The rescued castaways were furious with the American tug pilots who were supposed to take them to Sicily. These Americans left them to their own devices after the first gun fire, causing the unnecessary death of many airbornes. After the action HMS Beaufort dropped the rescued airbornes off on the island of Malta. When the survivors of the air landings on Sicily had subsequently assembled in Tunisia again, the operation turned out to have taken the lives of over a hundred men of the First Border Battalion. Many of them were killed at sea and Fred Terry was reported to have been wounded. In the

HMS Beaufort, the Royal Navy-vessel that picked up Lance Sergeant Jack Kimber and others out of the Mediterranean Sea after their glider had emergency landed in the water.

act of bringing the battalion up to strength again, Sergeant Fred Terry of 11 Platoon was transferred to the 13 Platoon and others, among them new recruits, would follow. Despite the losses, exercises were resumed promptly, for there was a war going on.

Italian intermezzo
In the autumn of 1943, shortly after the capitulation of Italy, the First Battalion, The Border Regiment received new orders. On September 11, three Royal Navy cruisers HMS Dido, HMS Penelope and HMS Sirius took the Battalion to the port of Taranto, in the heel of the Italian mainland. On their arrival the Battalion was ordered to take up defensive positions on the outside of the town. A few days later the airbornes went further inland, following the retreating German troops. During the march 13 Platoon was detailed to go on night patrol in a small village called Mas Girena, to check whether there were still Germans about. It appeared to be a dangerous assignment and it surely was a nerve-racking job. Dusk fell early and the monotonous sound of crickets and cicadas created a lazy atmosphere of Mediterranean calmness and safety. Yet, behind every tree a sniper or a Spandau machine gun could be lurking. How-

ever, their own comrades turned out to pose the greatest danger to the men. On a night patrol to the village they almost ran into a minefield their mates had laid and they were fired upon by their pals from a sister company. Anxious moments, but they managed to come through without casualties. Subsequently, the men lost direction a few times, but finally managed to reach Mas Girena. The men of 13 Platoon halted just outside the village for a quiet observation. After some time, it was evident that there were no Germans in the village, 13 Platoon returned to its positions near Taranto without further action.

Some time afterwards 13 Platoon moved with the Battalion to Brindisi, where guard duty at a depot awaited them. After the patrolling in Brindisi it was back to the port of Taranto again, where the exceptional picture unfolded of the many Italian naval vessels that had been captured by the Allied Forces after the Italian capitulation. The interned fleet filled both harbours of the city.

On November 17 1943, the Battalion embarked for a voyage to Philippeville in Algeria, where the men awaited their return to England. This time it was the SS *Duchess of Bedford* that was to take them home. The ship was nicknamed *'Drunken Duchess'*, as she tended to sway on the waves rather distinctly. The convoy that headed for England was huge. Under way on the Atlantic the *Duchess* sustained damage, when she was rammed by a ship sailing along side. The latter failed to react in time to one of the many zigzags the convoy made to shake off U-boats. At first everyone was ignorant of the fact that something was going on because the ship appeared to react to the change of course only a bit later. However, by the minute it became clearer that the other ship was not changing its course at all. To more and more people on deck of the *'Duchess'* it dawned on them what was about to happen. As if hypno-

Christmas card from Corporal David Patterson to his sister in England (1943)

tized they stared at the ship that was wilfully approaching. Until the demonic blow of steel crunching on steel broke the fascination. The *'Duchess'* had been rammed broadside on. The men were ordered into the life boats until it became clear how much damage had been done and whether it could be repaired. Fortunately, the damage turned out to be limited, and the *'Duchess'*, drunk or not, but definitely with a hangover of sorts, could continue her voyage home with the convoy. However, the other ship had indeed been damaged to such an extent, that it had to return to Gibraltar.

At 15.00 hours on December 9, 1943 the *'Duchess of Bedford'* moored in a wintry Liverpool harbour, bringing home the First Battalion after almost seven months. The Battalion travelled on two trains from Liverpool to Woodhall Spa, past snowy fields and frozen lakes. When taking up their quarters, every man was handed no less than four blankets to keep away the cold at night. Cyril put this pampering into perspective: "Yet, every morning we had to line up for our daily fitness training, dressed in shorts and shirt only."

Around Christmas and New Year 1943 many of the Battalion were granted a well earned two weeks leave. During all those long months overseas everyone had been craving these 14 days off. No one knew, but for some it was to be their last Christmas ever.

The New Year 1944 started with renewed and continuous exercises. 13 Platoon was, as a part of B Company, billeted in a camp in the village of Bardney in Lincolnshire. In March, General Montgomery and King George VI visited the camp. Other high-ranking officers made a tour of inspection as well, and on a number of these visits Cyril was the duty officer. On June 6, 1944 came the invasion of the European continent, anxiously awaited by all. However, the battalion that 13 Platoon belonged to, did not take part. It soon became clear the entire First Airborne Division was on stand-by for the landings in Normandy, but there was no necessity to bring them into action.

The summer months were characterised by an endless series of operations which were cancelled just as fast as they had been announced. Eddie Flinn recalled building a shed between times, together with Lance Corporal Ted Clague for a local farmer. "We were both carpenters, we enjoyed the change and the extra earnings", Eddie Flinn explained. He also remembered the fact that his bed was next to Eric Melling's whom he respected deeply because of his battle experience and fearsome fitness. During the last weeks of the summer of 1944, the First Battalion was relocated some 130 miles south from Bardney to Burford in Oxfordshire, as the frequent rain showers and resulting flooding caused unhealthy conditions in the camp. They were assigned to the Broadwell airfield as their starting point in case of an air landing. 13 Platoon was billeted at the pig-farm of a certain Charlie Silvertop. Cyril was amazed to find out that he knew that name and those sties. In this picturesque village he had been billeted once before while still in the Manchester Regiment. Back then, one of his duties had been to convert these particular animal shelters into sleeping quarters for soldiers. The sties had been in disuse for some time after a swine fever break-out. Cyril recalled that he and the other lads of 13 Platoon used to sneer that "the sties were still off-limits for pigs, but evidently they would do for us." These comments illustrated the growing frustration that kept pace with the steadily mounting number of cancelled operations. People in and around the division already started calling them the *Still borne* Division. Scornful comments predicted that they were going to be spared for the victory parade in Berlin, ended Cyril's elaborate account.

His account, with supplementary comments and quotations from others sources, made a fascinating overture to the experiences of 13 Platoon at Arnhem. I thanked him most kindly for his notes and then I asked him if he would be willing to check my list of names of the members of 13 Platoon. Did it contain names that evoked memories? Cyril told me that obviously the line-up of 13 Platoon changed during the course of the war. Not only because of casualties, but also due to the fact that people were transferred. Corporal Robert 'Bob' Ivison was a good example; he was transferred to the Anti Tank Group, where he became gun commander of the six pounder gun 'Cambrai'. And the platoon commander, Lieutenant John McCartney, went to join a Medium Machine Gun platoon in the Battalion.

Cyril was surprised to hear that I had managed to trace David Patterson in England, as he had assumed that David had left the country. Of the six names I had found with Patterson's help, Cyril did remember most. He also recalled that Albert Ashbridge was a member of a different platoon. A nice story came to his mind, involving the new platoon commander, Canadian lieutenant John Wellbelove. Cyril narrated:

> *"He joined our platoon in July 1944, and one of his responsibilities was to give theory lessons on various subjects. During one of those lessons the door of the classroom was suddenly jerked open. Major Armstrong, B Company Commander, legged in and interrupted the lesson to ask the Lieutenant a question on some, to him, important matter. But there was absolutely none of that with Wellbelove. Even before the Major could reveal the purpose of this entrance, John Wellbelove made clear in a calm but unmistakable way that he did not wish his lessons to be disturbed. Somewhat taken aback, the Major granted that his question might as well wait and slunk off empty handed. Imagine, reprimanding your commander in front of the men! Not surprisingly we all watched the scene with solemn faces but with a twinkle in our eyes. We never knew if he was later reprimanded by the Major for it. Wellbelove could also tell great stories about his survival trainings in the Canadian woods. About how to stay on course in the woods and how to survive for days on the things you find there. He also told about life on his parents' farm in Saskatchewan. He taught us many things. And he respected us for our combat experience, something he knew he was lacking. On that field he liked to listen to our advice. He was well-built and almost 6 feet 3 inches (1, 80 meters) tall and now and again he joked this would make him an easy target and would cause him to be the first one to be hit in battle."*

Cyril remembered other names as well. Privates 'Pip' Hulse and Tommy McDonald from his own scout section. And then there were Platoon Sergeant Fred Terry and Privates Edwin Ainsworth, Vincent Swarbrick, 'Johnnie' Walker, 'Gerry' Greasley and Norman Savage. About Savage Cyril recalled: *"Norman knew a magic trick that made it look as if he was able to swallow a razor blade. To this very day I don't know how he did it."* When I told him that I had managed to trace some of them, he instantly wanted to know who exactly and how I had achieved this.

The first one I could tell Cyril about was Philip Atherton 'Pip' Hulse from his own scout section. Ted Clague had been the first to mention this name. Much to my regret, Ted had not been able to put me on track of 'Pip's' story. The surname of Hulse sounded a bit Dutch to me, I mentioned this to Cyril, but it soon turned out to be a misconception. Namesakes in Wallasey near Liverpool, the town name that was linked to his name, told me that 'Hulse' was a name that was frequently found in that area. But they had never heard of a Philip Atherton Hulse before. I found that peculiar, as the place-name had been explicitly given. Written inquiries to other namesakes in Wallasey did not bring any clarification either. Only after broadening my search to other villages in the area, I found out – after many, many letters – that his parents had lived in the nearby village of Winsford. Again it was a local newspaper, the *Winsford and Middlewich Chronicle*, which was decisive. Through their reporting I came into contact with Bernard Hulse, a younger brother of 'Pip' Hulse, and Mike, a cousin. Bernard Hulse told me:

"Pip went to the St. Georges School in Wallasey, and afterwards he started to work as a junior office clerk with the General Electric Company in Liverpool. He enjoyed going to the cinema and loved to make model planes. He lived a life like anybody else until the heavy bombing of Liverpool at the end of 1940 ruined our house and a large part of its surroundings. We survived the attack because of the small air-raid shelter at the back of our garden. After the bombardment we moved in with relatives in Winsford. Pip was so angry about the German air-raid he volunteered for the Welch Fusiliers Regiment. But being only 17 years old, he was too young to join the army, hence he was not accepted. Not until he reached the age of 18, was he old enough. Pip's first Regiment was the Kings Own Regiment. He has been to North Africa, Sicily and Italy. 'Pip' was not a lover of the yanks, because when they invaded Sicily, the American tug planes dropped them short in the sea and his best mate drowned. For that matter, the name of 'Hulse' has no Dutch background".

Pte Philip 'Pip' Hulse volunteered for the army after his family home in Wallasey near Liverpool was destroyed by a Luftwaffe bombing air raid.

Bernard hardly had any details of Pip's experiences during the Battle of Arnhem. But the things he did remember, together with a picture of his brother, were being stored safely in my 'The Battle of 13 Platoon' file.

Much to my regret I had not been able to find any more information on Tommy McDonald, the other member of Cyril's scout section. Only the occasional mentioning by some other sources around 13 Platoon. Various posts requesting information on the website of the Manchester Evening News and other regional papers produced no result for many years.

The information I managed to retrieve on Joseph 'Joe' Winstanley was a bit clearer, but still rather sketchy. An article in the *St. Helens Star* had introduced me to his daughter. She told me that her father had volunteered for the army, despite the fact that he had been exempted because of his occupation as an engine driver. She wrote: *"He was 19 years old, not a worry in his life; he was cheerful, friendly and lively, and anything but truculent. Therefore his parents were very surprised to learn that he had not only volunteered, but had chosen an airborne unit as well! Perhaps he acted out of some sense of duty."*

Pte Joe Winstanley was a train driver when he volunteered for the airborne forces at 19 years. He married his Bridget when he was 26.

The memories of her father's experiences during the Battle of Arnhem were few and, as so many years had passed by, confused. I added them to my file, and hoped they would become clear when I tried to fit them into the stories from the others.

However, I was pleased that I could tell Cyril more about the story of Edwin Ainsworth. Initially it seemed an easy task, as combining his name with Blackburn resulted in only eight hits. It took little time to write the eight letters, but surprisingly they got me nowhere. Nationwide the combination E. Ainsworth indeed turned out to be equally rare, but this attempt remained fruitless as well. This caused a stalemate that lasted almost a year. Only when I discovered that approaching a newspaper sometimes presented amazing results, I made a fresh attempt and contacted the *Lancashire Evening Telegraph*. The editor was so interested he wrote an article about it in the history column *'Looking back'*. This was published in April 2003 and it caught the attention of one of Edwin Ainsworth's cousins. Through him I found out that Edwin Ainsworth was born on April 13, 1923 in Blackburn. Apparently he was a good student, as he was offered a scholarship for the Grammar school, but he joined the army instead. In 1940 he was admitted, even though he was not yet 18 years of age. Obviously he had 'administratively' advanced his date of birth somewhat.

He joined The Border Regiment straight away, where he developed a great interest in car mechanics. It was remarkable that not only his brother (by the Navy), but also his father (by the Army) was called up. To this Cyril added that Edwin Ainsworth had already been with The Border Regiment when they were in North Africa. He too had landed in the sea with his glider at the invasion of Sicily. However, he was not sure if Ainsworth was in the same plane as Cyril was. Thus the story of Edwin Ainsworth, built up by several sources of information, could be added to my ever growing file. It struck me that the other members of the Platoon were now providing information about each other as well. Often, these were only small details, but it was fascinating to see how the stories were now linking up.

At 17 years Pte Edwin Ainsworth declined a scholarship for grammar school because he preferred joining the Army.

Again through a newspaper, the *Grantham Journal*, I found the story of Charles Ernest 'Gerry' Greasley. His brother told me:

"Ernest was born in 1913. He was a silent man, who told very little about his experiences. Before the war he was in the building trade, and he worked as a caretaker of the horses of a retired colonel. He loved having everything shipshape. Even when putting on his hat, he would not go out before it was exactly right. Gerry was called up in 1940 and initially he was trained to be a gunner on the merchant ships that were being armed. But after a short while he volunteered for the airbornes. When I joined the forces myself, he taught me, his baby brother, how to look smart. This probably made me the best polished man on parade. He was a very dedicated soldier and cut out for the job of personal assistant/batman of the officer."

'Gerry' Greasley groomed the horses for a retired Colonel. He was trained as a gunner for the merchant navy, but switched to the airborne forces

When I sent Cyril the newspaper article, he sure enough confirmed 'Gerry' Greasley to being Lieutenant Wellbelove's batman.

More is the pity I had nothing new to tell him about the Platoon Sergeant Fred Terry and the Privates Norman Savage and 'Johnnie' Walker, due to either not having a place of residence to start my search, or I getting no response to my letters. For example: the name of Fred Terry yielded 74 hits, spread all over Great Britain. As additional information to reduce that number was lacking, a continued search was a hopeless case. Cyril, being a man of numbers, recognised the impossibility.

When mentioning the fact that I was afraid I would never be able to find something about 'Johnnie' Walker, for the very reason that this was a very common name, Cyril surprised me by telling me there was a photograph both he and Johnny Walker are in. Quite staggered, I consulted 'When

Dragons Flew', and indeed there was a Walker with Cyril in the picture. "That's him", Cyril said. But apart from this photo it remained silent around this man.

Trying to track down N. Savage seemed impossible because of the hundreds of hits my search had yielded for his name on the internet. Neither did my calls in various local and regional newspapers get any response.

Cyril admitted that he was already amazed by the amount of information I had found so far. Previously others had also made attempts to locate people for the purpose of a reunion, but their search had not produced much. Maybe it worked better this time because after 60 years some people had returned to their hometown, and because the inter-

Wiiliam 'Johnny' Walker

net facilitated the search. Moreover, I told him that my achievements encouraged me time after time to proceed with my quest for the remaining members of 13 Platoon and their stories, despite the frequent setbacks. The prospect that the next letter in the mail might reveal something special again was a powerful stimulus to take every next step. With some down-to-earthness, Cyril didn't expect there would be much more to find. Arnhem had been such a long time ago. I had to admit that this was quite likely, but as long as I kept receiving answers to my letters and newspapers were still willing to publish my messages, I never really considered quitting. On the contrary, I told him there was another new well I would like to tap into, the Municipal Archives in Renkum. To a large extent, the battlefields of the Battle of Arnhem lie within the municipal boundaries of this town, hence it was possible that this archive could provide me with clues. He agreed that this was an option yet to pursue. "I'm eager to know if you will be able to find anything", he said, and he asked me to keep him posted.

Old friends

One fine summer's day in July 2002, the registrar of Renkum, Geert Maassen, met me at the town hall in Oosterbeek, just after the lunch break. "Still in Oosterbeek", he said, "but soon this archive and I will move to the Gelders Archive in Arnhem."

I explained my search by telling him how Morley Williams came to ask me if I could help him retrace his passengers. I asked Mr. Maassen if he could assist me in my investigations. Mr. Maassen, who is considered to be an authority on the history of the Battle of Arnhem, showed me various documents to check for relevant information. He produced a list of the archives that the famous journalist Cornelius Ryan compiled for writing the monumental A Bridge too Far book. He also came up with several contemporary reports by German officers, fragments from earlier books and an overview of the Boeree collection.

Theodoor Boeree was a retired officer of the Dutch Army who personally witnessed the battle and afterwards did a lot of research on the events. I was also allowed to browse through a card tray that held the names and addresses of veterans who had been present at the fiftieth Commemoration of the Battle of Arnhem in 1994.

Maassen parked me in a quiet corner where I spent the rest of the afternoon searching through the files for clues on 13 Platoon and the glider pilots Williams and Blackwood. I started reading and making notes until, quite suddenly, it was five o'clock and the staff prepared to go home. Their shuffling about pulled me back into the present and I realised I was expected to leave as well. Still, my visit had proved to be very useful. Although I had not found specific information on 13 Platoon or its individual members, I did find a lot of relevant background information. I also discovered that photos exist of the place where 13 Platoon fought.

Geert Maassen advised me to contact the Friends of the Airborne Museum foundation (V.V.A.M.). The foundation has many members that do research on the various aspects on the Arnhem battle. One of them had specialised on the First Battalion, The Border Regiment and had good contacts with many Arnhem veterans. I remembered that I was able to start my search when one of the members of the V.V.A.M. had found that Morley's passengers belonged to this Border Battalion. This sounded promising.

I decided to approach this man, but at first found him rather reserved.

He, like others before him, started by telling me that most veterans were becoming rather fed up with people asking them about their Arnhem experiences. Also, he added, most of them were getting to a very old age now and he was keen to protect their privacy. However, when I told him that I got his name from Geert Maassen he was prepared to listen to my story. We made an appointment at the Schoonoord Restaurant in Oosterbeek, a historic place in the Battle of Arnhem.

I introduced him to the story behind my search and the results so far. Gradually, he became interested and gave me the names of several veterans with whom he was in contact. He told me that maybe the Platoon Sergeant of 12 Platoon, Wilf Oldham, and Private (later Sergeant) Johnny Peters of 14 Platoon might be able to assist me. These platoons, together with 13 and 11 Platoon, were part of B Company and fought in the same area. He also mentioned the name of Captain Patrick Stott, Second in Command in B Company. He added: "You would have to approach them yourself; I cannot do that for you. But I wish you every success and I am very interested whether they can add new information to your story."

I wrote my letters to Wilf Oldham, Johnny Peters and Patrick Stott with the utmost care. The chance to hear their stories first hand should not be treated lightly. I told them how I had got their names, about my research and its growing results. I also told them that I was in regular contact with Cyril Crickett, but that my knowledge was still very fragmented. I asked them if they recognised any names from my list with 13 Platoon members and, if so, whether they could give me any information about them. All three of them reacted very quickly to my questions. Wilf Oldham wrote that he was very glad to be of help. He was always prepared to help people who were seriously interested in the Battle of Arnhem. He remembered that Norman Savage came from Bolton, Eric Melling lived in Wigan and "Johnnie" Walker was from Blackburn. He suggested asking local newspapers to place a call for the people in question.

Also, Johnny Peters responded positively to my letter by email. He told me that he was in regular contact with Cyril Crickett, but thought that he would not be able to add anything new. He did, however, know Ted Clague very well and still had pictures showing them, together with Johnny Peter's future wife.

To my surprise, the answer of Captain Patrick Stott provided me with the address of Frederick Terry, the Platoon Sergeant of 13 Platoon. Stott added however that the address was about 12 years old. Checking it first proved to be a good idea, because no one by the name Terry was known there. I then discovered that the Northern Echo was the local paper for this area and through their cooperation, I was able to trace Terry's story. His son Bob answered my call in the newspaper and wrote:

Dear Sir,

I read in the Northern Echo, our local paper, that you were making enquiries after my father Fred Terry about his experiences during and after the Battle of Arnhem. I will do my best to help you. Before joining the Army, Dad left school at the age of 14 years and went to work in the local quarry, which was supplying limestone to the steel industry. That was in Leybum, North Yorkshire. When he was 15 years he began an apprenticeship with a local stonemason who was also a monumental sculptor producing gravestones. He completed his apprenticeship and did one year as a journeyman before he joined The Border Regiment in September 1939. Early in the war, he lost his brother Harry, who was in the RAF. From my father's pay book I took that he had also been in North Africa, Sicily and Italy. It seemed his glider was one of the few that made it to the island and did not land in the Mediterranean Sea. I do have a photograph of Dad in uniform which I will send you if you will let me know your address. This, I recollect was when he was a corporal, but I will check. I do have another photo of Dad in uniform with my late mother. I am also on the photo in Border Regiment uniform, which was made by a military tailor who was billeted next door to where we lived.

Bob Terry

Cyril Crickett reminded me that Sergeant Fred Terry had been first with another platoon. In January 1944, he became Platoon Sergeant in 13 Platoon. In this capacity he was responsible for the discipline and administration in the platoon, added Wilf Oldham, who himself was a Platoon Sergeant in those days. In addition, it was his job to make sure that the weapons of every soldier were in excellent condition. In fact, he was responsible for all the men in his platoon. He knew them all and discussed service or personal problems if they arose. The men of his platoon were under his command 24 hours a day. The typical Platoon Sergeant, therefore, not only had to be a strong personality with an iron discipline, but he also needed to be able to get along with the men. The Platoon Sergeant also had to be able to work very well with the commanding officer. Should the officer be injured or killed, the Platoon Sergeant automatically takes over command. According to Wilf Oldham, the Platoon Sergeant is a kind of father figure in the unit.

It turned out that at the same time that Wilf Oldham wrote his letter to me, he also contacted the papers that he mentioned. This proved to be successful, because in April 2003 I receive a letter from Norman Savage of 13 Platoon.

Platoon Sergeant Fred Terry worked in a local quarry in Leyburn that supplied limestone to the steel industry on Teeside(Middlesborough) before he joined The Border Regiment.

It was amazing to discover how a seemingly simple detail as someone's hometown could give so much result. In the case of Norman Savage, I lacked that information, which kept my searching fruitless. In fact I had given up hope to find him at all. However, with the help of his comrade Wilf, I did manage to contact him. This was what he wrote:

25 April 2003

Dear Sir,

Through a friend I learned about a call for information about me in the Bolton Evening News. I myself do not live there anymore. For a long time already. However, I am pleased to see that there are still people that are strongly interested in the Battle of Arnhem. I came from a family of five brothers and two sisters and was brought up in the bleak, grimy, smoky textile town of Bolton. I left school at 14 years and went to work for a local butcher for two years. I was 16 when war broke out in 1939. Most young men were drafted into the army and jobs got more plentiful. Therefore, I quit the butcher and went to earn more money at the tannery. At the age of eighteen, the war was still raging, I decided to sign up and fight for king and country. I was posted to the 70th Battalion, The Border Regiment. That was a young soldiers' battalion, where we did three months rookie training. One day I was checking the notice board at Headquarters. They were explaining that the 1st Battalion was being transformed into a glider borne unit. If you were accepted, your pay would be raised by a shilling a day. That was why I joined the Airborne Forces. I have also been in North Africa and Sicily, but then I was still in the Signals Unit at Battalions Headquarters.

I have not been back until the fiftieth Commemorations when Prince Charles was present. It was a very emotional experience to walk between the graves on the Airborne Cemetery. The names on the headstones brought back many overwhelming memories. There is so much to say about these events. However, I do not like to talk about them much, although I often relive these actions in quiet moments or when I am in bed and sleep will not come. However, I do urge you to continue your enquiries. Good luck!

With friendly regards,

Norman Savage
13 Platoon

Norman Savage worked in a tannery in Bolton before his army days.

I immediately answered his letter and told him that the call in the Bolton Evening News was placed through his old comrade Wilf Oldham. I gave him the outlines of what I had found out so far and with whom from his platoon I was in regular contact. Then I asked him for his personal story and a picture of himself in uniform. Norman Savage replied that in Signals he used to carry those big radios around as he was one of the stronger men. After the Sicily Operation though, on return to England, he applied for a transfer because he did not feel like carrying this heavy equipment about anymore. He found it difficult to put names to the faces on the list I sent him. Lieutenant Wellbelove, however, he remembered very well. He came at the same time as the other Canadian Officer, Lieutenant Aasen of 8 Platoon, he remembered. Although officers and men usually did not mix very well, the contact with them was very pleasant, he said.

The silence on "Johnnie" Walker's story wouldn't be broken until late 2017, some eight years after the first edition of No Return Flight. Not even Wilf Oldham's repeated letters to the Blackburn newspapers had established contact. It was not until Johnnie's granddaughter Sue Walker responded to a post in a Facebook group with a surprised "this man is my grandfather!" that the search bore fruit. Through her and her Dad Anthony, I learned that "Johnnie" Walker's real name was William Walker. He was born on 26 April, 1923 and raised in Blackburn, Lancashire. After leaving school, most likely at 14 years old, as so many others of his generation, William was a rope splicer in a local metal cabling/hawser fabricating works and a Labourer Metal Breaker Heavy Worker. That must have been hard work for the young man he was before the war.

William volunteered into the 1 Battalion, The Border Regiment in 1942, when he was 19 years old. Both the extra pay and the adventurous nature of an airborne unit will have appealed to him. His last name being Walker, he quickly acquired the nickname 'Johnnie', for obvious reasons. If there was an anecdote that gave him the nickname, it is unfortunately lost in time. Although his friends and relatives used to call him Billy. Until the invasion of Sicily which took place on the 9th -10th July 1943, Billy spent his time training. He became a radio operator, which meant extra studying, next to his training to become the elite infantry man that the airborne soldier was. During the Sicily operation, William was flown into battle in one of the many Waco gliders. Like so many, his glider was released too early and crash landed in the sea off Sicily. When it was still afloat, the heavily packed men quickly evacuated the ditched plane through the plywood roof. While

William tried to get out, he got stuck in the hole because he still had the radio set on his back. The webbing straps were cut off to release the cumbersome set. This 'friendly fire' cut to his shoulder was the only wound he was to receive during the entire war. He was picked up by a Navy vessel and evacuated to Malta. Here he was hospitalised for 24 hours after which he re-joined his unit in North Africa. Late in 1943, Billy's 1 Border Battalion sailed back to England and was brought back to strength. He, like Norman Savage, left his Signals unit and joined 13 Platoon as a sniper, fully aware that if the Germans would catch him, they would shoot him on the spot. Snipers weren't very popular. Billy's son Anthony believes he undertook 3 parachute jumps whilst in training.

Waiter in a trench

The year 2017 would also be the year that I found the first echoes on Private Frank Evans. In 2014 Airborne archives researcher John Howes sent me the *General questionnaire for British/American ex-prisoners of war* that Frank had filled in in June 1945 when he had been repatriated from his prisoner of war camp. This provided several leads. Frank was born in 1912. I realised that chances for him to be still alive were slim. So I focused on contacting several cemeteries and the local newspaper in 2017. This led me to the Cheshire Archives and Local Studies group who suggested I use Facebook, which had not been around for my previous research.

It turned out to be sound advice, because within 10 days his grandson Stephen Earlam was found and the story started unfolding. It gained further strength through combining it with details and general background information that I already had until it read:

Frank Evans was born in North Wales in 1913, in the coastal town of Rhyl. At some point he moved to Chester with his mother. He was an only child. Before the war he worked as a waiter in a number of the more upmarket hotels in Chester and along the North Wales Coast. Stephen Earlam said: *"He married my Nan (grandmother), Jane Bennion, in July 1938, in the Registry Office in Chester Town Hall when he was 25 years old. Their only child, my mum Beryl, was born in August 1939, just a month before the start of the war."* His Army number indicates that Frank directly enlisted in The Border Regiment. Presumably his pre-war occupation and his being a married father in his late twenties (28) qualified him for waiting-on in the Officers Mess. Here, he could have seen out the war in relative safety. But like many other men in their twenties that didn't suit him and at some point he volunteered into the First (Airborne) Battalion of The Border Regiment. This may have been in early 1944 when the depleted 1 Battalion returned from its Mediterranean campaign and needed to be rebuilt. No doubt, the extra money that came with qualifying for this glider borne unit will have been very welcome for his young family as well. Apparently he didn't mind losing his rank of Sergeant.

It was fascinating to see how the modern social media were helpful in retrieving these stories that outside of the family already seemed banned to oblivion.

Then the son of Platoon Sergeant Fred Terry sent me a copy of a very remarkable letter, dated 1995. In it, Captain Stott supplied Sergeant Fred Terry with a list of names of 13 platoon members. Stott told Terry that shortly after he had been captured in 1944, he made a list from memory with all the names of people that were in B Company and had it checked by Lieutenant Royall, the Lieutenant of 12 Platoon who was taken prisoner as well. Immediately I checked this with my own most recent list and saw that on 18 names there was a match. These names were:

Lieutenant John Wellbelove	Sergeant Fred Terry
Lance Sergeant Jack Kimber	Corporal Cyril Crickett
Corporal David Patterson	Private Edwin Ainsworth
Private ''Click' Fidler	Private Eddie Flinn
Private John Glenn	Private 'Gerry'' Greasley
Private ''Pip'' Hulse	Private Frank Jarvis
Private Norman Savage	Private Vincent Swarbrick
Private Jim Isles	Private Tommy McDonald
Private 'Johnnie' Walker	Private Joseph Winstanley

Lance Corporal Ted Claque, Lance Corporal Eric Melling and Private Frank Evans were mentioned by Pat Stott and by David Patterson. Private Bob Barnes was confirmed by his friend Jim Isles as a 13 Platoon member. This led me to believe that from 22 names it was now fairly certain that they were in 13 Platoon. The names of Privates Smith and Gibson were also mentioned on the short list as members of 13 Platoon. To get to a total of 25, as with the other platoons, only one name seemed to be missing on the list of 13 platoon.

The names Ivison, De Muynck and Ashbridge, mentioned in the Battalion Roll, Arnhem in the book ''When Dragons Flew'' did probably not belong to 13 Platoon, according to Cyril Crickett.

When leafing through all the information I had collected, I felt great respect for the friendly and selfless cooperation of those many people who had responded to my questions. The amount of information was impressive and still growing. Many contemporary and irreplaceable photographs were sent to me in good faith. I felt I was making progress.

The Lieutenant from Saskatchewan
As I went through the checked and renewed list, my attention was drawn to the name of the Canadian Lieutenant Wellbelove. Many of the people I spoke to, mentioned him with remarkably great appreciation. I had postponed looking for his story until I became more experienced in searching. There seemed to be a kind of symbolism in tracing the commanding officer's story last. Not until every effort had been made to discover the story of the men in his command, was it time to look into his. I finally seemed to have reached that moment.

I started looking for the name Wellbelove in a Canadian telephone directory on internet. There I discovered the addresses of four namesakes. I wrote to them, but the result was disappointing. According to Lisa Wellbelove, one of the Canadians contacted, they were all closely related to one another, but not to John. She also mentioned that a number of years ago she was approached by another Dutchman. Therefore, this trail did not seem to get me anywhere, but, experienced as I now was, I put my trust on other arrows for my bow, as a Dutch saying goes.

My next try was the association for Friends of the Airborne Museum and the website for Veteran Affairs Canada, but again, no results. I had learned that to keep going was the best remedy, so I did not lose courage. My last clue was the hometown, Eston, Saskatchewan, which was mentioned in the 'Battalion Roll, Arnhem'. A search on internet revealed that Eston was a small town in North West Canada. With some perseverance, I found the email address of the town hall. This should be a good starting point to find out more about John Arthur Wellbelove, I felt. For a number of days Canada remained silent, until on September 8, 2003, somebody from Eston by the name of Garnet Keeler, replied:

Dear Sir,
Your inquiry was forwarded to me from the Eston Town Office. Over the past ten years I have been involved in the research of those from our area who lost their lives in World War Two. I have some information of John Wellbelove and his military career, which I will share with you.

Some details I learned from my mother who was at Eston High School with John.
   Other things I gathered from John's sister Mary Spokes who lives in British Columbia. I will give you her address, so you could contact her directly. I will summarise my own information to pass on to you. Good luck with your investigation.

Gamet Keeler.
Eston, Saskatchewan

Intrigued by this solid information, I wrote Mrs. Spokes a letter. Almost by return mail she replied in an absolutely flawlessly typewritten letter. She wrote:

Dear Mr. Walburgh Schmidt,

Thank for your interesting letter. I would be happy to tell you a little more about the younger years of my elder brother John.
   The Wellbelove family bible records the birth of John and his twin sister Margaret on October 27, 1919. John had two younger sisters, Jean and myself. People used to think that I was his twin sister because of my resemblance to him.
   Our family farmed a 160 - acre homestead farm three miles North West of Eston, in a very fertile area of Saskatchewan. Our father had immigrated to Canada from England in 1906 from England, because of ads listing it as "The land of Milk and Honey."
   Homesteading means coming out to a very sparsely settled area of miles and miles of uncultivated land. In a period between 1890 and 1910 the Canadian Government sponsored new immigrants to come out from Europe to Canada to settle the untamed land and prove up an acreage.
   A homesteader had a year to prove up his claim of one-quarter section of 160 acres of land, build some type of residence and seed to some type

of grain crop. If he managed, he became the owner of the land. Dad's closest neighbour was three miles away. He drove a wagon and a string of oxen 45 miles to the nearest town for provisions. Quite an experience for a city bred lad!

I remember Dad telling us he was sitting down to dinner one day when a Native Indian appeared at his door in full headdress of feathers. The Indian carried a note from the Government saying he was a good Indian and he was to be given help where one could. Dad invited him to sit and have something to eat, and knowing my Dad, I am sure he gave him some money as well. Dad was still a bachelor at that time.

We grew up without electricity or running water on the farm and we had an outdoor toilet. When we were still small, Dad used to plough the land with a string of horses, but he progressed to a small tractor, which John drove. John was a typical farm boy who worked the farm and helped Dad where he could. His only hobby was stamp collecting.

We raised cattle, pigs, chickens, as well as turkeys and with our help Daddy also did some market gardening. The years of the "Dirty Thirties" brought many bad crops and great drought. We had to work hours on end just to get our food on the table. Still, we were luckier than most of our surrounding neighbours because of Dad's methods in farming. He was a comparatively strict English Presbyterian who never drank or smoked. But still a parent we all loved and admired for his guidance and understanding. In the same year that John went overseas, Daddy was elected into the provincial parliament of Saskatchewan.

John was always very well liked by his fellow students and teachers. One funny incident I remember when he was in Grade 10. He was 16 by then. The teacher asked him to stand and quote a poem he was to have studied for. Part way through John forgot some of the lines, but not to be deterred, he made up a few of the lines on his own. The teacher remarked that, while that was not exactly the way the poem was written, the class now had a budding Shakespeare in its midst. From then on until he passed through Grade 12, he was known by the rest of the student body as 'Shake'.

In 1937 John graduated from High School and enrolled at the University of Saskatoon, Saskatchewan, where he majored in Agriculture. His childhood at the farm gave him a good start and much background knowledge. He was very involved in the debating Team at the 'U' (university) and proved to be an outstanding student. In fact, he did well enough that he was offered a teaching post at the University upon his *graduation. However, four months before his graduation, on April 8, 1942, he went to North Battleford to join the First Battalion of the Prince Albert Volunteers of the Canadian Army.*

I was working at the local grocery store in Eston town and lived away from the farm during John's last year home before he went overseas. Therefore, I am not aware of any lengthy discussions between him and our parents about his plans to join the Canadian Army. He no doubt did it voluntarily, because he was the only son of farming parents and therefore would never be conscripted. I assume that he joined up because of a sense of pride in his country and possibly because he was influenced by his university chums' decision as well. Cliffy Aasen was one of them. Later in England they would join The Border Regiment together. Our family did have several military connections as the famous American five-star General Douglas MacArthur was my mother's second cousin. General MacArthur accepted the capitulation of Japan in August 1945.

Best Regards,
Mary Spokes

Only days after receiving Mary Spokes' letter, I obtained further information from Garnet Keeler from Eston. Together with the details I got from his platoon members, the story from John Wellbelove's sister could be completed as follows:

Still at university, John Wellbelove joined the S.O.T.C-class, an education for reserve officers. On October 26 1942, in Vernon, he was promoted to Corporal after successfully graduating for a course in bush fighting. Here he and Cliffy met Bert Ilsley

John Wellbelove

who would become a good friend of theirs. There he learned a lot about warfare, surviving in the wilderness and how to find his way about. Afterwards he did a follow-up course in Esquimalt where he received his officer's rank on 23 November 1943 and got a position as parachute instructor in Terrace. These cities are all situated in British Columbia. John was, however, not satisfied with his role as parachute instructor and foresaw that the war would be over before he would be able to get into action. He often tried to get a transfer to any regiment, but never succeeded. The need for people with his talent to educate others was too great.

In winter 1943, Garnet Keeler's parents were in Vancouver. One day his mother was bowling in the Marble Beach Hotel in Granville Street, when John and another soldier entered the hotel. As former high school mate she recognised him immediately and said hello. They spent the rest of the afternoon together and among other subjects talked a lot about home. Finally John said that he had to leave. Keeler's mum asked where he had to go, but he said he could not tell her, but that he would see her again in Eston after the war.

The British army in those days was suffering, due to heavy losses, from an enormous shortage of officers in the lower ranks. The Canadian Army offered to lend some of its own officers and this led to the Canloan-plan. John immediately saw his chance, applied and was attached as Canloan officer to the British army as were Cliffy Aasen and Bert Ilsley. In 2005 Bert Ilsley's wife Ruth commented:

Regina, SK, Canada, October 2005

Dear Mr. Walburgh Schmidt,

Thank you for your unexpected letter. I shall try to answer it to the best of my knowledge on behalf of husband Bert as his own memory is not its best anymore.

Bert met Johnny Wellbelove and Cliffy Aasen at Vernon BC, Military Camp in 1943. They became friends, all of them having come from Saskatchewan and being Lieutenants in the same unit. Here is a photo I found of I think the three of them, still as Sergeants. As volunteers with CANLOAN, they and Cliff Aasen were buddies. In England, when it came time to put the Canloaners into place, it was begun alphabetically. So Aasen was called first and he was able to take his two chums with him to the 1st Battalion, The Border Regiment. As luck would have it, Bert was assigned to R (Training) Company, the others to A and B Company. As R Company was held back on that run to Arnhem, Bert wasn't with Johnny and Cliff. Bert's Company was waiting to be sent, and then of course it was cancelled altogether.

Our very best wishes to you now and always,

*Very sincerely,
Ruth Ilsley*

In May 1944, in Halifax, they boarded the SS Empress of Scotland bound for the United Kingdom. As a Canadian prairie boy John probably felt completely at ease in the endless wideness of the ocean. They reached Liverpool on May 11 and in July 1944 he was assigned to the First Battalion of The Border Regiment. He immediately started training with the airborne battalion. 13 Platoon was assigned to him and Cliffy Aasen got 8 Platoon to command. As Canloan officers they wore a badge on both shoulders with the word Canada in white letters on a Khaki background. The Canloan badge was worn between The Border Regiment badge and the Pegasus emblem of the airborne division.

Lieutenant John Wellbelove (centre) with Albert Ilsley on the right and possibly Clifford Aasen on the left, still wearing sergeant's stripes in one of their Canadian training centres.

John Wellbelove probably joined the First Battalion, The Border Regiment around the time of its transfer to Burford in Oxfordshire. In all probability he, together with many other officers from the battalion, was billeted in the Priory, a well-known house built in Elizabethan style in that provincial town. Private 'Gerry' Greasley was assigned to him as his batman.

The Mess was also here, where the officers had their meals and gathered in their spare time to socialise or read a book. His platoon was stationed in a former pig farm, which had been transferred into army accommodation. John did not only immediately have to join in field exercises, he also had to give his platoon theory lessons on a wide variety of subjects. In those classes, he often told the men about his bush fighting course which he had done back in Canada and about life on the farm of his parents in Saskatchewan. While on field training Wellbelove found out about a remarkable plant that existed only in the vegetation of the old world. Johnny Grant from 14 Platoon told the story: "We were on a training that included some running through a nearby forest. Full gear and all. One of the instructors would suddenly shout INCOMING!! Then you had to dive to the ground as quickly as possible to avoid being hit by the imaginary shell. On one occasion Wellbelove did exactly as he was ordered, but unaware of the existence of nettles, dived right into a large patch of them. The others of course found patches that were free of these prickling plants. The point was that you were not allowed to get up before the signal all clear was given. That didn't happen for several minutes during which the Canadian Lieutenant had to stay put. Much to his credit he did stay down. And when he got up with a face and hands full of painful red spots from the nettles, we informed him ever so kindly of the danger of nettles. He muttered that in Canada these plants didn't exist and that he had never seen them before. But he didn't complain.

With the information about John Wellbelove, my folder 'The battle of 13 platoon' had received its last addition. I concluded that after more than so many years of extensive searching, I could hardly expect more information than I had now. Six years after I met Glider Pilot Morley Williams, I could finally give a fairly detailed answer to his question of who were in his Horsa 166. From almost every one of his passengers, I had been able to trace what happened after they had said goodbye on that field in Wolfheze on September 18, 1944. The search had transformed into personal stories told by the men themselves, their relatives and friends.

With these valuable jigsaw pieces I could now create the picture of their adventures during the Battle of Arnhem and of their lives afterwards. It was time to contact Morley and tell him what I had found.

Part 3

The Battle of 13 Platoon

Footnote:
In the next chapter German Army units were mentioned in italics to make it easier to tell them apart from the British army units.

Oss, 8 December 2003

Dear Morley,
My research on the fate of your passengers on the Horsa 166- flight has now progressed so far that I can finally send you some results.

I discovered that you and Blackie flew 13 Platoon, B Company 1st Battalion The Border Regiment to Arnhem. In the past few years, I was able to trace several of its surviving members. They usually were rather astonished to be asked about 'Arnhem' after so many years. Once past their surprise, they were more than helpful in recounting their experiences.

In other cases, I met relatives who were equally helpful. About some of your passengers I received very detailed information, about others sadly only very little or nothing at all surfaced.

For example, I am still not completely certain how many men were in 13 Platoon. From some 22 members I am confident that they were in that platoon and thus flew in your glider. However, I cannot guarantee that the list is accurate. Wherever possible I have checked the information to make sure that there were no internal contradictions in my researched version of the events. All the fragments l retrieved and every quotation from the literature I puzzled together into a coherent account of their experiences from the moment that they said goodbye to you until now.

I hope it brings you the answers you have been looking for, for so long. For me, the study into their fate has been an impressive and moving experience and I consider it an honour that it was me who you asked to fulfil your quest.

In friendship,

Haks

Day 1 Sunday, 17 September 1944

The story of 13 Platoon at Arnhem started at daybreak, when the soldiers climbed into the waiting trucks. The men were transported from Burford to Broadwell Airfield. Some 5 kilometres down the road, where their glider was prepared for take off. At the same time, tens of thousands of Allied soldiers all over England and Northeast Belgium were preparing for Operation Market Garden. In just a few hours a monstrous sledgehammer would savagely come down on the German defences in the southeast of the Netherlands and clear the way to the final defeat of the Nazi regime.

The Allied Airborne Divisions, of which 13 Platoon was only a tiny part, were to clear the bridges over the many waterways in the south of the Netherlands for the ground forces with their tanks and countless other vehicles. Once the ground forces crossed the bridges, the last natural defence line of the German Army on the Rhine would have been eliminated. Then there would be no way for the Germans to stop the Allied forces from pouring into the Ruhr zone, the heart of the German war industry. The road to Berlin would then lie open and hopefully, the war could be over before Christmas 1944. This scenario must have been an intoxicating prospect after nearly five years of war and destruction.

Upon arrival at the Broadwell airfield, the trucks turned onto the runway tarmac. Each one driving along the rows of waiting gliders until it arrived at the glider that it had been allocated to. The 42 Horsa gliders and 42 twin-engined C 47 Dakota tug planes were ready to airlift the Battalion to the operational area near Arnhem. The trucks of 13 Platoon had a long way to go before they arrived at Horsa 166, as it was one of the first in the queue.

The men shuffled to the tailboard of the truck, jumped down and walked towards the big glider. There they met their pilots, Morley Williams and Ian Blackwood, standing next to their glider. The handcart with extra supplies had already been stowed on the glider. The scheduled time of departure was approaching with the same speed as the likelihood of cancellation was diminishing. However, there was still doubt about the actual launching of the operation. So many times the whole thing had been called off at the last minute. Over the gliders hung a sensation of anxious excitement with an undercurrent of tension. The waiting soldiers were writing provocative and colourful comments on the flanks of the Horsa's. A jeep approached and a medical orderly jumped out. He distributed white tablets of Benzedrine. That would help to stay awake in the combat area should the fighting last too long, another sign that the operation had not been cancelled yet.

Then, at approximately nine o'clock am, the nerve-wracking order to board their gliders was received. The men of 13 Platoon entered their lightly built glider, which still smelt of glue and wood, and fastened their safety belts. The doors were closed and for a brief moment, no noise was heard. Then the boom of dozens of starting engines tore through the silence. Now it was final! They were going into battle!

At 0945 hours the first Dakota-Horsa combination took off from Broadwell and at 0950 hours it was Horsa 166's turn. It was a sunny and warm day. When the tug plane pulled the glider to a higher altitude, the sheer magnitude of the operation became clear. The sky was absolutely packed with aircraft heading east after having formed into large formations.

After about ten minutes Lieutenant Wellbelove, the platoon commander, got a startling message from the glider pilot. He was going to cast off from the tug plane. Something was wrong! A glance to the outside through the little windows of the Horsa showed that they were still flying over English farmland with a distinct possibility of hitting a stone wall or a farmhouse. The men put on their helmets for safety and braced themselves for an emergency landing.

The glider landed safely in a small airfield near Hatfield. The glider pilots told their passengers that the engines of the tug plane were overheating. Therefore, they had to release the glider and abort the mission. Another terrible disappointment! The tug plane returned to base, where it landed safely. For 13 Platoon and the glider pilots there was nothing else to do than to lie down on the grass, watch the armada fly over and wait humbly

A Horsa gliding down to land during a training in England (ABM)

for transport back to Broadwell. The only good thing about the landing was that it had taken place by day on solid English soil and not at night in the Mediterranean Sea, like in the Sicily Invasion.

It took until midday before an aircraft arrived to bring them back to Broadwell. By the end of the afternoon, the men were back at their point of departure, where they discovered that several other gliders of the battalion had been stranded in England as well. It was of little comfort. That evening the men of 13 Platoon listened closely to the first radio reports of the airborne operation in the Netherlands. They asked themselves how the rest of their B Company was doing in securing the landing zone for the scheduled landings of the next day, Monday, September 18.

Near the coastal village of Katwijk aan Zee in the Netherlands, on the still peaceful Sunday, recruits from the German *Wossowsky battalion* looked up at the enormous, seemingly unending air fleet that passed by overhead. This German unit was part of the *Hermann Göring Ausbildungs und Ersatz Regiment* of the Luftwaffe. The battalion commander was *Oberleutnant* Artur Wossowsky, who had originated from an anti-aircraft *(Flak)* unit and had no experience in conducting infantry operations. Not long after the aircraft had passed by, Wossowsky got orders to prepare his unit for departure.

Day 2 Monday, 18 September
Burford, Charlie Silvertop's pig sties, 0630 hours

Corporal 'Jock' Patterson of 13 Platoon woke up. First thing he did, was to look out the window to check the weather. "It's awful, it's drizzling and foggy", he called over his shoulder to the others who still struggled to wake up. After breakfast, Corporal Patterson and the others put on their battledress and gathered their gear for the operation. He saw to it that his Section was ready to go. The men were wearing Denison smocks, light marching kit, which included 24-hour rations, two mess tins, two ammunition pouches on their belts and shoulder belts. They were carrying a helmet and rifle and entrenching tools for digging and kept emergency dressings in their pockets. The snipers had their telescopic sights in a protective metal tube. Some men were carrying an extra ammunition belt. Patterson favoured a few hand grenades as extra. Every one of the battalion took as much ammo and hand grenades as he could carry. Finally, everybody went to the trucks which were already waiting with idling engines to bring them to the airfield once more. Patterson hoped for better luck than the day before. After so much hard training everybody was keen on going into action. He checked if everybody in his Section had boarded the truck. Suddenly something on the ground caught his eye. He saw a one-pound note lying between the first autumn leaves. He picked it up and put it in his pocket. Then he realised that he couldn't spend it in the Netherlands. Furthermore, being a superstitious Scotsman, he did not want to spend all his luck before the operation had started. He made a hard decision and gave the note to a surprised RAF ground service man, who happened to be passing by.

The bad weather in the morning delayed the second start for hours. Horsa 166 was now almost last in the line with a substitute glider in the second wave of Operation Market that would bring several thousand airborne soldiers more to the Arnhem area. The glider that had made the emergency landing was still near Hatfield and would be collected later.

Then finally, the weather improved and one after the other the tug-glider combinations took off in the direction of the Netherlands. When Horsa 166 was due to leave, a little bit of sunshine broke through the clouds. Once up in the air, the sun was shining brightly. The flight remained quiet and comfortable. Patterson was already convinced that giving away the one-pound note had been a good investment. During the trip he and the others made jokes about the lights of London that, for the first time since the war began, were not blacked out anymore. The danger of German bombing was past now, except of course for the V-1 and V-2 rockets. "The end of the war is coming near now and we are coming in to speed things up a little ", Eddie Flinn said to Tommy McDonald who sat next to him in the glider. He added that as far as he was concerned there was not much difference between flying in a glider and a bus ride.

Over the Netherlands, after they passed over the town of `s-Hertogenbosch, Flinn discovered a tiny hole in the fuselage of the glider. Apparently, some Flak fragment had penetrated the glider. Luckily, nobody was hurt and no vital parts of the glider were damaged.

Eddie Flinn said that, once in the air, flying in a glider isn't that much different to a bus ride(In this picture the airbornes are Polish(IWM)

At 1500 hours the Horsa released the tow cable and went into a steep dive. The landing area LZ 'S' near Wolfheze was cluttered with gliders from the landings the day before. A few craters were visible, leading to the worrying conclusion that there had been at least some German resistance. As the glider was about to land, Cyril Crickett saw a haystack approaching fast. He wondered if the pilots had seen it too. He and his mates were, strapped tightly in their quick release straps, tensed and ready to leave the glider as fast as possible after having come to a halt. The procedure had been rehearsed countless times. Horsa 166 made a safe landing and shakingly, screechingly and joltingly came to a standstill in the farthest corner of the landing area. The airbornes threw both doors open and burst out like lightning into the open. Forming a defensive circle around the glider, they dived to the ground. Only then did they start to take in the surroundings.

Cyril Crickett was one of the first ones out. He saw that their glider had stopped at a safe distance from the haystack. Eddie Flinn was directly on Cyril's heels. When he was lying on the ground and peering from under the rim of his helmet, he was vaguely disappointed for a moment not to see any windmills. Lance Corporal Ted Clague was looking tensely at the many gliders that came in to land between their predecessors that had arrived one day earlier. One of them miscalculated its landing and crashed in a row of trees at the edge of the landing area.

The task of helping the survivors of that crash had to be left to the medics and others who happened to be nearby. Apart from some sporadic fire exchanges in the woods, there did not seem to be any threat in the landing area from the enemy.

Looking back at their own glider, they saw their pilots having a well-deserved coffee after the arduous task of flying and landing their glider. Apparently indifferent to the threat of getting shot at in their unprotected cockpit.

However, it quickly became clear that it was safe enough for the passengers to get up too. After a look on the map to find the way to their Battalion HQ, the men of 13 Platoon said goodbye to their glider pilots. It would take 58 years before some of them would meet each other again in Oosterbeek.

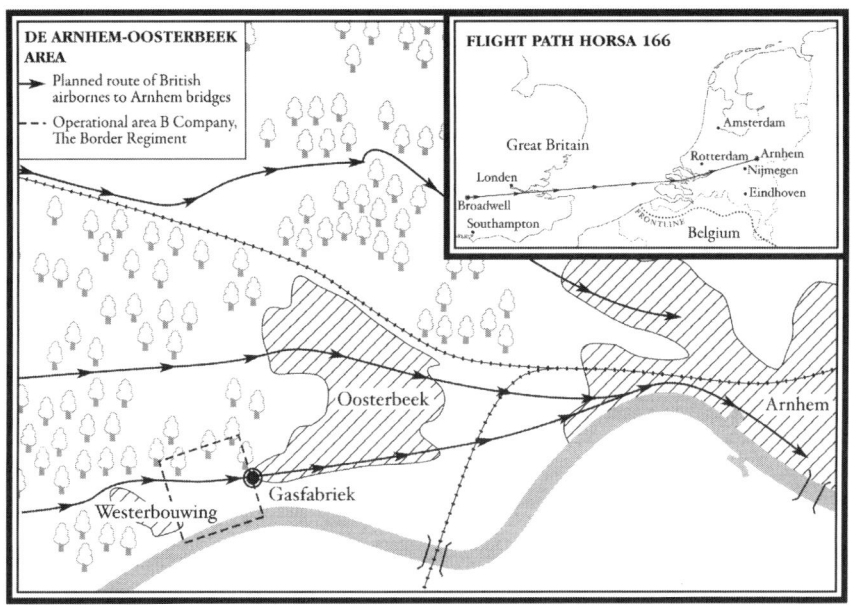

"The Arnhem-Oosterbeek region" and "Operational area B Company, The Border Regiment'

When 13 Platoon marched off, some of the men that had experienced the catastrophic sea landings in the invasion of Sicily told the rookies how successful this landing had been. Going to Battalion HQ, they passed a garden where a Dutch woman asked them in excellent English if they perhaps cared for a cup of tea or coffee. They thanked her politely for her friendly offer, but regretfully had to move on. Privates Eddie Flinn and Frank Jarvis were leading the way.

Battalion HQ was established in the Jonkershoeve, a farmhouse between Dropping Zone X (for the paratroopers) and Landing Zone Z (for the gliders). The Regimental Aid-Post of the Battalion had been set up in the house next door. Lieutenant Wellbelove and his men reported in and learned that they were going to be kept at HQ as a reserve. Contrary to what they had expected, they didn't have to go to the village of Renkum to help secure the Landing Zones against attacks from the west. This assignment had been taken care of by the rest of B Company who were to rejoin the Battalion later on. That night the Battalion would relocate to the planned positions on the western edge of Oosterbeek for Phase Two of the operation. There they were to protect the rear of the advance by the Parachute Battalions heading for the Arnhem Bridge, the main target of the entire operation.

While at Battalion HQ, 13 Platoon would help to protect the medical troops, who on the nearby Landing Zone, were taking care of the wounded of the second lift. It is quite possible that Lieutenant Wellbelove and a section of his platoon provided the escort mentioned in the incident described by the chaplain of the Glider Pilot Regiment, Captain Reverend Arnold Pare. He was amongst the medical staff in the Jonkershoeve. In his diary he wrote,

> *In the course of (Monday) afternoon a message arrived at the Regimental Aid Post saying that in a corner of the Landing Zone there were a number of injured men pinned down by enemy fire. The landed gliders around them were on fire and several of the men were wounded when they tried to reach the safety of the woods. They had to be evacuated from that spot urgently.*
>
> *A number of stretcher-bearers were ordered to fetch the wounded with two jeeps. For protection, they got an officer and seven or eight men. I (Padre Pare) offered to accompany them. Whilst we made our way to the designated area, we were met by several shocked and wounded air-*

borne soldiers. They told us that they had escaped, but there were many wounded still lying in a clearing, pinned down by enemy fire. Our side of this clearing was sheltered by woods. The escort group sneaked along the edge of the forest to scout the situation but they refrained from opening fire on the German side of the woods. I joined them and we decided to fire only when the enemy started shooting at the wounded and us. I took the Red Cross flag and signalled that only two stretcher-bearers were to follow me. I moved forward waving the flag with a thumping heart. I stepped out of the cover of the trees and I entered the open field, closely followed by two stretcher-bearers. I saw five gliders lie in ashes. The wreckage was still smouldering. Everywhere I saw killed and wounded airbornes on the grass. I wore my clerical collar and prayed silently for them. I came to a wounded man who, greatly relieved, thanked us for our being there. I called the bearers only to take those medical actions that were most necessary for moving him and went to the next victim. It seemed all rather quiet and I signalled the first jeep with the other bearers to appear. The wounded had all been hit in the back. The gliders were not unloaded. When the jeep was loaded with as many wounded as possible, it returned slowly to the woods. Then came the second jeep to take the others while I kept holding the Red Cross flag firmly. I told the men to take care only of the wounded and to leave the dead where they were. The second jeep departed and I returned to the woods edge, where the officer and his men were still lying in cover. I disappeared between the trees. Our worries had not been necessary, I thought thankfully. The enemy had probably left already. I had not progressed more than one meter between the trees when a well directed salvo of bullets struck the trees above our heads. I dived to the ground, for the first time thinking well about the enemy. All the time they had had us in their sights, but they never did fire. They seemed to respect the Red Cross flag.

We brought the wounded outside the range of fire and thanked our escort. When we returned to the medical post, we saw that preparations had already been made to move to another place.
(Paraphrased from Padre Pare's diary)

At approximately 1900 hours, The Border Battalion started to relocate to the area near Oosterbeek and the Rhine. Later on, the Germans would set fire to the abandoned gliders to prevent them from being used again.

Dusk also was the moment for the German *Wossowsky Battalion* to depart from Katwijk aan Zee. Travel by daylight was too dangerous for larger concentrations of troops because the Allied air forces dominated the sky. The half-trained non-commissioned officers (NCO's) of the German unit travelled by bike. It took them two days to arrive near the Ginkel Heath east of Ede and west of Arnhem. Together with other rapidly gathered German units, the *Wossowsky Battalion* was ordered to form a defensive line to the west of the battlefield.

Meanwhile, 13 Platoon was moving southwards as part of The Border Battalion, which was harassed by scattered enemy opposition. The men looked forward to rejoining the rest of their B Company. The task of the reunited company was to "establish a post on the Westerbouwing", on the north bank of the Rhine. At some time during the evening, the Battalion passed the crossing of the Wolfhezerweg and the Utrechtseweg and continued its southerly direction. Then 13 Platoon joined up with B-Company. 'Johnnie' Walker remembered passing the fallen body of General Kussin on the Utrechtseweg. United, they moved along the Van Borsselenweg to the Westerbouwing area on the north bank of the Rhine. Round midnight, the men began digging manholes and trenches. Sleep was out of the question. At 0515 hours, the complete B Company had put up a defensive position.

Day 3, Tuesday September 19
The Westerbouwing is a small wooded hill, 30 meters high, on the north bank of the Rhine looking down at the ferry of Driel. There was a small restaurant at the top of the hill. Westwards was the hamlet of Heveadorp and the village of Doorwerth. To the east, the hill sloped down several hundred meters, fading into grassland and then adjoining an orchard that belonged to a farm on the Veerweg. B Company Headquarters were housed at this farm. North of the Westerbouwing, the Oude Oosterbeekscheweg changed into the Benedendorpsweg. There was a strip of open grassland at the north side of this road that bordered on a forest to the west. On the southern side, the Westerbouwing declined with a very steep slope, overgrown with trees and ferns to the Veerweg. South of the Veerweg was a grassy meadow cut in two by the connecting road to the ferry. It was the task of B Company to keep possession of the Westerbouwing and control the Driel ferry.

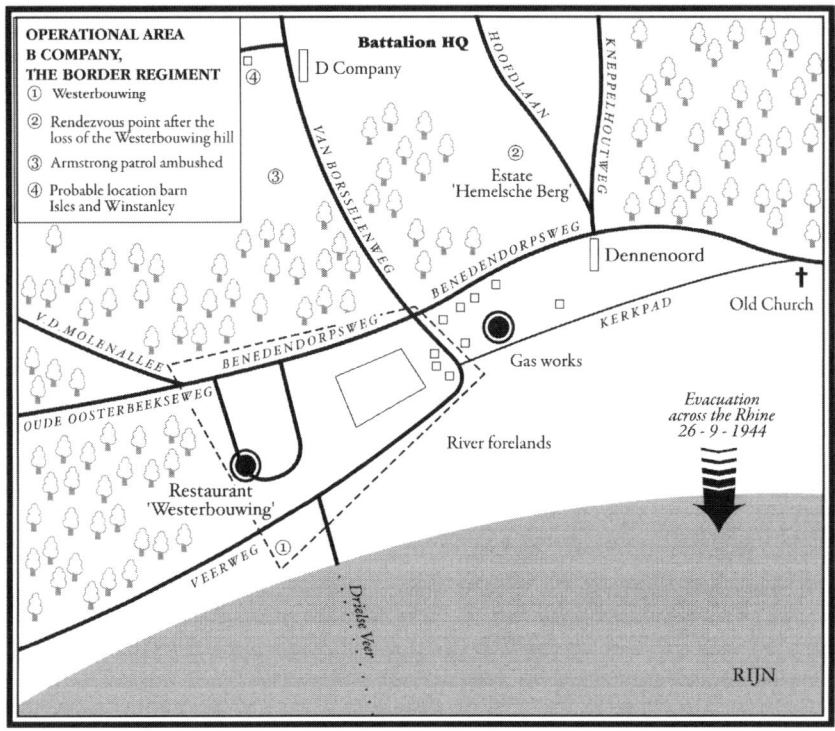

"Operational area B Company, The Border Regiment"

Upon arrival in this area of operation, in the early hours, the more than a hundred men of the four platoons and supporting mortar and machine gun crews were ordered to dig their slit trenches in the darkness of the night. With the entrenching tools every soldier carried, it took at least two hours until the pit was deep enough for him to stand in. A slit trench was usually manned by two men. One of them was on duty and the other could have a rest at the bottom of the trench. Corporal Cyril Crickett and Privates 'Pip' Hulse and Tommy McDonald of the Scout Section of 13 Platoon were assigned to dig their trenches along the connecting road to the Driel ferry, about 50 meters south of the Westerbouwing. Hulse was a Bren Gunner and McDonald was a sniper. In Crickett's opinion, the Section was rather unprotected with the open grassland to the front and the rear. Nor did the riverbank offer any protection. About five hundred meters west of his position, on the outskirts of Heveadorp, was a rubber factory. The Commander of B Company decided to position the rest of 13 Platoon provisionally on the Westerbouwing itself. He kept the other three platoons near the Company headquarters at the farm on the short side of the Veerweg for the time being.

When daybreak came on Tuesday morning, nobody had slept. German troops had not shown up yet, but noises of heavy combat came up from the direction of the Arnhem Bridge.

Later that morning a number of Dutch civilians walked past the trenches of Cyril Crickett's Scout Section near the Driel Ferry. These people wanted to use the ferry to reach the other bank of the Rhine, to get away from the war zone. Crickett found out that some of them came from the psychiatric hospital at Wolfheze. They had been sent home after the hospital had been bombed.

From the enthusiastic greetings and the "V"- signs these people were making, he understood that they were pleased with the arrival of the Allied Forces. Crickett's attention was drawn by one of the passers-by: "The man kept hanging around quite a while and kept turning round towards the forest areas nearly opposite to us. However, Pip, Tommy and I were not bothered by his presence and did not suspect anything at all. After a while the man disappeared heading north and because we were busy enlarging our trenches we forgot about him."

In the meantime, after their landing, Ian Blackwood and Morley Williams, the glider pilots of 13 Platoon, had also reported to their unit, F-Squadron of the Glider Pilot Regiment in Wolfheze. A little later, the Squadron had taken up position in the surroundings of Hotel Hartenstein in Oosterbeek, which had been chosen as the headquarters for the First Airborne Division. For the time being, the circa 250 glider pilots of F Squadron were held in reserve.

Around 1900 hours, on Tuesday evening, the British at the Westerbouwing heard the sound of engines from tanks or other heavy vehicles to their west; however, these did not seem to come any closer. There might not be a full scale attack imminent, the chance of running into a hostile reconnaissance patrol was increasing and the British started to prepare for the worst. 13 Platoon got orders to make a roadblock on the Veerweg by cutting down some good-sized trees and putting them across the road. For this purpose, they used the axes at their disposal. That should be sufficient to stop all enemy traffic on the Veerweg. Only tracked vehicles would be capable to cross the barricade. A bit further south was the position of the Scout Section, where Pip Hulse and his Bren gun were keeping an eye on the men who were working with the trees so he could cover them in case any Germans would try something. Lieutenant Wellbelove positioned a sentry of two men equipped with another Bren gun at the barricade. Sentries were changed every two hours.

At about 2100 hours that evening Eddie Flinn and five or six others were ordered to go on a reconnaissance patrol in the area. Eddie saw that 'Johnnie' Walker was in the same group. It seemed to be an uneventful patrol in the fading evening light until Flinn realised that he could hear people talking quietly nearby. He and the others froze on the spot and feared to have run into some Germans. After several hair-raising seconds, Flinn found that the language they heard was English. Still extremely vigilant, the patrol went straight towards the noise to discover a British war correspondent in the company of two glider pilots who had chosen this sector to have a look around.

By the time it was completely dark, Cyril Crickett and Pip Hulse were sitting at the bottom of their slit trench. Suddenly the evening silence was torn up by the ugly rattle of a German machine-gun. A salvo whizzed by; right between Pip and Cyril. Fortunately, they were sitting with their backs against the short sides of the rectangular trench, facing each other. Thankfully, the bullets passed between them without doing any harm. Had they been sitting in the middle of the trench, they certainly would have been hit. When it was quiet again, they remembered with a shock the man who kept hanging around their trench earlier that day. They suspected he must have marked their position for the German machine-gunner.

Several days before, on Sunday, 17 September, the proprietor of the garden restaurant "De Westerbouwing" and his family had seen the first British troops pass by on their way to the bridge in Arnhem. The proprietor's wife, Truus Giebing-Van Kolfschoten, wrote about this event in a letter,

> "On Sunday evening at half past six the English came past and we thought: war was over now, at least for us. We were pleased, of course. We had to sit almost all day in the cellar, because the Germans were shooting from Arnhem to Oosterbeek and soon the whole Benedendorpsweg

caught fire. We just plodded on those few days; often moving from the kitchen to the cellar and back again. We didn't have any gas, water or electricity and we didn't dare light the stove because of the fire-risk in case anybody would start shelling our house."

(Excerpts taken from the book: "Van Dollen Dinsdag tot de Bevrijding")

The last hours of Tuesday 19 September saw the Dutch family still trapped in their cellar while rifle fire was heard every now and then, possibly from German and British night patrols. Lance Sergeant Jack Kimber in his trench on top of the Westerbouwing could see some Germans attempting to find out where the British positions were. He didn't have a lot of trouble dislodging them with a couple of well aimed shots. Private `Click' Fidler who operated the light 2-inch mortar, was ordered to shoot a parachute flare, because of this hostile patrol prowling about. Fidler fired it in a westerly direction from behind the roadblock. However, the wind got hold of the flare and it drifted off eastward, illuminating the British positions as if in daylight.

The increasing noise of engines, and exchanges of gunfire during the fading hours of the day were an ominous prelude and everybody wondered how long it would remain calm. More than once, glances were thrown to the south bank of the river in the hope to see some reassuring tanks of relieving British ground forces arriving.

Day 4, Wednesday September 20
In the early hours of Wednesday September 20, B-Company rearranged the deployment of its four platoons. Now, three of them were situated on top of the hill. 13 Platoon took the south side and the edge of the wood that ran parallel with the Veerweg and the river. Cyril Crickett's Scout Section remained in position. Lance Corporal Ted Clague was assigned a position to the west of the buildings on the Westerbouwing and started digging new slit trenches with his Section. He took care not to have them too close to each other to avoid enemy fire making too many victims in a single explosion. Eddie Flinn was also digging his slit trench here. This was where he met his mate Jim Isles for the first time since the landing. He explained that he had not seen Bob

Barnes since the landing either. Isles belonged to Corporal Patterson's Section and was busy digging in the roadside of the Veerweg near the bottom of the stairs leading upwards to restaurant. Jim told Eddie that Bob was digging in just a little further on. Earlier that day, Lieutenant Patrick Stott, second in command of B Company, had taken some men from 14 Platoon on a listening patrol to the west. Shortly afterwards 14 Platoon, among whom Johnny Peters, went on a fighting patrol in the same direction. They discovered a tank in the woodland, accompanied by German soldiers. After a short engagement the British withdrew to the Company's positions.

In the meantime, their two glider pilots were now also committed to defending the British positions on the north-eastern edge of Oosterbeek. In the afternoon of the previous day the sector of the Dennenkamp woods, in the northeast corner of the British perimeter, had been assigned to their Squadron. The Germans launched an offensive at the end of the morning and the Squadron had to give up some ground there. Several Glider Pilots, Morley Williams amongst them, were made prisoner of war in the attack. Ian Blackwood and several others managed to escape. This has already been mentioned in Morley's story.

At the south-west end of the British perimeter in Oosterbeek, it was still more or less quiet. 11 Platoon under command of Lieutenant Barnes and sections of 14 Platoon led by Sergeant Thomas Watson were situated north and west of the buildings from the Westerbouwing restaurant. The 25 men of 12 Platoon of Lieutenant Royall had dug in in the orchard at the short side of the Veerweg. By doing this, B Company had created a position that due to its depth should be hard to overrun. Patrols were probably sent out regularly.

Two 3-inch mortar teams from 23 Platoon (S Company) had reinforced B Company, since the beginning of the battle. The first team was situated near the Company's headquarters and the second one could be found east of the restaurant buildings. Two Vickers Medium Machine Guns were in position on the northern and southern corners of B Company's line of defence. North was a six-pounder anti-tank gun that should stop German armoured attacks from the west. As B Company had lost their own two 6-pounder guns during the earlier fighting near the Renkum brickworks, it had become dangerously vulnerable to tank attacks. It was probably Air Landing Brigade Headquarters that helped B Company out. There, a 6-pounder gun towed by a jeep stood in reserve. It had emergency landed on 18 September south of the Rhine and the gun and its crew had managed to cross the Rhine on the Driel ferry unchallenged. The gun belonged to the South Staffordshire Battalion but had been unable to join them.

When Brigade HQ concluded that the 6-pounder was sorely needed in the Westerbouwing area, it was sent there. Probably on 19 September and likely to be manned by a Border crew (S Company) from one of the lost Antitank guns.

The day passed with little action and the men sat around, having a walk up to the southern edge to see if any tanks from XXX Corps were already arriving on the south bank. Syd Cringle from the mortar team near the restaurant said: "Alas! We never did see any movement. Those that smoked, smoked a lot. As a non smoker I didn't, but I almost envied them, for they had something to kill time with. All of us waited and waited."

In the course of the day, 13 and 14 Platoon suffered some probing attacks, but they weren't seriously challenged. The threatening sound of tracked vehicles could be heard, but no tanks or armoured vehicles were actually spotted.

Impression of the 13 Platoon positions. (The men on the picture are from 1 Para Battalion near Wolfheze- IWM BU 01167)

For the present, the Germans only continued their probing. Jack Kimber, whose Section was at the westernmost part of the Westerbouwing, asked David Patterson and Eric Melling in the trenches further down and left of his position, to come and help him to dislodge the enemy scouts. They succeeded without too much trouble. They even took a German Kriegsmarine (German Navy) soldier prisoner and Sergeant Kimber escorted the man to Company headquarters.

In the afternoon, some fifteen soldiers under command of Captain Heggie of the Royal Engineers (9th Field Company) arrived at Cyril Crickett's Section. They were instructed to go to the grounds of the rubber factory some 500 metres further west to look for boats or materials that could be used to make rafts. Crickett's Section was to protect them during their mission.

With the machine-gun incident of last night still in mind, Crickett, Hulse, and McDonald expected the enemy to have occupied the factory. It could even be that the machine-gun was still pointed at them, so they warned the Engineers to be very careful. However, the order had to be executed and the group set out with extreme caution. After a nerve-wracking expedition, they reached the factory. It took the Royal Engineers over an hour to search the factory grounds, but nothing useful was gathered and the group returned to their own lines, unharmed. The Engineers remained in the area to secure the ferry.

Later that afternoon, the men on and around the Westerbouwing saw Allied transport planes coming over, to resupply the now surrounded airborne troops. One of the supply containers dangling from a parachute, landed in the grassland behind the position of Crickett's Scout Section. Jim Isles and Bob Barnes were ordered to retrieve it. They crawled towards it as low as they possibly could, but on their way were discovered by the Germans who started shooting at them. However, Isles and Barnes managed to drag the container to safety without getting hit.

In the early evening hours, Captain Green, the Royal Engineers' Adjutant passed by the position of the Scout Section. He crossed the river by ferry and had instructions to make contact with approaching ground forces that, according to rumours, had been seen on the south bank of the Rhine. Later that evening, the area was intensively pounded by German artillery and mortars. This suggested that the German forces thought they knew enough about the position of the British on and around the Westerbouwing. The men of 13 Platoon, like everybody else, dived down in their slit trenches and prayed for the end of the shelling. That same evening the 75 mm guns of A Troop, from the Airborne Light Artillery carried out a bombardment on the area west of B Company's position. Captain John Lee, their Forward Observation Officer led the shoot.

Mrs Giebing-Van Kolfschoten, who was still in the cellars of restaurant "De Westerbouwing", wrote in her letter:

> *"It was in the afternoon when all of a sudden the English Major (Tom Armstrong) came to us. He told us that things started to look bad for them. The Germans were very near and the big army was still stuck near Nijmegen and could not come to help. So that same night we went back into the cellar and waited with our hearts in our mouths for what was coming. German shooting started around nine o'clock. Around our house there were heavy and light machine-guns, an anti tank gun and about four mortars. However, only the heavy machine-guns were shooting back. At half past eleven, it was quiet again and Wim walked out of the house. The English Major told him that they had repulsed the Huns, but if they came back tomorrow morning with tanks, we would be lost! As you will understand, that night was very worrisome for us. At six o'clock in the morning, we were already drinking a glass of Hollands (gin)."*

Jim Isles shared his slit trench with a mate who broke into a sudden panic during the shelling. The man said that he was going back to see his children and crawled out of the protective trench. Isles startled, jumped up and shot off after him. He jumped him from behind and pushed him quickly to the ground. At that very moment a mortar bomb landed square in the slit trench they had just left and exploded at the bottom. They looked at each other dazed. Convinced as they were that shells never land twice in the exact same spot, they both slipped back into their slit trench. After that, the mortar fire gradually ceased. Around midnight it was Norman Savage's and John Glenn's turn to keep watch at the barricade of felled trees on the Veerweg. Lieutenant Wellbelove warned them, just as he had the others, that the Polish Para Brigade would have landed that day on the other side of the river, near Driel. So, there might be Polish stragglers about in the Westerbouwing area. That was why everybody was ordered to be extremely careful and not to open fire straight away. Savage and Glenn once more rehearsed the password "Troop Carrier". In case anybody appeared in front of their position, they must call out "Halt, Troop!". Only if the answer was "Carrier", were they allowed to let them approach. Wellbelove didn't know that the Polish drop had been postponed till the next day.

Everybody had installed themselves in their slit trenches and Savage and Glenn stood guard behind the barricade in the darkness. Parallel to the Veerweg, on the south side of the Westerbouwing, was a narrow footpath. It was on that pathway that Savage heard twigs cracking, a sure sign somebody or something was approaching. It was well past midnight. The noise came from about four metres away from where he and John Glenn were positioned. He was faced with the dilemma that it must be either an enemy probing patrol or a Polish straggler. Savage wasted no time and pointed the Bren gun towards the suspicious spot. He shouted "Halt, Troop!" and waited for the obligatory "Carrier!" There was no answer, but Savage heard footsteps running away and more twigs breaking in the underwood. Savage immediately opened fire. "I must have emptied a whole magazine towards the noise. I suppose I got somewhat trigger-happy. Straight after that I heard Lieutenant Wellbelove calling, "Who is shooting?" Savage answered: "Private Savage, sir! I think we were stalked by an enemy patrol." Wellbelove replied to stop shooting. The rest of the platoon was alarmed as well and was ready to open fire immediately in case the enemy returned. It was dead quiet now, everybody was listening hard to detect even the slightest noise. Seconds turned into minutes, into five minutes, into ten minutes, into a quarter of an hour, but it all remained silent. Until daybreak.

Through the course of Wednesday 20 September, the German *Wossowsky Battaillon* arrived on the Ginkel Heath, west of Arnhem. Herbert Kessler, a 19-year-old non-commissioned- officer in training, heard that they would be held in reserve to fight further airborne landings, should they occur. One of their first tasks was to comb out a part of the forest where, supposedly, some isolated British paratroopers were hiding. They found nothing but dead British and German soldiers who had been killed in the fighting of the first days. At dusk, the *Kompanien* of the *Wossowsky Battalion* to which Kessler belonged, left the Ginkel Heath and headed south, towards Wolfheze.

Troubling news from the situation at the Arnhem Bridge led British Air Landing Brigade to strengthen its hold on the last potential river crossing at the Driel ferry. Suddenly the strategic importance of the Westerbouwing had become crystal clear. Late at night of Wednesday to Thursday, two sections of 17 Platoon South Staffordshires were sent to reinforce B Company and the Royal Engineers that were already in the area. The South Staffs were commanded by Lieutenant Donald Edwards. As they were approaching the ferry in the pitch dark over the open meadows on the northern bank, they came under heavy fire from German units on the south side. This forced them to give up their advance and they retreated to the church area.

Day 5, Thursday September 21, in the morning
At daybreak, Platoon Sergeant Fred Terry instructed Norman Savage and John Glenn to search the thicket in front of the barricade and to clear it from enemy soldiers that might be hiding there. Savage walked up the narrow pathway along the Veerweg, his rifle at the ready. After some five meters, he discovered bloodstained pieces of bandages on the ground and a German Schmeisser (sub-machine-gun) next to them. "Apparently, I hit someone last night who had been hastily dragged away by his comrades and lost his weapon", he concluded. Savage picked up the Schmeisser and took it with him. Just like the British Sten Gun, this German weapon fired 9mm bullets so it might come in handy, he thought. Then, he walked to the positions on top of the Westerbouwing and crawled into one of the slit trenches of his Section to the right side of a big tree, hoping for a bit of shut-eye.

Meanwhile, in the course of the night, the *Wossowsky Bataillon* had taken over the positions of a German Kriegsmarine unit, which had been positioned on the western side of the Westerbouwing. During the previous few days, the Germans had been carrying out reconnaissance missions. Around seven o'clock in the morning the *Wossowsky Bataillon* had arrived as relief party. Kessler's *Kompanie* had been instructed to move to the north bank of the Rhine and then, from 0800 hours onwards, to advance as far east as possible with the rest of the *Bataillon*. Should they encounter British positions, they were to attack them. It seemed likely that the *Wossowsky Bataillon* did not obtain accurate information on the enemy positions from the departing naval unit, because they approached the Westerbouwing apparently unaware of the British defence position.

As Kessler's Kompanie departed to the north bank of the Rhine, the soldiers on bike were preceded by the commander in his car. The German advance was to be supported by four tanks seized by the Germans from the French in 1940. The Renault "Char B" tanks belonged to the 224 Panzer Kompanie and they were already in the neighbourhood of Heveadorp.

Kessler's Kompanie reached the Oude Oosterbeekscheweg and crossed it unhindered southwards. At that moment, they were merely a few hundred meters west of the buildings at the Westerbouwing. Then the cyclists came on a small road, where they stopped to see which way to continue. It was quiet in the forest and there was no sign of any British presence.

The Germans continued cycling without worry, until the British on the Westerbouwing surprised them with a merciless barrage of machine gun fire. A number of Germans were hit straight away. Others dived, bicycle and all, to the ground and crawled away to safety. When the survivors looked up, they saw the small pavilion of the restaurant on the Westerbouwing, rising above the trees. They had encountered the British. This was probably also the moment that Jim Isles and his Section discovered a group of Germans in the distance from their positions down at the Veerweg. One of them was constantly walking up and down a forest track, obviously not aware of any danger. Corporal Patterson told Isles: "Jim, if you are really any good as a marksman, get that bloke!" Isles pointed his rifle, waited until the German came in his sights and brought him down with a single shot. Immediately after that, all hell broke loose when the Germans fired back and everyone around him started shooting as well. While all of them were diving away deep into their slit trenches one of his comrades shouted: "What the hell have you done now, Isley?!"

Practically at the same time, the rest of the *Wossowsky Bataillon* was running up against the main British positions on the Westerbouwing. British 11 Platoon, about 25 men, was the first to receive the German advance from the northeast. They saw how a mass of hundreds of enemy soldiers was approaching them at walking pace. They looked just like a crowd of football supporters leaving the stadium after a match. The roughly hun-

The Canadian Lieutenant John Wellbelove possibly helped several men of B Company to escape from the Westerbouwing by diverting the enemy. He himself never made it back.

dred and twenty five strong Border unit opened fire with everything it had and caused great losses to the enemy. However, after their first shock, the Germans managed to bring their own machine guns to the front. Together with their superior numbers, this enabled them to advance, inching in the direction of the buildings of the Westerbouwing restaurant. Although the three Border platoons received fire support from their mortars as well as from several 75 mm guns of the airborne artillery, it was not enough to stop the Germans. When these had come up to 40 meters from The Border position, 11 Platoon retreated with heavy losses to the Company headquarters via the south edge of the hill. Some dived straight off the steep slope. From B Company HQ, a number of men from 11 Platoon ran back up the hill to join the battle once more from the east.

About 14 men from 14 Platoon had entrenched themselves west of the restaurant and in the buildings, but it was hard to withstand the superior German numbers. The British position west of the buildings crumbled away, but withdrawal was perilous due to German fire. The western positions of 13 Platoon were now also under great pressure. Corporal Albert "Ginger" Wilson (11 Platoon) heard how the Canadian Lieutenant John Wellbelove, about 50 meters left of the positions of 11 Platoon, was encouraging his men. Wellbelove shouted, "Come on you Heini bastards" and was firing his Sten gun until his position was overrun and Wilson heard Wellbelove's Sten stop firing. It was the first time he heard the Lieutenant swear. With his action, the Lieutenant had been able to distract the enemy, which made it possible for a number of British to withdraw safely. However, the Lieutenant himself did not return to the Company Headquarters to join the regrouping.

The British 6-pounder anti-tank gun was destroyed by German fire even before it could come into action. That encouraged the four German "Char B" tanks to make their appearance. In the cellars of the Westerbouwing restaurant Mrs. Giebing writes,

> "It was just getting light when it all started. Pandemonium broke loose! A big German tank came out of the Valkenier forest. It crossed the playground, shooting all the time. Then it crashed through the children's toilets and the concrete slide. It stopped against the kitchen wall and fired again. It was dreadful! A little later, there were three monstrous tanks around the house, all firing away. The glass of the windows was

blown out, shutters and all. There was hand-to-hand fighting in our house. Behind the bar, there were three dead English and two Germans. In the kitchen, the attic and the toilets there were dead bodies. It was awful. Artillery were shooting at us. We got a direct hit in the hall, straight through the roof. It created a hole in the floor next to the pillar; two direct hits in the roof above the bedrooms brought the roof down in pieces. It was really bad! There were three English in the ice cellar and there was one amongst us in the beer cellar. The Germans threw the cellar door open and Dad went up with his hands in the air and had to tell them who else was in the cellar. When they found out that there were still some English left, they stuck a machine gun into one of the cellars and started shooting around. We were so terrified! The English surrendered and luckily, that ended it all. At midday, we were allowed to leave the cellar. Wim loaded a couple of bicycles and two old prams with clothes and things we didn't want to leave behind and we went into the forest. The tank near the kitchen stopped firing for a moment and we aimed to get on the main road to be able to reach Ede via Doorwerth-Heelsum. However, we could not cross that road, because the English were still shooting from up in the trees. In the end, the Germans sent a soldier with us to take us through the Valkeniers forest, away from the line of fire. However, on our way to Doorwerth they were still shooting heavily and we had to seek cover all the time. You cannot imagine how happy we were when we finally reached Heelsum. We got something to drink at a Red Cross post. We looked like vagabonds. The killed and the wounded, lying around at our home and lots more of them on our way out, it was horrible! Hannie, who was only a little girl then, thought that all those soldiers were sleeping. We also got a Red Cross soldier in our cellar that morning and all the wounded were brought there. First, an English soldier on his own came in and Wim helped him. He had a gunshot wound under his navel. The bullet had gone in a bit, parallel to his belly, and had come out 10 cm further. All the English carry morphine so Wim gave him an injection to make him sleep for a while. That boy was so scared! We had to take his wallet and sent it later to his mother with a letter to explain what had happened. Fortunately, he had a good chance of recovery. However, all those wounded, that was really awful. Some of them had five or six shot wounds or had lost some fingers. We had to help them because there was only one Red Cross soldier. I made them drink and talked a bit to them. When you have seen and lived through all that, you can't understand why they don't stop that insanity."

A third Section of 14 Platoon, the one situated near the British Company headquarters, was called in to assist in defending the buildings of the Westerbouwing. However, a number of Germans had reached that position earlier and captured some airbornes. When Kessler, the German NCO, saw them as they were taken away, he got very worried. These British were obviously a crack unit because he described them as `tall as trees, well fed and well equipped."

It was probably at this stage of the battle that Lance Sergeant Jack Kimber of 13 Platoon was wounded. He was hit in his ear by a bullet that flew out on the other side of his face via his cheek. Possibly, he had turned his face away instinctively as bullets kept on impacting closer and closer.

The section that came to help reached some trenches of 14 Platoon to the west of the buildings, but found them empty. Soon after, they saw that this position was untenable. The Germans were too strong in numbers. The airbornes threw a smoke-grenade and sought cover in the positions of 13 Platoon some 20 to 40 metres to the south.

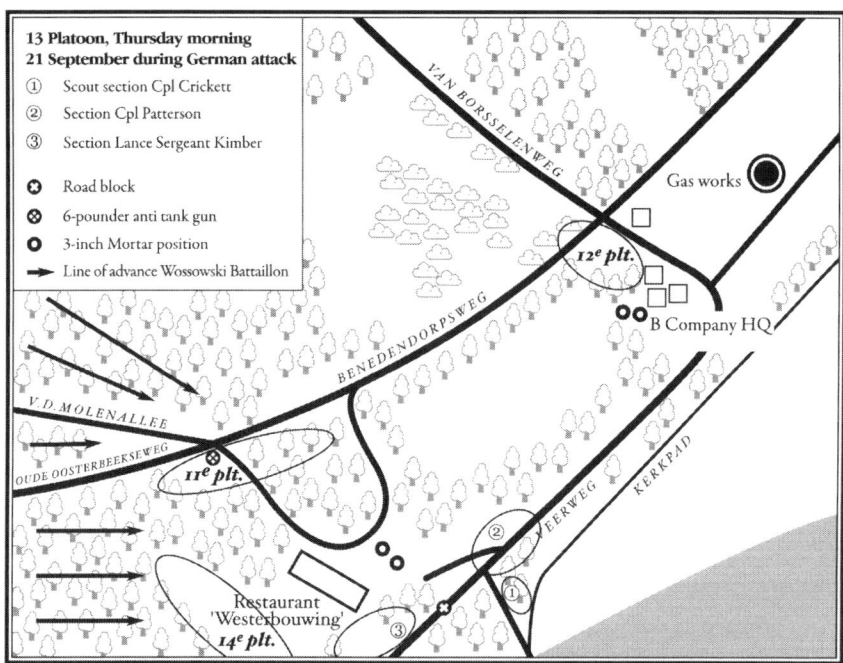

13 Platoon, Thursday morning, during the German attack on 21 September"

On the Veerweg

At the beginning of the German attack, Corporal David Patterson's Section were still in their trenches on the Veerweg, at the foot of the Westerbouwing. Cyril Crickett's Scout Section was also still in its trench along the connecting road to the ferry of Driel, anxiously awaiting developments. Patterson shared his slit trench with his friend Lance Corporal Eric Melling. To their left was Tommy McDonald's trench. North of them, on top of the hill, were the positions of Lance Sergeant Jack Kimber and his Section. At the Veerweg, close to the stairs, 19 year-old Jim Isles was in his slit trench. Bob Barnes' place was not far away from there either. It was around 10,00 hours and the German tanks were about to break through.

Cyril Crickett heard Platoon Sergeant Fred Terry shout that his Section should come up and reinforce the positions of the main body of 13 Platoon on the southern edge of the hill. Under cover of the roadblock on the Veerweg, he clambered up together with Pip Hulse and Tommy McDonald. They kept well to the left-hand side of the stairs on the steep southern slope. Once at the top, they saw German infantry approaching as well as four tanks. Even before they could come into action, an explosion quite near to Crickett hurled him off the hill again. Possibly, the shell was one of the first from the 4.5 inch artillery guns from the approaching ground forces (British 64 Medium Regiment) that had only just been contacted by the airborne forces. Tommy McDonald dived into a slit trench next to the one of Rifleman Eddie Flinn.

Major Armstrong then came to David Patterson's Section and ordered them to leave the Veerweg position and they hurried up the stairs. Edwin Ainsworth, who, acting on his own initiative, had come down to pick up the PIAT of 13 Platoon, went with them. The PIAT was an anti-tank weapon that could be operated by one or two men. Patterson mistook the three German tanks for Tiger tanks, the heaviest and most feared tanks the Germans possessed. The fact that they were the slightly lighter French Renault tanks did not make an infantryman on the receiving end feel any less naked.

When Patterson arrived on the Westerbouwing plateau, he saw another Border soldier at some distance, lying on the ground, firing a PIAT at the northernmost tank. The tank was hit, but immediately after that the PIAT-man was killed himself. Ted Clague also witnessed this PIAT-attack. David Patterson wanted to seize the precious anti-tank weapon, together with Eric Melling. This turned out to be impossible because of the intense German fire. Instead, they decided to stalk the middle one of the three tanks they could see. They crawled towards it in its dead angle. The tank in the middle could still move, but apparently, the other two were immobilized. This left the centre one with only very little manoeuvring space.

Melling and Patterson intended to yank the turret hatch open and throw a hand grenade in. They were only a few meters away from it when Melling was hit by a bullet in his head. He still said, "Pat, I got hit." However, Patterson couldn't do anything more than catch Melling's rifle before it dropped. Melling died practically instantaneously. When Patterson got up again, the tank gun fired at a target behind him. The shell flew past him only a few centimetres above his head. In a reflex, he dived away and ran off as fast as he could. The shooting tank rumbled slowly in the direction of the British company headquarters to the east.

Norman Savage, who was lying on the east side of a big tree on the southern edge of the hill, also witnessed the fall of Eric Melling. From the corner of his eye, Savage had seen him appear at his left, only a few minutes earlier. When Savage looked north again at the enemy, he saw a German with his machine gun jumping from behind one of the outbuildings. The German pointed his weapon at the area of the big tree where Patterson, Melling and Savage were and opened fire. While the sand of the impacting bullets sprayed up just inches in front of Savage, he saw how Eric Melling was hit. The German quickly ducked away behind the small building again, fleeing Savages revenge. Savage couldn't reach Melling because of the incessant fire from the rest of the Germans. The third, southernmost, tank had come to a stop at about ten meters beyond Savage's position. This tank was firing at the trees in the hope that the shrapnel would play havoc among the British defenders.

After the explosion that had blown him off the hill, Cyril Crickett managed to pick himself up and he started climbing the hill again. Pip Hulse and Tommy McDonald had vanished from sight. Savage heard someone calling for a PIAT and Cyril Crickett noticed the southernmost tank on his right being hit by a PIAT grenade fired by Edwin Ainsworth from a distance of about 12 meters from the tank. Platoon Sergeant Terry also saw how Ainsworth's first shot hit the target. The tank caught fire and the crew tried to abandon the vehicle quickly. However, a number of them, amongst them the tank commander, were killed by British rifle-fire.

German tank that was knocked out by Edwin Ainsworth using a PIAT. It may also have been destroyed by others from different positions as well. See also Photo 36, the map. (Photo Marcel Zwarts-Gelders Archief)

The same tank, seen from a different angle. (Photo Marcel Zwarts-Gelders Archief)

The Westerbouwing was now submerged in deafening noise and deadly chaos. Norman Savage felt that there hardly seemed to be any coherence left in the British positions. More and more, separate individuals seemed to be running around on their own initiative. The German troops had advanced to the buildings and the Benedendorpsweg. They were in the middle of the British positions but two of their tanks on top of the hill were on fire. The surviving German crew members were panicking and sought safety in flight. The middle one of the three tanks, which had escaped Melling's and Patterson's attack, was still rolling forward and was now threatening the positions of 12 Platoon in the orchard near the Company headquarters. Edwin Ainsworth had reloaded the PIAT and was choosing a new position to attack this tank as well. He managed to hit this tank too and there was probably another PIAT-grenade that hit the vehicle. In any case, this third tank was also put out of action, although it was not clear whether Ainsworth or another PIAT-shot was responsible. Possibly both.

The *Wossowsky Bataillon* suffered heavy losses, which caused the attack to peter out. The fourth German tank, driving further north from

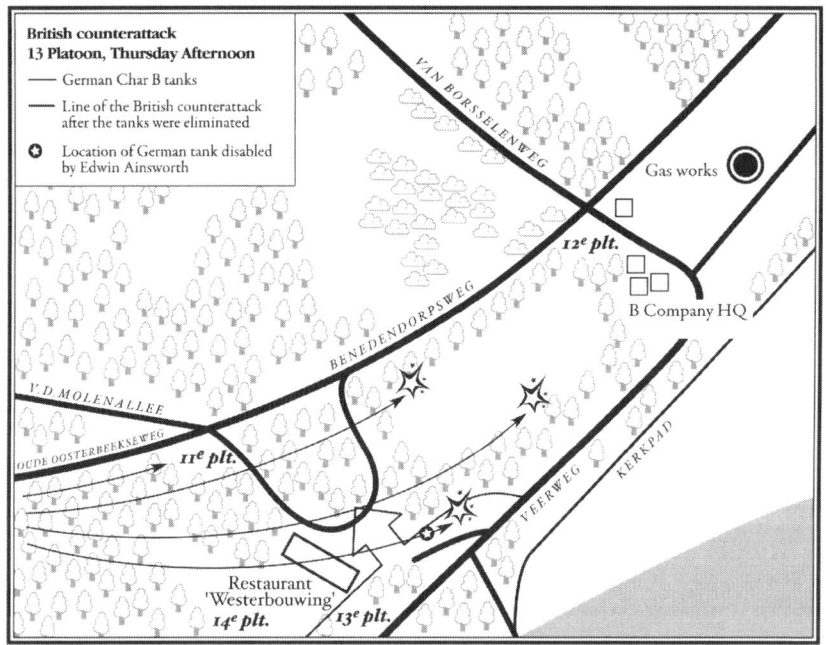

Map British counterattack

the other three, came to a stop and started to retreat, joined by the infantry. It proved to be a turning point in the battle. Another factor to help disrupt the German attack was the supportive shelling by 64 Medium Artillery Regiment from the Nijmegen area. Each of these guns fired ten rounds between 1000 hours and 1030 hours.

The British took courage from the German retreat. 13 Platoon, which had been pushed aside to the southern edge together with members of the other platoons, launched a counter-attack with fixed bayonets. This attack started at the east side of the buildings. Cyril Crickett, Platoon Sergeant Fred Terry, Private Frank Jarvis and countless others from the different platoons, machine gun and mortar teams chased the retreating Germans, screaming, swearing and raging violently. The direction of the counter attack was northwards, at right angles to the Rhine. Norman Savage said, "At that moment something happened to me. I got an enormous surge of adrenaline and I could only think of one thing. Get after those rotten Jerries! Screaming, cursing and yelling I started to go after them. I had only covered about 15 meters when a German potato masher (hand grenade) was thrown in my direction. It hit the ground just before my feet. I startled and it flashed through my mind, oh my God, I've had it! In a quick reaction, I dived into the bushes. The deafening din from gunfire and the many explosions was so intense that I never did hear whether that hand grenade exploded or not. However, I could not stay there and I sprinted away looking for better cover. I found a brick wall behind which I met Gibson from our platoon." Savage and Gibson could see the development of the situation; however, they were pinned down between the positions of 13 Platoon and the enemy and could do nothing but wait.

During the counter-attack, the Germans were beaten back over quite a distance, but Frank Jarvis was killed as Cyril Crickett witnessed. In their attack, the British reached a small elevation in the grounds of the Westerbouwing, probably near the Oude Oosterbeekscheweg. Heavy German machine-gun fire forced them to fall back to their initial positions. Cyril Crickett and the other Borders were "euphoric" because they had managed to keep their positions, in spite of the vastly superior German power in infantry and four tanks. However, to their amazement they received orders from Company Commander, Major Armstrong, to clear the Westerbouwing. Possibly because the Major felt that his force was now too depleted to keep its present position, but nothing further is known about this decision. Everybody was to gather at the headquarters near the farm at the bend in the Veerweg. Dispersed in small groups 13 Platoon started retreating. A group of men from B Company and mortar men from 23 Platoon were ordered to put in a delaying attack in a northerly direction. Syd Cringle was among them: "I think that we got about 50 metres into the woods before we were pinned down by machine gun fire. We made our way back towards Company Headquarters and had to cross the fairly open parking lot area. We were halted by fire from a tank on the road to the north that used its main armament and machine guns on us. We were caught above ground and our only protection was behind trees. There was a Bren gunner with us and he and another chap caught the blast of a shell that landed between them. I understood that they were both killed outright." Afterwards Syd Cringle felt that this incursion into enemy territory was only meant as a decoy to enable the Company to pull back and regroup at the HQ.

The 3-inch mortar team near Company Headquarters was also told that B Company were getting out. Mortar man Vic Banks (S Company) said: "At a given signal I stopped firing high explosive bombs and put smoke bombs in the barrel until B Company got out. Then we had to strip the mortar down and take out the firing pin to render it useless to the Germans. Then we made a run for it. Three of us were lucky to get out." When the Germans noticed the retreat, they retook the initiative and went in pursuit. Bob Barnes and Jim Isles had just reached the stairs to the Veerweg on their way out when Bob Barnes was fatally hit by the Germans who were at their heels. This happened right in front of his friend, Jim. While Eddie Flinn was crossing the open piece of land between the Westerbouwing and the Company headquarters, a volley of `Moaning Minnies' (heavy German rocket shells fired simultaneously and striking with a terrifying screeching noise) was exploding around him. Fortunately, he was not hit by the hailstorm of metal splinters. He managed to join the group which was reorganising at the headquarters.

On his way back, David Patterson met Sergeant Tommy Watson from 14 Platoon about ten meters east from the spot where Eric

Melling was killed. Watson had a wound in his leg and asked Patterson to get the morphine out of his back pocket. Patterson administered the morphine and Watson said to him, "Now we will have to get you out of here." Patterson answered: "Not before you are safe" and he moved Watson five or six meters to a small ditch where he would be safer from the bullets that kept coming in their direction. Patterson left him there, convinced that Watson would be all right. Then he ran down the hill past the slit trenches where he had started the day. There he met other men of his platoon and the company. However, he was instructed just like the others to retreat to the headquarters. He threw a smoke hand grenade first and immediately afterwards a High Explosive one. Then he sprinted towards the headquarters a hundred meters further east on the Veerweg. He found a growing group of B Company men. When the Germans subjected the area to more and more mortar fire the decision was made to retreat three hundred and fifty meters into the woods north of the Benedendorpsweg. The new rallying-place was the Hemelsche Berg estate. The survivors of B Company moved there in small groups. Amongst them were about 14 men of 13 Platoon. Lieutenant Wellbelove's batman, Gerry Greasley, who was slightly injured, seemed to have been one of the last to come from the Westerbouwing, because at the moment he stepped out of the orchard he bumped into some Germans who captured him immediately. Greasley feared he would be shot on the spot, but the Germans took him away to their own lines as a prisoner of war. A number of British wounded remained at the farm of the Company headquarters. More wounded were accommodated in the white house at the crossroads of Veerweg and Benedendorpsweg. After the withdrawal of the British troops, the inhabitants informed the Germans that there were only injured in the house. It is likely that, in this phase of the action the Engineers from 9th Field Company also gave up the ferry position and retreated east. The wounded from The Border Company group had to spend another full day in the house before they were evacuated to the Sint Antonius Hospital in Utrecht, where they were treated by their fellow prisoner, Medical Officer of the British 156 Para Battalion, Captain J.E. Buck, and a German doctor, Dr. Weber. The Dutch hospital staff took further care of them.

The utter destruction on the Westerbouwing, on the left are the ruins of the inn.

For now, the Westerbouwing had been given up by the British, but the inexperienced *Wossowsky Bataillon* had paid a terrible toll for its conquest. Half of their men and all but one of the officers were killed. Many were injured or were separated from their unit. The commander of the German battalion himself, *Oberleutnant Artur Wossowsky*, was killed in the area between the Westerbouwing and the former gas works of Oosterbeek. The German troops found it extremely difficult to locate the enemy in the wooded environment. British snipers caused heavy losses and the British automatic arms changed position so often that they could only be silenced with a lot of effort and heavy losses.

Around noon, the survivors of the *Bataillon*, Kessler amongst them, were withdrawn from the battle and added to another unit in the area. There is some speculation that the Westerbouwing was left unoccupied by the Germans until they had regrouped later that day or during the night.

Day 5, Thursday September 21, afternoon and evening
Meanwhile, B Company group was regrouping in the grounds of the Hemelsche Berg estate, several hundred yards northeast of the Westerbouwing.

Platoon Sergeant Fred Terry tried to get an overview of the number of survivors from 13 Platoon. He saw that Lieutenant Wellbelove was not there, which made him realise that he was in charge of the platoon now. Also missing were Lance Sergeant Kimber, Lance Corporals Ted Clague and Eric Melling, as well as the Privates 'Gibbo' Gibson, Norman Savage, Robert Barnes, 'Pip' Hulse, Frank Jarvis, Tommy McDonald, 'Gerry' Greasley and 'Click' Fidler. Cyril Crickett helped the injured John Glenn onto a stretcher, which was placed abreast on the bonnet of a jeep. Glenn was transported to one of the British Medical First-Aid posts together with several other injured. The remaining troops were counted.

Lieutenant Arthur Royall's 12 Platoon remained south of the Benedendorpsweg near the gas works where they dug in around a small farmhouse. This was close to the divisions' artillery positions. They were incessantly harassed with German mortar and machine-gun fire.

B Company stragglers who got off the Westerbouwing hill after the main group left for the Hemelsche Berg estate got sent through to that rallying point. This was where Clague, Gibson, Savage and Fidler turned up again. Somewhere in the course of the afternoon, it became clear that B Company Commander, Major Tom Armstrong, was considering a counter attack. It was not clear if he wanted to retake the hill on his

Platoon Sergeant Fred Terry took over command of the survivors of 13 Platoon when it became clear that Lieutenant John Wellbelove had not returned.

own initiative or if he got ordered to do so by Battalion headquarters. Major Armstrong asked Cyril Crickett if he could lead a patrol. However, shortly afterwards the Major decided to go with a large group of about 50 men to make a flanking movement and counter attack the Westerbouwing from the north. Platoon Sergeant Fred Terry, Corporal David Patterson and Privates Jim Isles, Eddie Flinn, Johnny Swarbrick, Joe Winstanley and possibly others from 13 Platoon were part of that counter attack.

After the Armstrong group had traversed a considerable distance, they came to an L-shaped open area of grassland, presumably to the west of where the Van Borsselenweg (see map) sloped gently down from the north to the south. The field was about 80 meters wide. They had only advanced about 25 meters into the open when the Germans, apparently from all sides, opened fire with machine guns at the practically unprotected group. At that moment, Jim Isles found himself at the forefront. Apparently, the machineguns still had to find their aim, because the stream of bullets flew quite low and Isles was hit in his ankle. Nevertheless he managed to reach the cover of the trees to his right. The gunfire swayed away from him in a curve towards the rest of the group. That was when Eddie Flinn came in the line of fire. He was hit in the toes of his left foot and there was no way he could escape. To his horror, he saw how about half of the patrol was being hit by the German fire. Joe Winstanley was hit by four bullets in his thigh, but he also reached the edge of the forest. Once among the trees, Isles, Flinn, Winstanley and others, amongst them an officer, found a barn where they hid.

Cyril Crickett ducked to the ground the instant the firing began. As soon as it stopped, he wanted to get up to find better shelter between the trees nearby. That was when he discovered that he was hit in his left hand. A bullet grazed the palm of his hand and made an almost surgical wound, exposing all the 'workings'. He tried to use his hand and all fingers still seemed to function. Sitting in the middle of the grassland he applied an emergency dressing to his dirt covered hand. The shooting ceased for the moment. Not far from Cyril Crickett Platoon Sergeant Terry was lying motionlessly on the ground. He looked seriously injured. Major Armstrong then came dashing past, probably to lead the patrol away from the danger zone. In the meantime, Cyril Crickett was crawling to the shelter of a small bush where he found Johnny Swarbrick who was hit in the arm. Johnny Brett from another platoon was hit in the throat and seemed to be in a rather bad way. Corporal David Patterson had found cover here as well. He had been lucky and was not wounded. However, they were pinned down there. It was as if they were on an island in the middle of a sea of open grassland. The total number of injured and killed was unclear and the counter attack as such was finished. Survivors sneaked back to British lines. Silence settled over the grassland until a raw voice in a thick German accent shouted "Come Out!" As there was no escape possible, Patterson waved with the only white object he had, a map. The Germans, commanded by an officer approached the little bush carefully and suspiciously. They captured the British they found there. Patterson had to say goodbye to his watch and to a pair of binoculars, which were a trophy of the Sicilian campaign. When Cyril Crickett's and David Patterson's small group was taken prisoner, they asked and got the assurance that their Platoon Sergeant Terry, Johnny Brett and the other injured men would be picked up and looked after. Terry was brought back by a German patrol of two men.

It turned anxious for a moment when a small, fat German officer started ranting and raving at the prisoners. He barked instructions at a *'Soldat'* who pointed his Schmeisser machine gun threatening at the unarmed prisoners. Fortunately, the officer calmed down and the group was taken away to a German medical post in a big black barn nearby the battle zone where they got a very, very welcome drink of water. Eddie Flinn, who was taken here as well after his capture, thought it was a Dutch farmer who was offering him the water. There is no indication whether the evacuated Giebing family was also in this barn. One of his uninjured comrades helped him to bandage his badly wounded foot. The men did not get anything to eat, although the Germans were well provisioned with food, due to the Allied supply drops. Most of all the Cadbury chocolate was looked at with longing and regret by the British prisoners.

Major Armstrong's patrol was annihilated and probably more than half of the men were killed, injured, or captured. The Major himself was also injured and made prisoner of war. Late that afternoon the Germans had gained complete control of the Westerbouwing. For them, the hill was a place that offered an unhindered view over a large part of the British sector and the Rhine. It could also be used as a springboard for an attempt to cut off the airborne forces from the river and thus make a future retreat impossible. 13 Platoon had ceased to exist as a unit.

At nightfall of that Thursday, the prisoners of 13 Platoon and other platoons were loaded in some trucks, together with a number of wounded Germans. Eddie Flinn was one of the last people to be taken away. They were taken from the battle area to the town of Apeldoorn, some fifty kilometres north of Arnhem. The truck was driving as fast as possible to avoid being fired at by the enemy. The German truck driver was hooting his horn in an irascible manner and flashed light signals at every crossroads. Probably to make clear to the German guards there that this truck, despite its speed, did not have any hostile intentions. The vehicle stopped at a sort of barrack building in Apeldoorn and the British were instructed to go inside. In spite of the appealing prospect of food, drink and rest, Cyril Crickett wanted somebody to have a look at his hand first. Some sort of sixth sense was warning him of the risk of his bullet wound. After some quarrelling with a guard, Cyril was allowed to go to the Saint Joseph Hospital where a nurse had a look at his wound. She did not like the look of it and insisted on an immediate examination of his hand. Crickett entered a waiting room where more Allied wounded PoW's were waiting for treatment. Another nurse also examined it and said "Good, no poisoning". He got the impression that the wound was not yet infected which was a great relief.

Meanwhile, a second truck took Patterson and several others to the town of Utrecht, which lies about 60 kilometres north-west of Arnhem. The wounded were taken to the Sint Antonius Hospital. The next day more wounded from the battle arrived. Lance Sergeant Jack Kimber was probably among them. He miraculously survived a hit by a bullet that went in through his left ear and came out through his right cheek. David Patterson saw him passing by and was shocked by the sight of the injuries to Kimber's face. In addition, Platoon Sergeant Fred Terry was taken to the Sint Antonius Hospital. He was hit on the left side of his neck and the bullet had left his body underneath his armpit. Terry assumed it had been a sniper that took him out. Pip Hulse was also taken to the Utrecht hospital. He appeared to have been hit in the back, probably while retreating from the Westerbouwing. He was paralysed and unconscious. To reassure Pip's family, a friend volunteered to send them this Red Cross card,

"*Dearest Mother,*

I hope you are all well at home. I am in hospital but I am O.K., so do not worry. A pal is writing this for me. I suppose I shall be kept prisoner when I am well but I hope it will not be long before I see you all again. So cheerio for now and God bless you.

Phil"

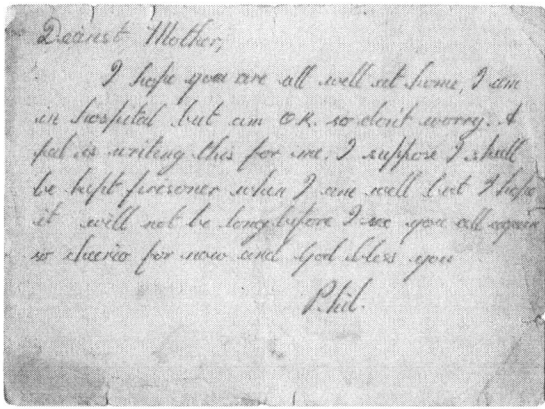

The Red Cross letter that a friend of the critically wounded Pip Hulse wrote to Pip's mother in his name.

At the same time the wounded airbornes were in Utrecht, Jim Isles and Joe Winstanley's group was still in the barn between the trees near Oosterbeek. To their horror, through a small window, they saw a group of German soldiers gathering around their barn and preparing a bivouac for the night. In the hope not to be discovered they kept as quiet as mice and realised that they were facing an endlessly long and anxious night.

Day 6, Friday September 22
After a cold night and a misty morning, the day turned quite sunny. The area around the Westerbouwing had changed into a desolate lunar landscape with the remains of burned out wreckage, fallen soldiers and destroyed equipment still lying about. Amongst the trees shattered by

the explosions, were the ruins of the restaurant "De Westerbouwing". The battle of Lieutenant Wellbelove's 13 Platoon and its sister platoons of B Company group against the superior power of German infantry and tanks was over. However, war was not over for those men who survived, whether they were prisoners or still in action.

That Thursday Ted Clague had lost contact with his comrades of 13 Platoon during the chaotic retreat from the Westerbouwing. He had found a group that entrenched itself west of the Dennenoord estate and some hundreds of meters east of the Westerbouwing hill. Besides some 11 Platoon members there were also some troops of the South Staffordshire Regiment, a sister battalion. The group was about thirty strong. By a strange coincidence, the estate belonged to a former Dutch Minister of War, Bonifacius Cornelis de Jonge, esquire.

Clague was instructed to operate a Vickers Medium Machine Gun. Although he usually carried a rifle or a Sten gun, he was trained, just like all others, to handle many weapons such as the Vickers machine gun or even German fire arms.

It was still dark when the British in front of Dennenoord heard the Germans prowling about in the garden of a house west of the lawn at Villa Dennenoord. They were obviously preparing an attack. Ted Clague pointed the Vickers straight at the gate, which was the most probable place for the start of an attack. The distance was about 60 meters. Dead ducks, floating in a nearby pond, seemed an evil omen, felt Clague. However, the Germans did not risk entering the open field and instead shelled the positions at Dennenoord from a distance with machine-gun and mortars.

In their barn, Jim Isles and others had spent the night among the oblivious Germans that had set up their bivouac around the barn. Everybody inside was praying that the Germans would leave. However, early in the morning they were discovered. With a lot of shouting and menacingly levelled guns, the airbornes were taken out of the barn by the equally terrified Germans. It looked as if they would shoot the British on the spot. The officer in Isles' group protested furiously and said that they should be treated as prisoners of war. That helped to calm the Germans down and they started to lead their prisoners away. While a German soldier was searching Jim Isles, he found a photograph of Jim's parents. The German was about to tear it to pieces when he saw who were on it. The German stopped, had a quick look at Isles and then returned the picture. To this very day, the photograph carries the small rip in the middle. Isles was taken to a hospital where he was examined and treated by German doctors. They were not able to get all the metal parts out of his ankle, but they advised him not to spare his ankle during recovery and to keep using it as much as possible. He should then be able to walk properly again in due course.

Eddie Flinn ended up in the Willem III barracks in Apeldoorn, where the British were allowed to run a field hospital under German command. The bullet wound in his left foot turned out to be so serious that all his toes had to be amputated.

In the Sint Joseph hospital, also in Apeldoorn, somebody came to pick Cyril Crickett up after a night of increasing pain to check on the bullet wound in his hand. The German doctor removed the bandage, which was an extremely painful experience. The doctor examined the hand, which by then was quite swollen. In perfect English, the doctor told Crickett: "Look, if you press here you can see small bubbles coming to the surface. That means that you are suffering from gas gangrene. If I do not take your arm off you will die. However, you are to decide yourself whether to keep your arm or not." Crickett did not really have an option because the injection he had been given a few minutes earlier was not meant to relieve his pain. It was a full anaesthetic, as it sent him straight into oblivion. When he came to again, he found his left arm amputated above his elbow.

He considered himself fortunate to have listened to his sixth sense. Had he not insisted on medical assistance, he would certainly have died from the consequences of the infection. However, his pain was not over yet. The first time the bandage was changed after the operation was so painful that morphine had to be administered. But the bandage had already been changed by the time the drug started to take effect. So, when the changing was done, Crickett made himself as comfortable as possible on his bed and lit a cigarette, waiting for the morphine to kick in. When it did he fell asleep with the cigarette still in his hand. The burning cigarette dropped from his fingers on to the flannel nightshirt he got from the hospital. When he woke up, the cigarette was out and underneath the ash cone on the nightshirt was a cigarette shaped scorch-mark. The German nurse grumbled and threatened that he would have to pay for the nightshirt. Ignoring the linguistic barrier, Cyril responded angrily that she should just take it out of his Berlin account. His first hospital dinner was a spoonful of mashed potatoes and a piece of meat the size of a stamp.

Day 7, Saturday September 23 to Day 10, Tuesday morning September 26, Evacuation

The British were still standing their ground in their positions in Oosterbeek while being permanently shelled. Dramatically, the ground forces of XXX Corps had still not shown up on the south bank of the Rhine. Only the artillery of the ground forces had been able to give some amount of support to the surrounded airbornes. It was getting more and more obvious that Operation Market Garden was failing to establish the desired bridgehead over the Rhine.

In the course of Saturday, the seventh day of the Battle of Arnhem, Edwin Ainsworth of 13 Platoon was made prisoner of war, but it is unknown where and under what circumstances this took place. That same day 'Click' Fidler, the 2-inch mortar man from 13 Platoon, was sitting in a trench in an open field north of the Benedendorpsweg close to the Hemelsche Berg. Not far from him was Private Johnny Peters, a sniper from 14 Platoon. Also 'Johnnie' Walker might have been in this area. Sixty years later Peters related:

> *"I was in the same area as 'Click', with Fred Jackson in a slit trench. We were fired upon, and all of a sudden, Fred said that he was hit in the neck. Fortunately, it did not seem a serious wound, but as he was quite shaken, I offered to go and get him a drink. I left, leaving my rifle behind and went searching for something drinkable. I succeeded in getting hold of a mug of tea somewhere. Just when I was about to go back, the Germans started shelling the place where Fred was. Therefore, I had to wait before I could return. When I came back to the slit trench after the shelling, I did not see Fred anywhere. The tea that I had brought him I threw away, because it was full of soil. I started looking for Fred and came by Fidler's trench, near a house. The occupants had probably been killed by the shelling, because they were covered with airborne smocks. Upset I went to size up the situation. I recognised one of them from his black curly hair. It was 'Click' Fidler from 13 Platoon. Fidler, being 28 years old, was older than most of the members of 13 Platoon. He had probably been in the army from the beginning of the war. He had a good sense of humour and he used to make a joke of his name. He said, "I am called Fidler by name, but not by nature." He possibly earned his nickname 'Click' from the full denture that after two or three beers he*

used to take out and put in his pocket so he would not lose it.

In my quest for my mate Fred, another bombardment took place. I ran from this place and found refuge in a proper air raid shelter, underground and made out of tree trunks cut into blocks. I can only assume that this was made by some Dutch residents who lived there. A clue to this was that it was near the Battalion HQ, I say this because after the bombardment ceased, someone called out to me asking who I was. At first I thought it was a German, speaking English, but when I answered, it was Les Fielding, Company Sergeant Major from HQ Company, who knew me as he was at one time in B Company. He asked me if I was all right and I replied yes, but I have no arms. He asked sharply what I meant, but quickly understood that my arms were still there, but that I was without my rifle.

I have not been back to this place, but I have heard that Fidler and the other two are still missing. It is possible that their trench was buried by later shelling which could have caused them not to have been found yet. My mate Fred turned out to have been made a prisoner of war."

                                                                                       X
                                                                                       Battalion HQ

                   X
       Purpose built wooden air raid shelter

                                                         X slit trench
                                           where I found Click
                                           Fidler and another
                                           2 soldiers dead
                                                           >
                                          opposite this> I
                                        believe stood a house
                                             where 3 officers were
                                          killed in doorway by
                                          Shell or Mortar blast

                            X
                   My slit trench
            shared with Pt.Fred Jackson

                                     x
                            another slit trench
                          were I found soldier dead
                          laying on top of his trench

Rough sketch of the location where Pte Click Fiddler was killed in action by Johnny Peters. He is still missing in action.

Savage and Gibson with A Company

Norman Savage and Gibson were in a trench close to `Click` Fidler's. When the heavy shelling was over, they too saw that Fidler had died. At some moment during these days Ted Clague must have passed the spot where Fidler died, because he also described the situation of the fallen, including Fidler, covered with an airborne smock.

An officer addressed Savage and Gibson. He asked them what Company they belonged to and instructed them to report for duty to Major Montgomery, Commander of A Company. They were instructed by the officer to pass the position of the Glider Pilots and then The Border mortar positions on the Utrechtseweg. After that, they would find A Company Headquarters in a big house. Savage and Gibson got on their way. When they arrived at the big house, they reported to the Major who instructed them to dig themselves in at the end of the garden. He also warned them that the Company was attacked every day so that they would have to take good care. "Gibbo" Gibson carried a welcome Bren gun that he was cleaning all the time. They found their way to the end of the garden and Savage started digging a slit trench while Gibbo was next to him with his Bren gun, ready for firing.

They surveyed the surroundings and saw an open field with a small copse behind it, straight in front of them. All of a sudden, Savage saw a German sniper climbing down from a lone tree and disappearing into the copse. He said to Gibbo, "Get that bugger!" Gibbo took aim, pulled the trigger but nothing happened. He changed the Bren quickly to automatic fire, but still, nothing happened. Eventually Gibbo cursingly took the magazine off to remedy the defect. By then, the German sniper had disappeared in the bushes. Savage decided that they should not keep digging here, in full view of that sniper. A bit further away was a trench that was already finished. It was even covered with a door that offered some protection against shrapnel. They crawled towards it and discovered the trench to have a comforting depth of a full three feet. Gibbo and Savage crept in and fell fast asleep, for the first time in at least four nights.

They were woken when pandemonium broke out. It looked like morning and apparently they had slept all night. They peered carefully out of their trench and saw the enemy shooting whilst they were creeping from tree to tree. This made them check to see whether any comrades were near. Savage and Gibbo only saw a number of fallen strewn across the garden. It seemed they had been abandoned. The only British answering fire came from the house. Gibbo and Savage decided not to stay in their trench any longer, as the danger of getting a hand-grenade thrown in was increasing. That would certainly be their end. So a quick dash to the house was what was necessary. Although the bullets were flying all around them, the two men from 13 Platoon were lucky and reached the house unharmed. The house turned out to be full of wounded comrades. An officer told them to get out, because the house was used as a hospital and it was against the Geneva Convention to arrange a military position in it at the same time. That was when Savage and Gibbo realised that the battle was only a matter of bare survival now. There was nobody in command or giving instructions any longer. The two of them went running from one garden to another diving away from the incoming mortar grenades. They entered a house and dropped in on an elderly Dutchman. He spoke English and told them, "Don't be afraid, you should only be afraid of the SS. These are worse than tigers in the jungle. A tiger only kills for food, but the SS kills, kills and keeps on killing!" Shortly after that, the old man said abruptly, "I think I'll go for a short walk". He left the house, leaving the bewildered British behind. Savage never did see him come back again.

Unknowingly, Savage and Gibbo had come close to the position of F Squadron, the unit of their Glider Pilots. However, they would not have found their Horsa 166 Glider Pilots there, because on September 24 Ian "Blackie" Blackwood had been hit in his thigh and was taken away on the bonnet of a jeep, probably to the medical post in Schoonoord. In that hotel-restaurant, Doedie Minderman's elder brother and sister were among various other civilians helping the British medical troops. This circle would be completed in the eighties when Doedie Minderman offered Morley Williams a place to stay during the commemorations.

Evacuation across the Rhine
On Monday September 25 Gibbo and Savage were somewhere in one of the besieged houses in the perimeter. They had no idea at all of their exact position. Probably somewhere north or east of the Division Headquarters at Hartenstein. They had been stuck in the home of the elderly gentleman for about three hours because of enemy fire, it was late in the day and they did not have the slightest idea of what was happening around them. At a certain moment Gibbo said to Savage, "I'm going outside to ask somebody what's going on now." When he returned half

an hour later, he reported amazed that, "Guess what, we are pulling out tonight. As soon as it gets dark we are to gather at the tennis court behind the division headquarters." Savage gave him a bewildered look. Had everything been in vain? Then they settled to wait for nightfall.

Soon after sun down, they set out. It was raining incessantly and the night was pitch dark. When they arrived at the tennis court, they met about 20 other airborne soldiers. The small group got on its way and Savage saw many German and British dead in the surroundings. Gibbo never knew that his cousin Joe, who was the driver/batman of Major Montgomery of A Company, was killed close to that location but a few days earlier. They stepped carefully over the fallen on their way to the river. Sneaking through the woods, the airbornes moved in line like shadows to the river. To avoid losing each other in the dark, they held each other's smock tails. Occasionally, they heard some machine-gun fire to their left, mortar bombs were coming down every now and then, but fortunately nothing came really close. Savage had no idea how long he had been walking, but all of a sudden, he stepped into the meadows near the northern bank of the Rhine. Gibbo was still with him. There were about 50 men waiting for a boat at that spot, while the Germans were firing flares to illuminate the evacuation area. The men were extremely disciplined and very quiet. That was until a boat moored close to the group. A slight panic broke out when all 50 men wanted to go on board, while there was only room for about 20. The men steering the boat urged them to remain calm and told some of them to get out again and wait for the next boat. Savage never knew if there really was a next boat. He was very happy when he turned out to be one of the fortunate who were allowed to stay in the boat and escape to the south bank. Although he did not see him, Gibbo seemed to have escaped too.

They were not the only 13 Platoon members that are said to have reached the evacuation area. Frank Evans had survived the cauldron as well, but it isn't known where he went after the German attack on 21st September in the Westerbouwing area. He wasn't wounded and remained in action right till the evacuation orders came on the 25th. Unfortunately, reaching the evacuation area didn't lead to safety for him. As he was a non-swimmer he needed a boat to cross the Rhine. But he wasn't wounded and possibly because he was a 32-year old father, he may have felt that younger men deserved to go first. Anyway, he stepped back from the boats, letting others go first. If so, that was a truly impressive gesture.

Once on the south bank, the evacuees were sent to a nearby barn. Here they got a mug of hot tea. It was the first time in about a week that Savage had had tea. He enjoyed it as if it was champagne. Some time later, he was loaded on a truck with other survivors and driven to Nijmegen. It was already getting light when the truck crossed the bridge at Nijmegen. Savage saw American paratroopers along the road staring at their British colleagues from their slit trenches. He wondered what they must be thinking as they saw this mud stained, unshaven and bedraggled party of exhausted British that had crawled out of the witches' cauldron in Oosterbeek. In Nijmegen, Savage and others were lodged in a school. He had stayed there for two days, when his group was brought to an airfield near Eindhoven. From there he flew back to England. He did not see or speak to Gibbo again.

Ted Clague and others near him were instructed long after midnight to abandon their posts in the surroundings of Dennenoord to set off for the Rhine to evacuate. They tried to find their way soundlessly and desperately tried to pierce the darkness to discover the pieces of white guiding tape that hung at irregular distances on branches and gates. This marked trail was their lifeline to the river. If they missed a ribbon, they could easily end up in a German field of fire. After the trees, they crossed a flat piece of grassland and vaguely saw grotesque shapes of dead cows with their legs in the air, scattered everywhere in the meadow. On his left Clague could see the little church dimly silhouetted against the only slightly lighter night sky. That was where the British airborne artillery positions used to be. After a while, he arrived at the north bank of the Rhine and joined a silent queue of dark and drenched shadows. There was a boat waiting which took him and as many others as possible on board. The boat pushed off and Clague reached the liberated south bank. It did not make him feel any better though. He was too soaked, cold, tired, and hungry to realise that he was out of danger. With others he followed the directions of some British troops from the ground forces that guarded the area. He kept walking on the road heading south and came to an unattended jeep. With a calm and determined contempt for the trivial matter of ownership they got in and drove away, following other British vehicles, personnel and evacuated airborne soldiers that were moving towards Nijmegen. Upon arrival in Nijmegen, Clague was offered something to eat, for the first time in days. However, he declined; he was simply too exhausted to be hungry. The only thing he really wanted was a bed to sleep. In a last furious attempt to harass the escaped airbornes, the Germans started shelling the quarters where Clague had been billeted. Beyond caring, Clague didn't wake up and just slept through the night and came to no harm.

Equally exhausted, wet, hungry and cold from the rain but still on the northern bank of the Rhine, Frank Evans waited morosely for first light of Tuesday 26th. Like many other men that didn't make the crossing, because they were wounded or got lost, he couldn't do much more than wait for the Germans to take him prisoner. Which they did sometime later that morning. The captured airbornes expected that captivity probably wouldn't last very long with the vast Allied armies resuming their advance into Germany shortly after 'Arnhem'.

After the evacuation
After the evacuation, still in Nijmegen, 'Johnnie' Walker was photographed together with Border Regiment soldier John Hamer from 24 MMG Platoon. That picture would appear in the regimental book When Dragons Flew (page 167, on the left). Why he is wearing a Glider

On the left is 'Johnny' Walker in Nijmegen after the evacuaton.

Pilot helmet is not known, but it caused him to remain unidentified for decades. The radio head phones around his neck might indicate that he, as a former Signals man, had been working a radio set. Despite his broad smile, he still seems unshaven. So he will not have been in Nijmegen for more than a day.

In England it became clear that 121 of the 788 men of The Border Battalion had been killed, 432 were missing and only 235 men had managed to come back across the Rhine. As the sight of so many empty beds could easily affect the morale of the survivors, the battalion was very soon moved to another location. The new encampment was in Boston, Lincolnshire, where the rebuilding of the First Battalion started. This was where Johnny Peters of 14 Platoon took the photograph of Ted Clague, just outside the town, when they were going out with two girl friends from the Woman's Royal Naval Service they had met in the pub. One of his friends of B Company, Johnny Peters, told about Ted Clague:

> *"When we were still wearing those leggings Ted always took painstaking care that the creases in his trouser-legs were kept razor sharp. He did that by sowing in little lead weights in the crease, just above the legging. Also his shirt and battle dress he kept immaculately ironed. He always looked spick and span."*

Walker and Clague were also part of the policing forces sent to Norway on 10 May 1945 to put the German surrender in effect and to disarm the German occupation forces after capitulation. The Norwegians welcomed their British liberators warmly and the British experienced their stay there as a treat. Clague's stay in Norway was only of short duration though. He suffered a serious motor accident when he took a motor bike which had been confiscated from the Germans for a spin and took a nasty fall. He got back to camp on his own, but was put in hospital right away. He had to be flown back to England.

Beside Savage and Clague, 'Johnnie' Walker and `Gibbo' Gibson were the only ones from 13 Platoon who had come back safely across the Rhine.

However, my quest did not produce any new details about the after Arnhem experiences of Gibson. Up to now my search hasn't yielded any results. So it isn't known if he was in Norway or if he was transferred to another unit.

Behind barbed wire
When the Battle of Arnhem was over, the outlines of the catastrophe started to become clear. Almost 1500 British and Polish and an unknown number of Dutch civilians had lost their lives. More than 6500 airbornes had been made prisoner of war, over 2000 of them were wounded and only some 2400 men had been able to make their way back across the Rhine. The Bridge near Arnhem was lost, the First Airborne Division was virtually wiped out and the hoped for breakthrough into the German heartland to Berlin had gone up in smoke.

The figures on 13 Platoon are equally shocking. As far as is known now, only four men (Savage, Clague, Walker and Gibson) of the Platoon had returned across the Rhine. It must be assumed that six people had been killed, Lieutenant Wellbelove, Lance Corporal Eric Melling and Privates Bob Barnes, Telford Fidler, Frank Jarvis, and Tommy McDonald. Besides, 13 men, whether wounded or not, had been made prisoner of war. These were Sergeants Fred Terry and Jack Kimber, Corporals David Patterson and Cyril Crickett, and Privates Eddie Flinn, Jim Isles, Gerry Greasley, Pip Hulse, Joe Winstanley, Edwin Ainsworth, John Glenn, Johnny Swarbrick and Frank Evans. Their stories are, as far as they have been recovered, grouped into the different PoW camps they were held in and are presented next.

Stalag XIIA Limburg, near Koblenz
Fred Terry, David Patterson, Jack Kimber and Pip Hulse were interned in the Sint Antonius Hospital in Utrecht. The Germans wanted to get their prisoners of war as quickly and as far as possible removed from the warzone. They checked strictly and regularly those of the wounded who were not yet fit to be taken away to the PoW camps further east in the Reich. Neither Fred Terry, Jack Kimber nor Pip Hulse was fit for travelling yet. Pip Hulse's health was very worrisome. The wound to his spine had become infected, which eventually led to meningitis. Without recovering consciousness, Philip Atherton Hulse died on Tuesday, 3 October 1944, 8 days after the Battle of Arnhem. His family in Winsford, England, only got Pip's Red Cross card after he had passed away. In it, a comrade had written that Pip was relatively okay and that they

shouldn't worry too much. Together with several other airbornes who succumbed to their wounds in Utrecht, Hulse was buried at the local cemetery Soestbergen.

Fred Terry was on his way to recovery and the Dutch nuns in the St Antonius hospital who nursed him managed to delay his transport repeatedly by insisting to the suspicious Germans that he was still far too weak to travel.

Jack Kimber, whose face was badly injured, was getting better after an operation but he too needed to recover further before he could leave the Utrecht hospital.

After a few days in Utrecht, David Patterson, who was unharmed, was put on transport together with other non-wounded airbornes to the prisoner of war camps in Germany. While their train was still in the Netherlands, a sanitary stop was ordered somewhere near a field with tobacco plants. The prisoners were allowed to get off to relieve themselves. David Patterson was studying the tall stalks of the crop with growing attention. Just when the plan to disappear with a few quick paces into the tight-packed stalks was ripening in his mind, one of the guards looked at him and smiled watchfully. Patterson's chance for an escape had gone. After this stop, the prisoners did not get outside of the train until they arrived at a Stalag in the town of Limburg, near Koblenz and Frankfurt. Stalag XIIA `Limburg' was very overcrowded and Patterson's group was put in tents where they had to sleep on straw. He described the food as outright disgusting. Many other airbornes were sheltered in these tents. It is plausible that Patterson was in this camp at the same time as his Glider Pilot Morley Williams and it was even probable that they had met there. Unfortunately without having recognised each other. Morley Williams had been taken there around the same time but came from Apeldoorn in a train full of British prisoners from Arnhem. Frank Evans also arrived in Stalag 12 A. He stayed there from the 30th of September until the 6th of October 1944. He spent 24 hours in solitary confinement, but the cause of this punishment is unknown. Neither is there any mentioning of him meeting either Patterson or Williams.

Stalag VIIIC Sagan, Poland
A few weeks later, probably near the end of October 1944, David Patterson was, together with hundreds of others, transported in cattle trucks to Stalag VIIIC in Sagan, Polish Upper Silesia. After five nights and four days, the train made its last stop at a tiny station somewhere in an un-

known forest. Everybody was told to get off the train. German guards sent them along a winding track that disappeared into the trees and darkness. The isolation seemed ominous, but when the forest got less dense, they could see a large PoW camp materialising behind the trees. They had arrived at their destination. Quite soon, Patterson found that here, hygienic conditions were a lot better than in Limburg. They even had the opportunity to play football because in the centre of the camp there was a big open ground. Sure, the Germans used it for the daily roll call, but at other moments it was a first-class football ground. To Patterson's relief old airborne friends were regularly arriving at the camp, during the first weeks after his arrival. After a while, David Patterson saw Jack Kimber arriving at the camp and when the occasion arose to talk to him, Kimber told him that the German doctors in Utrecht had done an excellent job and had actually saved his life. Though his face was still swollen, he seemed quite healthy. David Patterson also caught a glimpse of former 13 Platoon member Bob Ivison in another block of barracks but he didn't get a chance to talk to him. Patterson only had one blanket and in the winter, it was not unusual to find icicles as thick as an arm in the barrack. There was no glass in the windows so when the wind was blowing towards the barracks, the inside was not much warmer than the outside. The newcomers soon found out that they had to pay careful attention to their rations and that the only safe place for food was their own stomach. This was what Patterson wrote to his wife in December 1944 in a Red Cross letter:

> *"It won't be long before I get back home to you. I am longing to see you and I dream a lot about you. Last night I dreamt that you were cooking for me, but when I woke up you were not there and I had to do it myself. When I am back home l can show you some amazing things with cooking. Things you would not even have dreamt of that could be cooked or eaten. Fortunately, my health is good. I love you. Give everybody my regards,*
>
> *Your loving Pat"*

Stealing food was punished as the gravest crime imaginable. A thief who got caught was put into a ditch and everybody present urinated on him. In another variant, the thief was simply thrown into the latrine. The food supply was scanty, but with help of the essential Red Cross food parcels the prisoners managed to keep alive. However, with the Nazi regime crumbling, the food supply got more and more dire and even the Red Cross parcels arrived with great difficulty. As a consequence, the food parcels had to be shared with more men and the prisoners visibly lost weight. At the end of January, the approach of the Russians became noticeable in the Stalag. Large numbers of refugees streamed by the camp and rumours about an evacuation of Stalag VIIIC were becoming stronger.

Pushing on to the west
On 29 January 1945 David Patterson, Jack Kimber and former 13 Platoon member, Bob Ivison noticed that the inmates of the neighbouring POW camp for air force officers were being moved to the west. Still, there was little change for the airbornes until February 5, 1945. Patterson, Jack Kimber, Bob Ivison and the other PoW's in Stalag VIIIC were told that they would soon be sent westwards by train because the Russian Red Army was advancing.

At about five o'clock on the morning of 8 February, around 2000 the camp was abandoned. The prisoners of war were taken with their humble possessions to the nearest station in Mariasdorf, 23 km further on. They walked because the German camp Kommandant did not have enough means of transport. The weather was not too bad at first, but upon arrival at the village station it turned out that trains were unable to reach the station at all. The German train service in this area had practically come to a standstill because of the approaching front line. Therefore, the thousands of prisoners of war had to travel further west and the only way to get there was on foot. They stayed the night in the local glass factory. Many of the PoW's were in bad shape because of the poor food supply or because they had not recovered completely from their injuries. Many were extremely worried about how things would develop. On 9 February, the column arrived at the village of Friebau, after a march of 23 km in the rain. But again, there was no train here either. This time they slept in the open air under the blankets they carried with them in a wet forest just outside of Friebau. The next day the column moved on to Bad Muskau, 15 km further west and it was raining again. They were slowly loosing confidence in finding a train and their worries about their future were increasing. How long would this journey last and how would it end?

David Patterson was 'lucky' enough to sprain his ankle after a couple of days. He showed his swollen ankle to a German officer and the latter sent him, and some others who had fallen out, with a carriage to the Stalag IVB somewhere near Mühlberg. Patterson had no idea that his glider pilot Morley Williams was in the same camp. Williams had also been moved from Stalag XIIA Limburg and landed in this camp. To his pleasure, David met some Scots Guards here, the regiment he had joined on entering the Army.

He also saw many Americans who had been captured at the Ardennes offensive late 1944- early 1945. Patterson's stay at Mühlberg was a short one. As soon as he was able to walk again, he was sent to the next camp. He ended up at the PoW camp Colditz, which became famous in later years through a television series and a film with the same name. This was where he met Captain Cleasby from his Border Battalion. He was asked to help cutting trees for fuel, but being a non-commissioned officer, he had the right to refuse, so he excused himself for the job. After a little while, Colditz also sent him on his way again. It was a camp for officers and as he was a Corporal, regulations forbade him to stay in Colditz. Eventually he ended up in Stalag VII Moosburg, where Jim Isles from his own Section was too. They did not meet, however, as it was a very big camp with several satellite camps.

In the mean time, the column coming from Sagan was moving further and further westwards. The prisoners spent the night wherever the column came to a halt. Football grounds, barns, a bricksyard, even the shed of an old castle. No place was too exposed or too uncomfortable. Weather conditions like snow, rain or freezing cold were simply irrelevant. The men huddled together as much as they could and tried to keep themselves at least a bit warm with the help of all the blankets and clothes they had. Jack Kimber woke up after one frosty night and found himself frozen to the ground. The food supply was miserable and the prisoners grabbed every opportunity to find or steal food on their way. They would eat really anything that was vaguely edible: cattle-fodder from a stable they were passing, old bread or sometimes something they got from the villagers they came upon, anything would do. However, when the guards saw civilians helping the prisoners, the civilians got punished severely and the food was taken away or even thrown away. The inhumane march continued all through February and innumerable prisoners fell ill. The deprivations after the injuries and the bad circumstances in the camps were the final blow for dozens of them. Finally, the march ended after 605 torturous kilometres in Stalag IXB in Bad Orb near Frankfurt am Main in southern Germany.

On 14 March, the survivors set foot in the camp. From this column, which originally started with some 2000 men, 53 did not survive the march and 173 had been hospitalised. The remaining were dazed and exhausted, covered in dirt and lice. Many of them did not have any shoes left or they missed pieces of clothing. There had been several similar marches, some of them also ending in Bad Orb. The wanderers were deloused and they were shown a place to stay in the already overcrowded camp. The barracks were originally meant for 100 men, but now there were 500 in each barrack and everybody had to share his plank bed with several others, taking turns. The food situation was also stretched to the limit due to the overcrowding. Red Cross parcels had to be shared with more and more men and there was queuing for the potato peelings thrown away by the Germans. Jack Kimber explained: "We used to wash them and then cook them in an empty butter tin from the Red Cross parcel. When we had any condiments, like salt or pepper, we added them and we would compliment each other on a fine meal. Sometimes we got potato soup, but only the first 24 men in the queue would find something similar to a potato in their soup. The others were just drinking water with some taste in it."

On April 2 the camp was finally liberated by the American 6th Armoured Division. After liberation, the prisoners of war were advised to take their rags off and have a shower. The Americans managed to put up the necessary showers in no time. Although there was only cold water, it was a feast for the prisoners to be finally able to wash themselves with real soap. Their old clothes were so infested with fleas and lice that these were still moving when they were lying on the floor. After the shower and delousing the liberated prisoners of war got American uniforms to replace their old rags. The cigarettes which were supplied also received a warm welcome. The extremely undernourished prisoners were advised to be very careful with food for some time to come, because they would not be able to digest much food yet. Some, who disregarded the warning, became seriously ill. After this first relief, everybody wanted to go home as soon as possible, but it still took a while before the logistics were arranged. The fact that the Germans had not surrendered yet was also delaying repatriation. Finally, on April 20, departure day arrived for Jack Kimber and he returned to England by plane, landing at the air base in Oakley near Basingstoke. From there he travelled on to a reception camp in Leeds. On his way, he met David Patterson and Bob Ivison. Ivison had also been at the march from Sagan to Bad Orb. All were strongly emaciated. Shortly after their arrival at the reception camp, Kimber continued his journey to Llanelli in Wales, where he knew his girlfriend Nancy Morgan was waiting for him.

Stalag XIB, Fallingbostel
In October 1944, Cyril Crickett was still in hospital in Apeldoorn. Because of the amputation of his forearm, he was automatically considered for repatriation. While awaiting his repatriation and only ten days after his operation, the Germans sent him for the time being with several

Prisoner of War Camp Stalag XIB Fallingbostel (Photo ABM)

others in a cattle-wagon to the PoW camp Stalag XIB in Fallingbostel near Hannover. The journey took three days. All that time there was no medical or sanitary attendance and they got water only once. In the sickbay in Fallingbostel the doctors diagnosed that the injury was not healing well. However, this was no obstacle to send him on transport again after a week. Together with some others, he was moved to Stalag IXC Mühlhausen/Obermannsfelt this time. The reasons for this transfer were not clear and nobody bothered to explain anything either. It probably had something to do with his expected repatriation. He was only informed that he was going to be moved. As a prisoner of war that was all he got to know.

During the journey, the train ended up in an air raid in Hannover. At the time of the attack, the guards took shelter and abandoned their prisoners, who were locked up in the wagon. As soon as the bombers had gone, the guards came back to check how their prisoners had stood the attack. Fortunately, the locked up British were unscathed. The doctors in Stalag IXC found out that the reason the injury was not healing was that there were still some bone splinters in Crickett's arm wound. After removing these, the wound finally started healing properly.

Platoon Sergeant Fred Terry had also been taken to Utrecht, after having been captured at the Westerbouwing and having stayed the night at a German medical Dressing station (MDS), in the Renkum area. His injury looked serious at first glance, but things could have been worse. Once in the Sint Antonius Hospital Terry recovered quite well. Time after time, the Dutch nuns that nursed him managed to convince the Germans that Terry was still too weak to be transported to a permanent PoW camp. However, then the inevitable happened. During a surprise visit, the Germans found Terry sitting straight up in bed. For that reason they declared him fit enough to be taken away to a hospital in Bocholt where he arrived on 5 October. 26 November would see him arrive in Stalag VI F in Bocholt. Next stop turned out to be Stalag XI B in Fallingbostel, near Hannover on 1 December 1944. Three days later Terry was moved to Stalag Xb in Sandbostel, near Bremen. Then back to Fallingbostel and on 22 February to the neighbouring Stalag 357, where many Arnhem PoW's would end up. In April, with the German collapse approaching, Terry was taken from the severely overcrowded Stalag 357 camp. The huts were designed for 150 men each, but by then they housed 400. Still in April, some 12,000 British from the camp were marched to the east, away from the advancing Anglo-American forces in columns of some 2000 men each. They passed by Lüneburg and then after 224 days of being PoW, Fred Terry was freed when the column he was in, got stopped by an armoured unit of the British Dragoon Guards in the village of Salem, some 250 km east of Hamburg.

Terry wrote in his little diary that he was liberated on 2 May, 1500 hours. This was, by coincidence, the exact time that their glider had started its descent into the 'Arnhem' battle September 1944, some 8 months earlier. The little notebook contained among several others, the address of Squadron Sergeant Major Ian 'Blackie' Blackwood, the Glider Pilot of Horsa 166, that had flown Fred Terry's 13 Platoon to Arnhem. Remarkably, it appears they met again after the battle, among the thousands of PoW's that were being transported away from the Arnhem battle grounds. They will have recognised each other and, while in hospital, become better acquainted as they shared many comparable responsibilities and experiences. As senior NCO's, both were in responsible positions, they may have had to work together when the glider landed prematurely in England, both were wounded and they may have been in some of the same hospitals somewhere along their way to the PoW camps. Also both of them were in Stalags XIB and 357. Furthermore, it seems likely that Terry appreciated his (fellow British) glider pilots for putting him and his platoon safely down in the right spot for the Arnhem operation. Unlike in the Sicily landings where so many gliders were ditched by their American tug plane pilots in the Mediterranean. That had resulted in many Border men drowning before they even reached Sicily. On 5 May Fred Terry was flown home.

Eddie Flinn, after the amputation of the toes of his left foot, was put up for a week in the town of Munster near the Dutch/German border, but he also ended up in Fallingbostel. Although he saw Fred Terry there, he never got a chance to talk to him.

Preceded by dire warnings in bold capitals that relatives should write very clearly on the lines to avoid delay in censorship, 13 Platoon member Vinnie Swarbrick received a Prisoner of War letter from his parents on December 7, 1944:

Dear Vin,

Just a few lines hoping to find you alright. Everything is alright at home. Your mother sends her best love. I am home for a few days. I was down at your grandmother's yesterday and she sends her best wishes also your granddad and Bernard. We have not seen nor heard from Ted Joss for some time now but I think he is alright and you maybe having a letter from him. Well then if there is anything you want, do let your mother know and she will see what she can do. Joan is still at the same place. Do you know anybody there called Jack Place or Charles Blesdale? Well Vin, I must close now all the best love from mother and Joan,

Dad

Edwin Ainsworth seems to have been taken to Fallingbostel as well. He was, at least after a while, healthy enough to be put to work in the salt mines. A German civilian, who happened to work quite often near Ainsworth and several other prisoners of war, secretly brought them food every now and then. It was an enormous risk for the German to take, because if he was found out he would be accused of aiding the enemy and would be shot. At the beginning of January 1945 Edwin Ainsworth's mother wrote him a letter:

Blackburn, 6 January 1945

Dear son,

I am writing you to tell you that I am fine and I hope you are fine too. Your brother Bert had had an appendicectomy in Blackburn hospital and had to have a 28 days rest. Old Bert (Edwin's father) was shortly starting work in Blackpool. Your brother Bert had given Kath the sack again and was now meeting someone from Leeds. Old Mrs Cowell had a grandson who was with you. His name was Leslie Cowell. You met her the last time you were home. She asked me to send you her regards. Mrs Alberts said that you are having sing-alongs in the evening. I am glad to hear that you are trying to make the best of it that way. Do you get the Red Cross parcels every week? Albert was sending you cigarettes every fortnight. We were sending you a large parcel with woollen underwear and slippers through the Red Cross. Could you please let us know when you received the parcel? I hope this annoying war will be over soon. Orris was also writing you a letter one of these days. He came to visit us on New Year's Day. Take good care, probably it will not be long any more I hope. Your brother Bert was quite angry about what they did to you. You should hear him talk about the army!

All my best wishes,

Mum

Weeks later, the letter returned unopened. It was not clear why the letter never reached Edwin Ainsworth. Somewhere in April, Ainsworth and two others escaped, possibly from one of the marches eastward from Fallingbostel to Salem. Unfortunately, it has remained unknown how they managed that. Ainsworth and one of his fellow fugitives arrived in Berlin where they were kept hidden by prostitutes. The third was killed during their escape.

As soon as they had recovered sufficiently from the privations of their flight, probably shortly after the surrender of the Germans at the beginning of May 1945, they continued their journey to the coast, possibly Hamburg. In doing this, they made their way back to England. It is not known whether they made contact with British troops or if they got passage on board of an Allied ship returning to Great Britain. Back in England, Edwin Ainsworth reported to his Battalion. After a medical examination, he was sent on repatriation leave. After three months he rejoined the First Battalion of The Border Regiment again for active duty.

Soon after his capture, Joe Winstanley's parents to their horror received a letter from the British Ministry of Defence telling them that it regretted to have to inform them that their son Joe was missing and presumably killed in action. Some weeks later, to their immeasurable relief, they heard through the English speaking German propaganda radio station of Lord Haw Haw (a British Nazi collaborator) that Winstanley had been made prisoner of war. Also a nun is mentioned as having sent a postcard to his parents reassuring that their son was all right and explaining that he would be home soon. This probably took place when he was still in the Netherlands, shortly after he had been captured. It is not clear if his parents ever got the postcard. At some point, Winstanley was sent to a hospital in Linz near Innsbruck (Austria). After another one of the PoW marches Winstanley presumably washed up in Fallingbostel, some 700 kilometres to the north. Having recovered only recently from the shot wounds in his thigh, he couldn't have been in a good condition when he was forced to join the march to Fallingbostel. The horrible expedition caused him to get several sores and he got lice in his beard. He also started to suffer from asthma which would bother him for the rest of his life. During the journey, the itching from the lice was driving him so mad that he took the first knife he could find, unfortunately rather blunt, and shaved his beard off rigorously. The fact that he cut himself severely did not stop him from finishing that shave. He just wanted to get rid of those lice. After the march, he was registered in Fallingbostel as a prisoner of war.

John Glenn from 13 Platoon had also been taken to Fallingbostel. On 2 October 1944, he was taken away on a stretcher in a cattle truck from the Willem III barracks in Apeldoorn to the camp in Germany. Gerry Greasley, as one of the walking wounded, was put on a train to the same camp the day after.

It was not odd that those from 13 Platoon in Fallingbostel did not meet each other or their Glider Pilot Sergeant-Major Ian "Blackie" Blackwood. The camp was huge and had several satellite camps. Fallingbostel had become so overcrowded, particularly in the last weeks of the war, that merely finding a place to sleep was hard. The hygienic conditions and food supplies were extremely bad.

The liberation of camp Fallingbostel, which everybody had been looking forward to so desperately, came somehow like an anticlimax. When the prisoners woke up one April morning, they saw the watchtowers were empty and all the guards had gone. From a distance, to their surprise, they heard the characteristic and familiar stutter of a Bren gun. Shortly after, British army vehicles appeared on a nearby hill. Only a few minutes later these entered the camp under bursts of jubilation. Although the liberation itself passed off unspectacularly, it didn't diminish the explosive joy over the end of their captivity. Still, the men had to wait several days before they could be flown back to England.

During the wait, Fallingbostel inmate Eddie Flinn used his newly recovered freedom to search for food outside of the camp and in a nearby village. Of course, he was not the only one. Everyone else was. So, when Eddie Flinn could finally leave the German camp, he experienced his homecoming as one big treat. He found it marvellous to see his family and friends again and enjoyed being able to freely go for a 'pint' with his friends at home in Cleator Moor. Of Fred Terry's and John Glenn's homecoming similar stories were told, but of Johnny Swarbrick and Gerry Greasley nothing specific has been found.

Stalag IVC Wistritz
After the battle in September 1944, Frank Evans arrived in Stalag IVC in Wistritz, Sudetenland, now Dubí in the Czech Republic. The date was Sunday 15 October 1944. In this PoW complex tens of thousands French, British, Polish, American and Russian prisoners of war were detained. He was put to work in the mines, excavating brown coal. This was used for producing synthetic petrol for the motor vehicles of the Third Reich. Frank was kept in Working Camp Kolumbus, one of the satellite camps of Stalag IVC. While he was there, the facilities were bombed several times. But again, he survived unscathed. Grandson Stephen Earlam says: "*I know little about his time as a PoW, but at some point there was no food to eat. He was reduced to rummaging in dustbins and reckoned he only survived when he found some mouldy rice pudding at the bottom of a bin. Another story was of a fellow prisoner who managed to catch a sparrow and was roasting it over a candle. Then there was an air raid and the Germans turned all the lights out. When the lights came back on someone had stolen and eaten the sparrow.*"

After some 7 months in April 1945, the German guards suddenly fled the camp because the dreaded Russian Red Army advanced into the area. The Germans left the prisoners to their fate and hurried west. Then in early May the Russians arrived. They weren't too quick with repatriating the thousands of prisoners of war, so many of them didn't wait, but walked out themselves, on their way towards the American forces in southern Germany. That would have been a walk of some 100 to 140 km, among the many thousands of refugees fleeing the Russian army.

HEILAG IVD Annaburg
Somewhere in November 1944 Cyril Crickett was sent to yet another camp. Via Stalag IIB he ended up in Heilag (*Heimkehrer Lager* or repatriation camp) IVD in Annaburg (between Berlin and Leipzig) a transit camp for people who were to be repatriated. These soldiers were wounded so badly that they weren't expected to be able to join the allied army again.

Crickett received Red Cross parcels here that made him suffer less from hunger than in the weeks before. Lack of fuel during those harsh winter months meant it was extremely cold in the buildings and the available blankets were quite thin. The repatriates slept with their clothes on and their feet in empty Red Cross boxes, thus trying to keep as warm as possible. Their uniforms were British made and had been supplied by the Red Cross. Crickett spent Christmas in Annaburg. During one of the walks, as always accompanied by some guards, the British prisoners brought a small Christmas tree from the nearby forest with them. They decorated the tree with some coloured paper including an angel in the top. They organised some crackers for a meal and made a small present for everyone in the room. An American Christmas Red Cross parcel brought a tin of turkey and plums wrapped up in red wax paper. The red paper was used to make a lantern and a self-made plum cake increased the Christmas mood, although the plums turned out to be none too good for digestion.

It was in the beginning of January 1945 when Cyril Crickett was told to prepare for departure. Together with many other repatriates, he was leaving the German transit camp by train. This time, the journey took place in decent coaches through the south of Germany to the Swiss border crossing near Konstanz/Kreuzlingen.

After many time-consuming formalities and delays that were extremely frustrating for the repatriates, the train crossed the Swiss border and left the war behind. At the same time, a train with repatriating German prisoners of war went the other direction, into Nazi Germany. The British were shouting and waving for joy, but hardly got any reaction from the gloomy German train. Undoubtedly, the repatriated German prisoners of war were seriously worried about what they would find back home. They knew their country was in ruins and they were probably asking themselves how their families were doing. It was also possible that they were scared for reprisals from the Nazi authorities. It was quite special to see the Germans wearing British uniforms.

The Swiss supplied the British with food and drinks, some chocolate and even a small present. Cyril Crickett got a handkerchief. There was also a wash-place. He met a Red Cross nurse who helped him and they exchanged addresses. Finally, the train left Kreuzlingen and took Crickett, as if in some marvellous dream, into a fairy winter wonderland. The weather was bright and clear and the Swiss mountains were covered with freshly fallen snow.

At every railway crossing there were people cheering. At every stop the Swiss came aboard, eager to talk to the British and offer them cigarettes. It was already dark when they arrived in Geneva.

Again, the repatriates had to wait a long time for the locomotives to be exchanged. Eventually, when this was done and the train was ready to leave the station, the platform was packed with nurses and other people from the Red Cross singing "Auld Lang Syne". Tears of emotion were trickling down the cheeks of both the Swiss and the British by this warm and unforgettable gesture.

After Geneva, the journey continued to Marseille through the strange new world of liberated France. Upon arrival in the French seaport the train passengers were treated to liberal amounts of DDT for disinfection. After that they were allowed to board an American hospital-ship. On board, they all got a small, light meal. In order to help their digestion getting used to normal food again, they were regularly served small meals. Everybody was marvelling at the luxury of hot showers and good beds. After a day or two the British changed to the British hospital ship SS Arundel Castle. The ship was sailing under the Red Cross flag for this particular journey. Cyril Crickett came back home to Liverpool on 5 February 1945 after a wonderful cruise. His father was waiting for him on the quay. After a short stay at the military hospital in Chester, Cyril Crickett was sent home on 8 February. The same date on which several of his 13 Platoon comrades started their march from Sagan. He got measured for an artificial arm/prosthesis and was dismissed from the service in October 1945. But what was he to do next?

Stalag VII in Moosburg

This large PoW camp was in a rather flat area surrounded by hills, one kilometre from the village of Moosburg, and 35 kilometres northeast of Munich. The camp had a rectangular shape and consisted of three parts. The first part was the so-called Nordlager, where new prisoners were lodged for two days to be searched and registered, have medical examinations and be deloused. From there they went to the Hauptlager. In Hauptlager Sud (South) there were only Russians. There were seven watch towers and the camp had a double barbed wire fence on the outer perimeter.

In October 1944 Jim Isles was taken to the Moosburg camp. Later he was relocated to Stalag VB in Villingen, also in the Munich region. This Stalag complex, comprising of several camps, held between 20,000 and 30,000 prisoners of war. Some of them were already there since 1941.

Because of his injured ankle Jim was kept in hospital at Rottenmunster where conditions were a little better than in the camp itself. Early November 1944 he wrote home that he didn't mind being there at all and that his family shouldn't worry about him. His early optimism lasted till late in November when a 'good bit' of snow announced winter. He wrote his girlfriend that he didn't know what to write about as the things that he wanted to write about probably would not pass the censor. Instead he asked her if she had been to any shows lately in Blackpool and strongly hoped that there would be some good ones when he would get home again to help make up for the time that Jim was a prisoner of war. He also mentioned the photos he had managed to rescue from his captors at Arnhem. Shortly before New Year's Eve he was discharged from hospital, which, in the end, was a relief.

Just as with the other camps, everything was in short supply. The diet consisted of black bread and clear potato soup. The Red Cross parcels supplied the British with some very welcome extra food and anxiously awaited cigarettes. As long as they could share the Red Cross parcels between three, life was still more or less bearable. However, the more the Allied Forces advanced, the more the German logistics disintegrated. Fewer and fewer parcels made it to their destination. These had to be shared with more and more people. And not every nationality had the luxury of these parcels. The Polish and the Russians hardly got anything extra. Jim Isles saw a Pole pulling some straw from a mattress, rolling it in a piece of paper and then smoking it as a cigarette. The resulting stench was unbearable. Isles was irritated by the constant complaints from some Americans about the hardships. There was a war going on, so they just would have to cope with the circumstances, he felt.

As Isles was a Private, the Germans were allowed to deploy him for activities that were not related to the war effort. He was assigned to a party which had to clear away rubble in the nearby city of Munich. When they left the camp they were searched, but none too rigorous. Simply by keeping the contents of their pockets in their hands, which they were ordered to put up in the air, they managed to save their possessions. In town the British were called names and spat upon, which was very humiliating. Once, while clearing rubble, they suffered an air raid. One after another, the planes dived down and sprayed the area with bullets. Isles could only find shelter behind a headstone at a nearby cemetery. He ducked behind it and made himself as small as possible.

Everywhere around him the bullets hit the ground, but he was saved by the headstone. "Finally, one Jerry who's helping me," Isles thought bitterly when he got up after the attack.

On 20 April 1945, the American Third Army arrived at the village. The camp direction surrendered without any resistance to the liberators, in fact to General George Patton himself. During the time he had to wait for transport back to England after the liberation, Jim Isles made the mistake to have a look at one of those concentration camps he heard so much about. He would never be able to put the terrible images out of his mind again. He had no words for it other than that the stench was horrible. Jim had walked into Dachau, shortly after its liberation...

Dear Morley,

These were the details I have discovered about the fortunes of your Horsa 166 passengers during the Battle of Arnhem and the subsequent captivity of the survivors. Beside the above-mentioned names two more had come up during my quest. It is possible that they were also from members of 13 Platoon. These names were Private Leo Smith (35 years old) from Manchester and a Private called Bill Sloane from Cardiff. Both did not survive the battle. As I have not been able to find anything specific about them that could confirm this supposition, I have left out these names. In the correspondence with the survivors or their family I also have gathered information about former 13 Platoon members returning to civilian life. These stories turned out to be equally fascinating. As they are also an answer to your question of what happened to them I have put these facts to paper as well. At first glance, they are everyday stories about work, getting married and

Lance Corporal 'Ted' Clague back in England, shortly after the Arnhem battle.

sometimes having children. But as you are a fellow veteran yourself, you will agree that they are a moving contrast and indispensable sequel to the stories you just read. Just turn the page, like they and you yourself did some 60 years ago, and find the concluding parts of their tale.

With kind regards,

Haks

Part 4

Civvy Street

In the early months of 1945, the Nazi regime was crumbling under the burden of looking after its prisoners of war. Allied air raids on roads and railways hampered the provisioning of the Stalags, and the resulting food shortages led to severe rationing. The excitement among the PoW's over the approaching liberation was thus considerably tempered by the worsening living conditions. Not until the Allies liberated the camp, did improvement set in for the prisoners. Some German guards surrendered on the spot when Allied army vehicles came, sometimes literally crashing, through the gates. Others vanished like thieves in the night, leaving the prisoners to their own devices. Sometimes freedom only meant the disappearance of the guards. In the western camps the food supply and sanitary conditions improved considerably after liberation, occasionally even resulting in the appearance of complete shower installations.

After the initial celebration of the end of their imprisonment, the soldiers had only one desire, to be returned home straight away. Repatriation was put in motion as quickly as possible. However, as this involved moving hundreds of thousands of people of many different nationalities, a huge logistic operation with much preparation and organisation was needed. All through April 1945, liberation also arrived for the survivors of 13 Platoon and their two glider pilots. In the first days after their liberation, they happily took the opportunity to roam freely outside the fence. Still, to their taste, the long awaited day of departure from their hated camps was a bit long in coming.

Despite the seemingly endless wait, the majority of the men returned to Great Britain in April or May, usually by plane. Upon arrival, the men of Horsa 166, as the others, had to check in for registration at an assembly point, and were submitted to medical examinations. They all had lost a lot of weight and still suffered from malnutrition, but the relief over their liberation and the ending of the war was powerful medicine for many. After registration, the men were sent home for a three months repatriation leave. Then, they had to report again to their Regiment. Unfortunately, coming home to family and friends was not the glorious journey so eagerly awaited for everyone.

John Glenn
In May 1945, 21-year-old John Glenn was still bedridden, after being wounded in 1944 and sent to Stalag XIB in Fallingbostel on a stretcher. Due to the nature of his injuries and the bad medical conditions

Months after the war, Pte John Glenn, still fell victim to the effects of the battle at the Westerbouwing

in camp Fallingbostel, he had not fully recovered. On his return, he was so alarmingly weak, that he was admitted to a British hospital immediately. Sadly, recovery didn't set in. Well over one year after the Battle of Arnhem and more than five months after the war had ended, John Glenn was the last member of 13 Platoon who tragically passed away as a direct result of the fighting. In 2004 his sisters Claire Duffin and Mary Edmundson wrote:

"Dear Sir,

John was our oldest brother in the family of nine children. He was born in Salford on 26 May 1924 and was a caring big brother for us. He attended St Catherine's Church of England School in Collyhurst, Manchester until he went to work as a salesman on a fishmongers stall. Some years later, he got his second job. That was at Mather and Platt Engineering, Manchester. From there he joined the army in 1942. He quickly volunteered for the Airborne Forces because of the extra pay, which he intended to use to support our family. In 1943, he went to Italy as a member of the First Battalion, The Border Regiment. Here, he was wounded, but he recovered enough to be sent to Arnhem in September 1944. In this battle, he was wounded again. He probably spent the last four or five days of the German siege of the Oosterbeek cauldron in a British Medical Aid Post. After the British positions had been given up, John was taken to William II barracks in Apeldoorn as a prisoner of war. He was seriously weakened by his injuries and the lack of medical treatment during the Battle of Arnhem. This made his PoW-time even harder as the harsh conditions in the camp took their toll from his recovery. We, his sisters, want to take this opportunity to thank all his comrades who looked after him in the camp and covered for him when he was too sick to work. They enabled him to get to England and see his family once again. After the liberation in April 1945, he was flown back to England. He was straight away sent to the Ashridge Military Hospital in Berkhampstead. His medical condition proved to be very serious. This cast a dark shadow over his return. Even though it was a great burden on her budget, his mother Hannah Carr visited him every week.

His girlfriend came to see him soon after his return to Manchester, but she was so shocked by his frail appearance that she did not have the courage to visit him again in the hospital. Then, after having been in hospital for several months, John fell victim to pneumonia and passed away on 24 October 1945. He had a military funeral with full honours. His head teacher, himself a World War One veteran, led the sermon to the full church, with family, friends and the people of Collyhurst paying their respect. John has a military headstone at Philips Park Cemetery in Manchester. His medals were The Ribbon and Star, The Italian Star (wounded), the French Star and the Service Medal-wounded at Arnhem.

God bless you.

Clair Duffin and Mary Edmundson

David Patterson

David Patterson returned to England in April 1945. When he was demobilised after his repatriation leave, the issue on how to make a living arose. The first thing that came to mind was to take up football again, as he felt that, at 26 he was still young enough to pick up his football career from where he had left off. He was quickly disappointed when he found that he had been out of the game too long. He couldn't earn himself a place in Bedford Town's first team. He came to the tough conclusion that he had to focus on another type of job. Eventually he found work as a joiner.

Work was only the first step towards coming to terms with his war experiences. During the first few months after his return to England, he found it hard to concentrate, and for two years after the war, he suffered blackouts. He also continued to be extremely alert for a very long time. For instance, when he came home in the evening, he never switched on the light before the curtains were drawn. He knew that this was no longer necessary, as there was no danger anymore to get shot at, but the ritual still had a reassuring effect. But little by little, David relaxed and the memories of what had happened in Holland and Germany diminished. It was not that he forgot about it, but it dominated his thoughts less and less, especially when he and his wife had a son.

Now that he was no longer able to make it his profession, football became his big hobby. He joined the amateurs of *Hornchurch & Upminster Football Club*. A contemporary newsletter from the club described one of his actions on the football pitch as follows:

> "Our reserves on Saturday kept their unbeaten record intact. They travelled to Stevenage and drew 3-3. When the score was 1-1, David Patterson put us in the lead again with one of his specials. However, in the end Stevenage managed to reach a draw, much against our having the best of the game."

Later in, in 1954, a local newspaper report said of him:

> *Latest to join (the non-playing staff) was burly, bighearted David Patterson, the Scotsman who stayed south of the border. With Ted Miles resigning from the post of trainer, David had stepped into the breach. His holidays this month had been spent at the Carnegie Centre in Leeds, where he had taken a six-day trainer's course, including radio physiotherapy and at the Leeds Centre Hostel, where he was given practical coaching lessons. David is one of the 'old brigade' in the Hornchurch and Upminster club, having been first introduced as a player in the Upminster side by Bob Luchford in 1946. Born in Kelso, Scotland, the new trainer is known to the local fans as a 'canny' centre forward with a terrific shot. It might surprise them to learn that he started out as a goalkeeper! He played for the Patrick Thistle reserves and as left half for Bedford. Then he came to Upminster. David, a family man, now lives at Barkingside, and was a PoW during the war. His age? Well, they say at the stadium that he had been 32 for the past few years.*

David Patterson, centre-forward in the Hornchurch & Upminster Football Club in the early Fifties

When his son was old enough, David every now and then told him something about Arnhem. The incident when the tank fired only a few inches over his head or about the ambush that led to his capture. "It was so incredibly stupid to simply set foot on open territory with so many men. Particularly, as there was a wood very close to us, which would have offered far better cover", he said to his son Kerry. David never understood why the patrol acted in a way that went so completely against their long and hard training. Why did they fail to have scouts to go on ahead? Why did it not cross anybody's mind to protect the advance with their own machine guns from the shelter of the woods? He also told him about the one-pound note he found on the street just before his departure to Arnhem, which he gave away out of superstition. Occasionally, he spoke about the situation in which his friend Eric Melling fell. Kerry Patterson considered the fact that his father and his fellow soldiers were repeatedly deployed for new operations to be one of the most trying aspects of his father's stories. No matter what one had gone through, it did not prevent them from being deployed again in a new mission. David found it hard to accept that the efforts and sacrifices he and his mates made during World War Two were so little appreciated. He kept having flashbacks about war situations in North Africa, Sicily, and Arnhem and about the hardships in the prisoner of war camps, which, in his view, he only survived by sheer chance.

No wonder he was very surprised to find a letter from me, a total stranger, on his doormat chance, some 57 years after the event and for no apparent reason, inquiring after his experiences during the Battle of Arnhem. He wrote back, thus starting a correspondence in which he recounted much of what he and his comrades had gone through. The exchange of letters and the telephone conversations even aroused his intention of returning to the Westerbouwing area, together with his son Kerry. However, Kerry felt that his father's health was too delicate for such a trip. Still, David did renew his contact with Cyril Crickett. I gave Cyril's telephone number to David, which enabled them to talk to each other again after 58 years. Although they had not spent their time off together in those days, they did remember each other. They talked about what happened on the Westerbouwing, and the course their lives had taken after Arnhem. It pleased David to tell Cyril that Johnny Brett, the man who was wounded in the throat when they were captured, had also survived. Much to his surprise and pleasure David met him once again in the Sixties at a building trade fair, somewhere in England.

David was shocked to hear from me that Sergeant Watson had not survived the Battle of Arnhem. David was convinced that Watson was reasonably safe where he had left him. Besides, he only had an injury to his leg which did not seem to be life threatening, as far as David remembered. In several telephone conversations, he expressed his difficulty to understand what might have happened to Watson. "It keeps haunting me" he said.

In July 2002, I wrote him a letter asking him if he was able to make a drawing of the situation at the time of Eric Melling's death. Over half a century later, Melling was still missing in action. David's drawing arrived in August. I was unaware that this would be his last contribution to the book on his platoon.

On august 21, 2002, David Patterson passed away unexpectedly at the age of 83, when he did not wake up from an anaesthetic after an operation. Much too soon, I had to do without his invaluable help with my search. It was sad to realise that David would not learn more about the way the project had developed and many of his fellow platoon members had fared in life.

One might call it coincidence, but in the first months after his passing away, I suddenly came into contact with Ted Clague, for whom David and I had been searching fruitlessly for such a long time. And in October, I even managed to trace Jack Kimber's story.

Ted Clague
In May 1945, after having recuperated from Arnhem, the Battalion was sent to Norway. Ted Clague was one of the Arnhem veterans who were part of this mission. There they supervised the disarmament and internment of the German occupying army. The Norwegians welcomed the liberators warmly. In Norway, Ted was involved in a serious road accident. He had taken a German motorbike for a spin and had missed a corner on a slippery road. He managed to get back to the base by himself but was immediately put in a plaster corset and was sent back to England to recover. It took several months before he was fit for duty again. During his convalescence news arrived that Ted too would be allowed to return to civilian life fairly soon. In anticipation of his demobilisation, he was transferred to Stanley Park, an army base in Blackpool. He became batman for a Captain. In this period, he met his future wife

Ted and Elsie Clague on their motor bike, in the late Forties.

Elsie, who was from Oldham. She was five years older than Ted, and she was the widow of a British soldier killed near the French town of Caen three weeks after the invasion of Normandy in June 1944. After Ted had left the Army, he and Elsie stayed in Blackpool for a while. With the war only just over, there was little work for carpenters in the area, as the available timber was designated for repair works in the areas that had been damaged the most by the bombings. He was provisionally hired by a coach company, where he helped to build coach work for buses. Elsie started work at the Ministry for War Pensions.

Ted and Elsie never realised that Ted's fellow 13 Platoon member, Cyril Crickett, had also got a job at the same Ministry. This was not as strange as it may seem, as there were around 4000 people working there at that time, and Elsie was using her maiden name, Sheridan.

After a couple of years, daily life in England became a bit easier, and Ted and his wife moved to Oldham, where Elsie still owned a modest private home, which was being let during the war. Shortly after their move to Oldham, their son Doug was born. Ted and Elsie's choice for Oldham also related to Oldham Borough Council's plans to build a new residential area, which could produce a lot of work for carpenters like Ted. He did actually find a job there. As the months went on, he got more and more work as a carpenter. He was even promoted to foreman at Eric Cockin's building company. This enabled Ted to replace his motorcycle and sidecar with a real four-wheel car and, later on, even a small van. Once he had established his reputation, he became self-employed and had his own little workshop. During the following years, he acted as a subcontractor for companies building houses in the area. He was doing well, and after some time worked as a building contractor himself. It was quite successful too, carrying out various house building projects in Oldham and the surrounding area.

The success allowed Ted and his wife to build their own home in the early fifties in Chadderton Fold, a little village near Oldham. Their son Doug was then seven years old. They built the house on the grounds of an old farm, which they first demolished for the greater part. As a hobby, the Clagues kept poultry and cattle in the barns of the former farm, just as Ted's parents had done. For Doug, this meant that he, both before and after school, had to help feeding the horses, pigs, one hundred chickens, geese, ducks and turkeys. Neither could he escape cleaning the stables. Some years later, the barns had to be knocked down in order to make room for new houses in the village, and the livestock was reduced in numbers. When he turned 21, it was time for Doug to live on his own. After he had left, and when retirement was coming closer for Elsie, she and Ted decided to change their large home in Chadderton Fold for a smaller house in Oldham and a second home in Blackpool, 60 miles away. Once retired, Elsie went ahead and moved to Blackpool. Ted kept working in Oldham during the week for another 10 years. The reason being that, according to British Pensions law, men had to continue to work for at least five years after their wife had retired, before being able to claim a government pension themselves. They were both delighted that after those ten years they were finally able to spend all of their time together in Blackpool instead of meeting only at weekends and holidays.

Ted was very reticent about Arnhem and the war. He was of the opinion that what had happened in those days was best forgotten about. In October 2002, I got in touch with him. Initially, he was very suspicious about these unexpected questions about his past, but once he understood the reason for all these inquiries into his Arnhem adventures, he was willing to talk about it. He told me that his memory was failing him more and more, and he added that he did not remember everything about those days." If you had asked me ten years ago, I would have been able to tell you much more". I painfully agreed. Fortunately, his son Doug could add information on several matters. However, when it came to the war Doug knew fairly little, as his father rightfully did not think those stories were fit for children. It was Doug's guess that his father had already told me more than he had ever told him. With regard to the post war period, Doug's help was invaluable.

He remembered: "As a little boy I was always very disappointed each time my father refused to take me for a swim when we were on holiday. Yet I knew he did know how to swim quite well. When I was a bit older, I asked him why he did not want to go into the water. Rather curtly, he replied, "I have spent more than enough time in the water of that bloody Rhine River. I understood that he was referring to his escape over the Rhine. And as he said it with a voice so full of emotion I did not dare to ask any further. Only over the last few years, his son Doug's and even more, his grandson's pride in him, made him talk a bit more openly about what happened back then. Reading the book "When Dragons Flew" on the history of the First Battalion helped Ted somewhat. Doug said, "In the book he found out what happened to many of his comrades. This enabled him to better place his own experiences, which had a calming effect on him."

Ted even became eager to return to Arnhem. He was planning to attend the fiftieth Commemorations of the Battle of Arnhem in 1994, but then Elsie fell ill and he had to give up his plans. Ted himself had always felt that he was indestructible, and that there was nothing to fear in life.

Ted Clague, with his brother and two sisters in the Seventies

One of Ted's business relations once told Doug: "I was visiting Hamburg with a couple of fellow building contractors at the start of the Seventies to attend a construction fair. Some of us were in a bar, your father was not with us. We got into an argument with some shady characters who were hanging about there. Things got increasingly out of hand and at a certain point, knives were drawn. At that stage, your father entered the bar, as he was looking for us, his colleagues. He took stock of the situation and rapidly made out that it was too late to settle the argument with words. He then legged it towards the two quarrelsome groups, jumped between them and spun a chair around. The German wranglers recoiled, which allowed us to leave the bar safely. We then returned to our hotel and your father silently joined us, at the rear of our little band." Doug only found out about this story twelve years after the event, when he was employed by the same business contact.

I had given Ted the telephone number of Cyril Crickett and Ted called Cyril: "You probably do not know who I am" he said to Cyril's wife Beryl, who had picked up the phone. When Cyril took the receiver, Ted was very surprised to learn that Cyril remembered him very well. Cyril was even able to tell him that, just after the war the two of them had met at the railway station in Preston, where they had chatted for about ten minutes. Back then, Ted had only recently returned from Norway, and he had just recovered from his motorcycle accident. Both proud and pleased, he told Cyril that, being a contractor, he was sometimes asked whether he could think of names for the new streets that were in the development plans he was participating in. Ted was always glad to assist, and a number of streets owe their name to him: "Elsted Road" in Greenfield, Oldham, which was a combination of his own first name and his wife's. And there was "Danisher Lane" in which he combined his second Christian name with his wife's family name Sheridan. To this very day, both streets still exist under these names. There actually is a street called Elsted Road in Greenfield, Oldham.

Cyril Crickett
When Cyril left Chester Hospital in early 1945 he knew he would be dismissed from the army quite soon and was pondering over what kind of work he wanted to do now the war was over. Back to the building trade was no longer an option due to the loss of his lower arm. He had been promised an opportunity to start studying Quantity Surveying at

the University of Cardiff, but as the weeks passed without any news about this promise, his worries increased that it would not happen. Cyril was haunted by the memory of a one-armed World War One veteran who, obviously on the dole, was often seen hanging around a sweet shop in his home town of Wigan. "Am I going to end up just like him?", he asked himself and tried to shrug off this dreadful prospect. In October 1945, Cyril was dismissed from the Army. Searching for work, he found a job as temporary administrative employee with the Civil Service in Blackpool. As he lived with his father in Wigan, this meant he had to move to Blackpool. He worked five and half days a week in the Civil Service. After work, he went to evening school to prepare himself for the exams to get a permanent job as a Civil Servant. Used to hard work, he studied with full commitment, passed his exams and got a permanent job in June 1948. Cyril got stationed at the War Pensions Department for disabled ex-service men from the First World War.

From then on, his life settled slowly into a moderate pace. Daily life did not leave him much time to look back on Arnhem, even though he kept in touch with his regiment and with the Swiss Red Cross volunteer nurse whom he met in 1945 while on the repatriation train from Germany. They had exchanged addresses and over the years the correspondence developed into a pleasant friendship. This probably helped Cyril and his wife Beryl in developing a taste for Switzerland as a holiday destination. The annual journeys to Switzerland seemed to offer a natural opportunity to make a stop in the Arnhem area and in 1967 Cyril and Beryl decided to finally make that stop. They stayed for a couple of days in Arnhem and Oosterbeek. Cyril found his way to the Westerbouwing area and as they walked around, he was surprised that he could still recognise the trenches that he and his Scout Section had dug near the "Drielse Veer ". The visit made a deep impression on them both. One unexpected effect was that they both stopped smoking after leaving Arnhem again.

Apart from seeing Ted Clague shortly after the war, Cyril had never met any comrades from 13 Platoon for decades. That was until one rainy day in the early Eighties, while going home from work, a fellow bus passenger surprisingly called out a name. Cyril, who was deep in his own thoughts after a long days' work, did not pay much attention. The man then started shouting loudly through the bus "Joe! JOE!" The other passengers all looked his way. Cyril began to feel uncomfortable and turned around in the direction of the shouting. Then he saw and recognised the man. It was Jim "British" Isles from David Patterson's Section. Cyril then understood that he himself was "Joe", as Jim recognised him by his army nickname 'South American Joe'. To their utter surprise, it turned out that Cyril and Jim had been living less then two miles apart for several years. After their coincidental encounter, they saw each other regularly and talked about their own experiences.

In the last year of his professional career, Cyril was in charge of the World War One Pensions department. When Cyril started to think about his own retirement, the number of war invalids from the First World War in his administrative care had of course drastically diminished. "At the time it was a very quiet department, well suited for someone on the brink of retirement", he remembered with mild irony. He retired on his 60th birthday on 5 April 1981.

With more spare time on his hands, their Switzerland holidays became a little longer. Each year they went to the mountains in Interlaken and had one week at Bodensee where the Red Cross volunteer nurse and her husband lived. They continued to do mountain walking tours of 20 km or more until they were well into their seventies.

They also liked to go by cable car to the top of a mountain, sit on a big stone overlooking the "Eiger" and "Jungfrau" and simply enjoy the view. When fresh snow had fallen on the ice-covered parts, the mountains twinkled like jewels and Cyril was taken back to his wondrous train ride in the winter of 1945, which took him past these same snowy mountains towards freedom.

Cyril visited The Border Regimental meetings where he met several of his old comrades, but unfortunately no one from the 13 Platoon from Arnhem. When Cyril and Beryl went back to Arnhem in 1994 for the 50th Commemoration, the landscape had drastically changed since his last visit in 1967. There was an island in the Rhine now and the old ferry had been replaced by a small passenger ferry. Also, the old rubber factory had disappeared. When he was walking around in the Westerbouwing area it all looked different. He did not succeed in retracing the field where he was wounded. Trees had grown taller, new ones had been planted and old ones felled. He found it difficult to orientate himself. At the Westerbouwing he was approached by a veteran of D Company, who, during the Battle of Arnhem was positioned just a couple of hundred meters north of the hill. He asked if Cyril had been in the battle at Westerbouwing. When Cyril nodded, the man told him that where they were dug in, D Company could see how heavy a beating Cyril's company took that morning. "We all thought that it was a miracle that anyone of you chaps got out of there alive," recalled the former Border Regiment soldier. In 1995 Cyril received the address of his Platoon Sergeant Fred Terry from Patrick Stott, one of his old Arnhem comrades. Cyril and Fred exchanged letters about their experiences. Cyril told Terry about the finding of a missing British soldier in the Westerbouwing area in 1995. Considering the location, he asked Terry if it could be Frank Jarvis from 13 Platoon who had gone missing in the area. However, there was not enough evidence to confirm this and to lead to a positive identification.

When Cyril received my letter about the haystack in October 2001, he took a great interest in the research on his platoon. I gave him the phone number of Morley Williams, his glider pilot. They seemed to like each other, because they wrote and phoned each other regularly. Also, David Patterson got in touch with Cyril and they had a long and interesting conversation. Sadly, this came to an end far too soon with David's sudden death.

Cyril checked much of the information I gathered and even though he did not know everything, he cleared up a few misunderstandings. The project also brought him new knowledge. He had always been in doubt whether Ainsworth or Savage had eliminated the tank at the Westerbouwing. He thought it had been Ainsworth, which Platoon Sergeant Fred Terry confirmed in their correspondence. However, Jim Isles thought it was Savage who fired the PIAT. From the stories I received from Norman Savage it now seems likely that Edwin Ainsworth was the one who put the tank out of action. "You must realize that we wanted to make ourselves as invisible as possible during the battle and therefore it was difficult to see what the others were doing", explained Cyril. In September 2003 and 59 years after their first encounter, Cyril Crickett and his glider pilot Morley Williams met each other again in Oosterbeek. Morley shook Cyril's hand and, glider pilot to the core, asked if Cyril and his comrades from 13 Platoon had had a pleasant flight, back in 1944. Cyril smiled dryly and answered that the flight was quite pleasant but getting safely to their destination was Morley's and Blackie's most important achievement. He added that since then, when visiting Arnhem, he preferred to book return flights.

Corporal Cyril Crickett (left) meets his Glider Pilot Sergeant Arthur 'Morley' Williams in 2003 after 59 years. (picture by Tim Rogers)

Morley's godson and travel companion, Tim Rogers, who was a journalist with ITN TV News, took a picture of the renewed acquaintance, which now adorns the cover of the Dutch edition of 2004. The reunion between Cyril and Morley continued in the garden of Morley's hostess Doedie Minderman, and as soon as the veterans started talking about Arnhem, there was an almost audible click when their intense stories met. In seconds, they travelled back 59 years in time. Their faces looked solemn and, just for that moment, it was Glider Pilot Sergeant Williams and 13 Platoon Corporal Crickett from 1944 sitting opposite each other, lost in memories and out of the reach of everyone who had not been there at that dreadful time. They themselves were unaware of the effect of their sudden time travel on the other people in the garden. Tim and I were reduced to distant but fascinated listeners from a different era.

Jim Isles

Jim Isles returned home in April 1945. During the months her son had been in captivity, Jim's mother had gone to church every day to pray for him. Jim's girlfriend and future wife soon after his homecoming saw that the war had changed him. He had become more brusque and curt. Several times, they split up and got back together again. Initially she blamed herself, but, later on, her suspicions grew that Jim's experiences during the war might well be the cause. During such a phase, he frequently had nightmares and drank heavily. PTSS was still unheard of.

Still in his repatriation leave during the spring of 1945, he departed for Cleator Moor to inform the parents of his mate Bob Barnes, killed in action, about what had happened. On his way to Carlisle, he bumped into his old mate Eddie Flinn. They agreed that Jim would come round to the Flinn's home after his visit to Bob's parents, as Eddie lived in Cleator Moor as well. Jim could stay with him and his parents for a few days. Together, Eddie and Jim, neither of them older than 20 years, went to visit Bob Barnes' parents to tell their sad story. At the Barnes' home, they related the events at the Westerbouwing, as well as the situation when Bob was hit. Bob's mother then told them that her son had originally applied for the Navy and that he asked her to put the application in the mail. However, instead of posting his Royal Navy application, she had made it disappear in the fireplace, without telling her son. "I was afraid he might drown", she explained. Now that her son had joined the Airbornes instead and was killed in an airborne operation, Bob's mother couldn't escape the horrible idea that she might be to blame for his death.

After their taxing visit to Bob's parents, Jim and Eddie went back to Eddie's family home. Jim stayed there for a week, happy to be in the company of a friend who knew exactly what it had been like. When this week was over, Jim returned home. As Jim's brother kept asking him about his experiences during the war, Jim told him that throughout the time he was in Arnhem, he was waiting for the bullet with his name on it. He really did not expect to get out of there alive. When he and his mates were taken away as prisoners of war, he passed by a long line of German tanks in the city, ready to be brought into action.

Jim looked for work, and after having gone through several jobs he finally found regular employment as an operator with ICI Chemicals in Thornton Cleveleys, where he would continue to work for 30 years.

He never knew that the son of 'Johnny' Walker from 13 Platoon was employed there too. He got married, had a son and a daughter, who painted him as a nice father whom they were very fond of. Gradually, Jim's crises diminished and he learned to live with his memories. He was grateful to his German doctors for their advice to keep using his foot as normally as possible. He noticed that his heel had healed well. Life resumed its normal course, the children grew up and Arnhem became part of the past. In the Sixties, he finally had the last remainders of the bullets removed from his ankle. His son John kept the point of the bullet that was removed, in a small glass jar. Sadly, later on in life, Jim was yet again confronted with his memories of what had happened at Arnhem and in the prisoners of war camps. He suffered from depressions and consequently withdrew into himself.

In 1979, Jim, his son John and several other members of the First Border Battalion returned to Arnhem. It was the first and only time Jim made the journey and he was the only one from 13 Platoon present. In the early morning of the first day of their stay, they visited the Westerbouwing restaurant, which had been rebuilt several years previously. While strolling through the surrounding area, they looked around, and Jim told his son that during the fighting in 1944 the woods on the west side of the buildings were absolutely swarming with Germans. As they spoke, the travel group descended via the Benedendorpsweg towards the crossing with the Van Borsselenweg/Veerweg. They walked back and forth and gesticulated busily in an attempt to retrace the barn where Jim, Joe Winstanley and others, had been hiding. Jim was frustrated when they did not succeed in finding it. When I discussed the story of the barn with Geert Maassen of the *Gelders Archief* (the archives of the province of Gelderland in which Arnhem is situated), he felt that the farm at 41, Van Borsselenweg (see map) was the most likely spot. The family that lived there had been sent away from their home one day prior to the attack on September 21, 1944, because the conditions had become too dangerous for civilians. Jim and the others followed the Veerweg parallel to the Rhine on their walk back to the Westerbouwing. By then, the day had turned pleasantly sunny. Jim pointed out to his son that in 1944 his trench was right next to the stairs that lead to the restaurant. Via these stairs on the south side of the Westerbouwing the company climbed the hill, which was about 30 meters high. John kept a close eye on his father, who was visibly reliving the events of Septem-

Jim Isles revisited the spot of his trench on the Veerweg on his visit that he and his son John and several other veterans, made in 1979 to the Arnhem battlefields.

ber 21, 1944. After having climbed almost one third of the stairs, his father suddenly stopped dead in his tracks. He was silent and appeared to be looking for something. A tense silence lasted painful seconds, half a minute, an unbearable full minute. Then Jim said, with a smothered voice: "That was where Bob Barnes was killed." pointing to a spot, only a few yards away from where they were standing. Immediately thereafter Jim abruptly turned away and without paying attention to his son, he continued on his way as if he had never stopped. He joined the conversation of the other members of the group, who tried to pin their memories to specific spots. Jim still stood rooted to the spot because of his father's barely suppressed outburst of sudden raw emotion and its instant disappearance again. During the remainder of the walk up the stairs, John did not feel like talking, almost punch-drunk by the event. After the stroll, they visited the Airborne War Cemetery, where Jim took pictures of the graves of Bob Barnes, his lieutenant John Wellbelove and the other men he knew.

However, the visit to the former battlegrounds did not cure Jim of his melancholy moods, something he had hoped for. John remembered for instance a sunny, quiet Monday in September 1984, when he had taken the day off to paint the outside of his home. His dad had promised to give him a hand. John had been painting for about a quarter of an hour, when the silence was for no apparent reason disrupted by his father's choked voice: "On the day we went to war, we had the exact same weather!" John startled, looked down and saw in his father's eyes that he seemed to be back in Arnhem! John quickly climbed down the ladder and asked his father whether he was okay. The flashback had already passed and Jim was himself again. Once more, John realised that his father had been through some terrible experiences. To be sent to war at an early age, having to watch friends being killed, himself getting wounded by machine gun fire, being captured, only just evading an execution and seeing at first hand the concentration camp Dachau - all this in a period of just 10 months – is an extremely great burden for anyone to bear, John thought. All the more difficult, as Jim had to get to work immediately after the war was over, without having been given the time or help to deal with his experiences.

Jim was surprised and delighted when he bumped into Cyril Crickett, who turned out to be living almost on his doorstep. The encounter offered them the rare opportunity to discuss the events, which united them. Back and forth, they paid each other visits until Jim suddenly died of a heart attack on January 5, 1987.

Eddie Flinn
The memory of his homecoming made Eddie Flinn smile for many years to come. After all the hardships and horrors, it was a real treat for him to meet his family again and just to have a peaceful pint at the pub with his mates. Eddie thought that it was just by pure chance that he returned alive and well, and that it was 'just' his toes that he lost as a result of the combat. He enjoyed his return to everyday civilian life, and slammed the door shut to his Arnhem past. "Arnhem was my first and fortunately also my last war experience", he said with whole-hearted relief, bordering on disgust. The only thing he missed about it was the companionship of his mates from the Platoon and the Company. "We have been through such a great deal together. The demanding training, the fatigue, the cold and the hunger, the fighting itself and the captivity and the drinks in the pub as well: we experienced it all together", he related. It did not take long before Eddie could take up his old profession of carpenter again as construction in the area was booming. Life resumed its normal course and Eddie minded his own business. He tried hard not to attract attention and to

As a joiner Eddie Flinn left his Arnhem experiences far behind

remain out of the picture. He maintained that he was not troubled by his foot, which was lacking all five toes since Arnhem. He did not talk about Arnhem, but the images of what happened there remained in his head. He still envisaged how he was sitting in his trench on the Westerbouwing, while the Germans were close enough for him to hear them talk. He tried however, to think of the past as little as possible. To continue working hard was his cure to clear his mind of the memories of war. In 1989, at the age of 65, he retired. Eddie and his wife Eileen had two daughters and a son, all married. They were very proud of their six grandchildren. During the first interviews I had with Eddie, he was reluctant to go into detail. However, when I spoke with him on later occasions, whilst he continued to keep his distance, every now and then I detected a glimpse of appreciation for the interest shown in him and his fellow soldiers. He asked me how many people and stories I had managed to trace so far, and said, "Many people will be grateful to you for the results of your quest". Perhaps he was referring to himself as well. In 2007, Eddie passed away at 82 years old.

Jack Kimber
Long did the search for Jack Kimber yield little more than that he had passed away in 1992. Not until I found relatives of his in Newcastle, was I able to record any details. His Newcastle relatives put me on the trail of family members of his wife Nancy and subsequently to a former colleague from his job in Wales. This led to a richly detailed portrait of Lance-Sergeant John "Jack" Kimber, including his life after the war.

On April 10 1945, Jack Kimber returned to England by plane. After having been registered as a returned Prisoner of War he travelled by train to Llanelli in South Wales for his repatriation leave. He rang Nancy Morgan, his girlfriend and wife-to-be, to tell her that he was on his way home to her. She delightedly promised to pick him up at the station. Together with her sister, she was standing on the platform when the train arrived. They walked along the train and stopped every few meters. They were stretching their necks and standing on their toes trying to look over the crowd getting off the train, hoping to spot Jack. They arrived at the last wagon, but they had not seen him. Puzzled, they walked slowly back as the platform quickly emptied. Then, Nancy's eye fell on a tall, strongly emaciated man who looked at them in bewilderment. Silent tears were running down his cheeks and with a shock, Nancy recognised her boyfriend Jack. She understood instantly that it must have been a cruel blow for him that she passed him by without recognising him. In a flash, she decided to pretend as if she had played a trick on him. Walking towards him with outstretched arms and her head slightly to one side, she merrily said, "I bet you were thinking I did not recognise you?"

During the first days back at home, Jack ate with great difficulty due to his malnutrition. His digestion still couldn't cope with large amounts of food. Nancy could only give him a teaspoonful every hour, 24 hours a day. Slowly, he raised the quantity his digestion could handle and step by step, he regained his strength. Jack stayed with Nancy in Wales. With his recovery well under way, it was time to start thinking about a job. His first job in Wales was as a construction worker on an estate of newly built houses in Felinfoel, near Llanelli. He and Nancy got married on 11 November 1946, at 11:00 a.m. Armistice Day. The choice for that particular day was symbolic, "because", as Jack said, "on that day my life started over again". They stayed together their whole life, but to their disappointment, they did not have any children. Every summer they went together to Newcastle for a couple of weeks to visit Jack's family. Jack was not the only Englishman who returned to Llanelli after the war, married a local girl and took up permanent residence there.

His niece Rose Ball from Newcastle remembered that Jack (as he was called in Wales and John, as he was known in Newcastle) had been wounded by a bullet in the face. It had hit his left ear and had passed through his mouth and right cheek. That was why he was deaf with one ear and he missed part of his ear lobe. "Those were the scars you could see from the outside," she said. She did not know anything about his period of recovery in Wales. She remembered her uncle as a caring and friendly man who, like his wife Nancy, was very fond of their nephews and nieces from Newcastle. It was not until my quest that she realised the symbolic meaning of Jack and Nancy's wedding day. By marrying on Armistice Day, they symbolically pledged their alliance to peace.

As a result of my questions, Rose Ball remembered another remarkable story about her uncle Jack: "Several years after the war somebody called at Jack's parental house in Newcastle. His mother found one of his airborne comrades at the doorstep. He explained a little embarrassed that he had come to express his sympathy with the death of her son Jack. The man was extremely surprised to find out that Jack had survived the war and was living safe and sound in Wales. His mother gave the man her son's address in Wales. But I do not know whether the man ever got in touch with him."

After some time Jack found another job as a barrel carter at the Felinfoel Brewery in Llanelli. It did not take long before he got promoted. At first, he was a driver of one of the Lorries and eventually he got appointed as Transport Manager. He kept working at the brewery until his retirement. As a true former Sergeant, he was appreciated by the factory men and the management alike. The brewery still exists and when I sent them a letter asking if anybody remembered Jack Kimber, I got the following letter from one of his old colleagues, John Reed:

Llanelli, 24 November 2003

Dear Sir,

I am writing to you from Llanelli regarding your search for information on L/Sgt John Matthewson Kimber. Your email to Felinfoel Brewery was passed on to me by the manager, Mr. Philip Lewis. I am only one of two employees at the brewery who remember Jack Kimber during the time he worked there.

As you were probably aware from the brewery website, we are a small firm and in the thirty years, that I had worked there, it had seen many changes of personnel, many of whom have since died. I had endeavoured to make enquiries about Jack's military service from local people who knew him but it would appear that Jack never talked about the war or his own experiences. What little I knew and what I have been able to find out I am more than happy to pass on to you.

I was aware that he was in the Airborne and that he had been wounded in action but where, I did not know until your e-mail arrived. Jack carried some scars to his neck and to his ear lobe so I presume these were the wounds that he received at Arnhem. I also seem to remember that he carried a wound to his stomach.

One story may be of interest to you. When I first started working in the brewery it had a large maintenance department, employing a number of carpenters, painters and decorators, etc.

One of the painters, a man by the name of Arthur Evans, served during the war in the Royal Navy in the Mediterranean. He was part of a rescue party that pulled Jack Kimber and others out of the sea. As you are probably aware, large numbers of glider borne troops took part in the invasion of Sicily. Many of whom were cast off too far away from the land and were forced to ditch in the sea resulting in large loss in life. I think therefore, that it was safe to assume from these two incidents, that Jack was part of that invasion force, although I never heard any explanation as to why the emergency landing had occurred. I had always assumed that he had been on a troop ship and that it had been torpedoed.

Why Jack came all the way from the North East of England to settle in Wales, I do not know, but it was extraordinary coincidence that both men, from different ends of the country, should end up working in the same small company.

I remember Jack as a man who carried the air of one who had served in the armed forces, always well turned out and dapper. He spent the majority of his working life as a foreman in charge of the transport department at the brewery. I found him to be a kind and caring person. The death of his wife was a great loss to him, which I think he never got over. You say in your email that it seems that he was relatively well treated during his time as a PoW. I was told that he was very malnourished because of his captivity, but of course, that was nothing out of the ordinary for many of the prisoners of the Nazis. I think Jack was like many people who fought in the war, quiet, brave and humble. An unsung hero. It was good to know that there are people like yourself who are striving to acknowledge their heroism.

I am sorry that I have taken so long to get in touch with you and have so little to tell, but I wish you every success with your book and hope that it would be published in English as well.

With best wishes,
John Reed

Together with my email to the brewery, I had also asked the local newspaper, The Llanelli Star, to place a call for information on Jack Kimber. This call sensationally also reached the Mr. Evans who was mentioned in John Reed's letter

Llanelli, 4 December 2003

Dear Sir,

I write to you as an answer to your recent call for information in our local paper, The Llanelli Star. My name is Arthur Evans and I was A.B. (Able Bodied) Seaman aboard HMS Beaufort (L14), a Hunt class destroyer in the Royal Navy. That happened to be the very ship that pulled Jack Kimber and several fellow Airbornes from the Mediterranean Sea in 1943. Their glider had ditched during the Invasion of Sicily. I had never seen him again after the Sicily-operation until my dad asked me for no apparent reason if I still remembered the name of the ship I was on in the war. That must have been in 1948. I was just coming home from work and did not understand why he wanted to know. Dad was already working at the Felinfoel Brewery. He explained that a new man had started work at the brewery that day who mentioned that during the war he had been rescued from the sea by HMS Beaufort.

"*Well, that was my ship!*" *I answered quite surprised. I had served on that ship for two years and 10 months and I do recall picking up some glider borne troops from the sea. Still in 1948, I also found work at the brewery, in the maintenance department as a 'sign writer', painting signboards and things like that. That was when I met Jack again. I was in the firm canteen during my lunch break, when Jack walked in. My father introduced me:* "*Jack, this is my son who was on the ship that rescued you from the sea.*" *Jack took a few big steps towards me and greeted me quite jovially. Jack happened to be a very big lad and I measure only 5 foot and 3 inches. I was a little afraid that he, in his enthusiasm, might crush me to pieces. He said,* "*Arthur, tell these people all about how you saved us.*" *It was quite emotional.*

During the Sicily invasion, my position was in the Transmitting Station. I was there day and night. Therefore, I did not actually see the men being picked up. I just got a glance at some of them, wrapped in blankets, during a visit to the toilet. I did not speak to them until later.

During the time that they were on board, our ship was used as a decoy for a big German gun that was located on the island. It caused a lot of trouble to the shipping and landings in the Syracuse area. Our task was to sail up and down that area to draw fire of the German artillery. This worked rather well and we had a couple of very unpleasant near misses. We even had some casualties. Anyway, Jack referred to that time, pardon the expression, as the time that 'he filled his pants.'

Still, the tactics worked, as the flash of the German gun enabled our planes and monitor HMS 'Lord Roberts', to pinpoint the location. Then, our bombs and 15-inch shells from the Lord Roberts quickly silenced the gun. I remember the Airbornes were more than annoyed, I can tell you, of being dropped in the sea by the towing pilots. I seem to think they were Americans. I had given Jack a picture of HMS Beaufort, because he liked to have that as a souvenir.

Everybody in the canteen in Felinfoel was amazed about Jack and me meeting again after so long in such a different spot. We have always kept contact during all those years that we worked at the brewery. When we ran into each other, he always greeted me with 'Hi Kidda!' When it was holiday time in August he always said to me: "I am going home, Kidda!" He would then visit his relatives in Newcastle in England to which he was always looking forward.

I think that he was some five or six years older than me. I have known Jack at work to be an open and forthright man who rarely spoke about his wartime experiences.

Arthur Evans
Formerly A.B. Seaman HMS Beaufort

Jack's niece Joyce Marryfield from Swansea, explained that he was very reluctant to talk about his war experiences. When people asked him about what he had witnessed he often said, "You don't want to know." He was a bit solitary, but sometimes, after a glass of whisky, he narrated something. She remembered a story about a march from the Polish PoW camp to the west when he discovered one morning, lying amidst the other prisoners of war, that he was frozen to the ground after a frosty night and that he had difficulty pulling himself free when he tried to get up. After the war, Jack never ever went abroad again. He felt he had seen too much, and too much had happened to him to make him leave Great

Jack Kimber (on the left) in the Seventies. Together with his brothers Oswald and James.

Britain ever again. He felt much more comfortable in his own country. The box with his service medals he received passed on to Joyce Marryfield without having been opened once. In all those years, Jack Kimber had never ever taken the medals out of their casket. In turn, she handed them to her youngest son who had the same name as his great-uncle. Jack did not want any souvenirs from the war. He used to say, "I'm not a hero, I just served my country, so what do I need any medals for?"

'Pip' Hulse
It was the *Winsford and Middlewich Chronicle,* which informed Bernard and his son Mike Hulse at the end of June 2002 about my search for the fortunes of Bernard's elder brother 'Pip' Hulse. Pip died in October 1944 in the St Antonius hospital in the Dutch city of Utrecht as a result of his injuries. Mike Hulse was touched by the coincidence that he had been in the Netherlands with his wife just two months before the call in the newspaper. They had been looking for his uncle's grave but to their disappointment, had not been able to find it.

They were very interested in my quest. As they had very little on Pip's adventures during Arnhem, they were both very pleased with the additional information that the search had revealed. For Bernard this turned out to be a great support during a period of serious illness. They explained that the Red Cross card from Utrecht, sent by one of Pip's comrades in his name, did not reach the family until after Pip had passed away. To this day, they don't know who wrote the card. Comparing the handwriting in 2019, it became clear that it hadn't been Platoon Sergeant Fred Terry. After the war, Pip and Bernard's parents were visited by one of his comrades who told them he had been with Pip when he got hurt during the retreat across the Rhine. "We did not remember his name. We only knew that he was from Norwich, a town about 10 km from here. We actually think that this man was the one who wrote that card", Bernard and Mike explained.

'Gerry' Greasley

The war and camp experiences also left deep scars in 'Gerry' Greasley, Lieutenant Wellbelove's batman. His younger brother Ken, with whom I got in touch 21 years after Gerry had passed away, talked about him coming home from Stalag XIB Fallingbostel. Gerry was physically in poor condition and mentally he was not his usual self either. He had lost much of his former self-confidence and gave a nervous and restless impression especially immediately after his return. After his demobilisation he picked up his former work in the building trade. Together with his wife Lena he settled in Fulbeck in Lincolnshire. As time went by, Gerry recovered but he remained a man of very few words. Therefore even his closest family knew next to nothing about what had happened to him during the war. In 1965 he started working for his younger brother Ken's building company in Grantham. He was employed there until his retirement in 1983. Sadly, he would not be able to enjoy his pension for a long time, for, that very same year, at the age of 70 he passed away unexpectedly.

Joe Winstanley

Joe Winstanley also returned home in an emaciated state from Fallingbostel, but coming home gave him new strength and he recovered well, although he kept suffering from asthma for the rest of his life. During his repatriation leave he met his future wife, Bridget, at a dance hall in St Helens. After his leave he was sent to an army unit in Italy. He was no longer with the Airborne Border Battalion, probably because of his asthma. War in Italy was also over and he was deployed there with the task of disarming and interning the surrendering German units and collaborators who were stranded there. In his letters to Bridget he wrote that the service in Italy was not too hard because there was no fighting. Obviously there was also time for some relaxation, because during his stay there he developed a lifelong taste for foreign food. When the job was finished, Joe was demobilised and returned home permanently. On the 4th of August 1946, Joe (26 years old) married Bridget in the Saint Anne's Church in St Helens. They had four children and Joe returned to his job as a locomotive-driver. His children remember him as a friendly and loving father who, despite of periods of poor health, remained cheery and happy. Only too quickly this came to an end with Joe's sudden death in 1972. He was only 52 years old, recalled his daughter Lorette in April 2004.

Vincent Swarbrick
After his repatriation leave Vinnie "Johnny" Swarbrick rejoined the 1 Border Regiment until August 1945 when he became a Royal Engineer. Here he seems to have remained on active service until February 1947. Then he was transferred to the Royal Engineers Army Reserves. He married and had two daughters. After having left the army, he started work in Meadows Street Fishmongers, more or less continuing the role as shop assistant he had had before he joined the Army. Sometime after that he owned a fruit and a fish shop in Longton. In his last years before retirement Vinnie drove a bin lorry. He rarely spoke about his wartime and PoW-memories. It was only clear that he didn't like Monty at all, possibly because Vinnie blamed him for the failure of the Arnhem Operation. Vinnie passed away in 1995, he was 71 years old. His daughters and others remember him as a quiet and friendly man.

William 'Johnny' Walker
On 6 January 1945 Billy, as 'Johnny' was known in civvy street, married Edith. They got two sons. In October 1945 his assignment in Norway ended. At the same time The Border Battalion ended its airborne role. A book with (many snow) photos of Norway was presented to members of the battalion by the King, as the inscription said. The Battalion was sent to Germany to become part of the British Army on the Rhine (BAOR) in Dortmund. Billy was there too. It seems he was still train-

Edith and William Walker 1945

ing in the shooting teams. He still was in contact with Quarter Master 'Uncle' Barnes, who had taken care of the evacuated men in Nijmegen. He brought home a metal shoehorn as a war souvenir. On the back it says *Fritz Sanders, Grösste Auswahl, moderner & solider Schuhwaren, Duisberg, Ludgeristr. 12,* but if there is a story behind the object, it intriguingly enough, didn't survive.

Billy never talked of his experiences during the battle, as his son Anthony recalls. He did not seem to suffer from what latterly was identified as PTSD or indeed had any flash backs. He was open to the suggestion of the 'spy' theory as to the reason the operation went so badly wrong.

Son Anthony remembers: "He was quiet and unassuming and not easily made to sing his own praises. Whenever as a young family we would go out on picnics – say to a local beauty spot like Ribchester, I remember he would play a game with me and my brother. One of us would be made to cover our eyes, or turn round, and the other would be told to walk down the field to a certain spot that dad would designate and then would be told to lie down. When I turned around or uncovered my eyes – sure enough my brother had 'disappeared'! Clearly a skill which came to be of use when in battle. He was also a crack shot at any fairground shooting galleries – and readily passed on the techniques of lining up the sights. We never knew that he was called Johnnie. He never used it or was called it after the war as far as I am aware."

In civvy street Billy became a public transport bus conductor in Blackburn in 1947. Every now and then he would see Wilf Oldham of 14 Platoon. Wilf had become a policeman, directing traffic at a crossroads in the town center. They would greet each other as the bus passed by but never got to talking to each other. Once Billy was witnessed helping a frail lady courtly from the bus. The witness happened to be the Lady Mayoress of Blackburn. An illuminated address once resided in the Blackburn transport office testifying to his kindness. Anthony hopes it's still there as a memory.

Anthony recalls: "This employment may have lasted until the late 40's when Dad joined Mullards, part of the Dutch (!) Phillips Group. From there he was employed by English Electric and engaged in the manufacture of insulators for Electricity Pylons, possibly related to his experience with radio's and electronics. He went on to be employed by Singer Cobble and travelled within Europe and elsewhere, installing machinery for the manufacture of tufted carpet. During this time I know he was in Holland and Belgium and I seem to recall he may well have taken the opportunity to visit the Oosterbeek / Arnhem area. He then rejoined Blackburn Transport, his first love. Once again as a conductor, rising through driver/one-man-operated buses eventually to be promoted to Inspector."

Anthony continues: "One memory among thousands is the occasion he felt badly about not being able to help me when I was studying, as a 19 year old, for my Higher National Certificate in Business Studies (Economics and all that). I said not to worry … However when it came to the time for him to take his Inspectors exams, he asked me to give his work and essays 'the once over'. So, I picked up the red pen and it goes without saying, he passed!"

When the Richard Attenborough film - A Bridge too Far - was premiered in 1974 at Blackburn, it was Billy's wife who had to respond to the local paper when they asked for anyone who had experience of operation Market Garden. Dad would not push himself forward, it was down to Edith to contact the local newspaper…..although he did tease the Army cadets who were paraded with the veterans prior to the film being shown. One of his pet gripes concerned the famous film footage of the mortar team of 23 Platoon, S Company, attached to C Company. The gripe was that the footage was shown whenever any particular battle was being illustrated – 'D' day etc. He always mentioned it, and always said – 'it was at Arnhem!' Once, while out shopping with Edith in Blackburn, Billy met someone in town and had instantly recognised him as an ex comrade from Arnhem. When she asked him how he could remember someone from some 30 years previous, he apparently said "you never forget anyone you've eaten tree roots with!"

William Walker sadly passed away far too early on 12 May 1982 of a heart attack whilst at work. Anthony says: "Mum decided to take the funeral procession via the town bus station 'The Boulevard'. I have never seen so many broken-hearted faces of all nationalities lining the route. Truly loved. Without doubt he was one of the top 20 percent of the top 20 percent."

After having compiled Billy's story from his son's notes I wondered how remarkable contacting the Walker family was. In more than ten years of research, with the help of newspapers, countless letters and even with support from Border comrade Wilf Oldham no contact had been made. And now through modern age Facebook, Billy's granddaughter Sue Walker found my call for information and filled another void on 13 Platoon.

But just as I thought Billy's story was done, Anthony Walker wrote: "An extraordinary revelation was that of 13 Platoon member Jim Isles (and his son John) who worked at ICI Thornton-Cleveleys. Guess what, ... so did I! Jim, as I recall, was a Chemical Process Operative on the PVC area and John was a Mechanical craftsman (fitter we called them) on the Vinyl Chloride Monomer Plant (VCM). I was employed by ICI for 30 years at Hillhouse, working ultimately as Site Personnel Manager in the Personnel (HR in modern speak) Department, until early retirement in Feb 1999. Not retirement as such, as I still do some tasks for the local College in the Management and Business Apprenticeship area.

William and Edith Walker 1976

Sue Walker's words sum it up wonderfully: *"A small update from me, Haks, this has been an incredible journey for me and my sisters learning more about grandad. It's really opened my dad up to talking about him and brought tears to our eyes learning about what an amazing man he was. My dad is truly enjoying learning about the other veterans and men connected to Grandad Walker. What a fabulous journey!"*

I replied: *"It is very rewarding to hear that our research has such wonderful effects. Thank you for letting me know. It is quite fascinating to discover that people from different countries, ages and eras without knowing each other are still connected in one way or another."*

Edwin Ainsworth

Edwin Ainsworth, who was involved in the destruction of two tanks at the Westerbouwing, was demobilised in 1946. His Certificate of Service described him as:

"Military conduct very good. This extremely smart soldier who returned to the Battalion after having been captured at Arnhem in September 1944, is very capable, amiable and thoroughly efficient at all duties in connection with his work."

Edwin Ainsworth as ambulance driver in the Fifties

In September 1947 Edwin joined the army again, this time in the Royal Signals Regiment. He was only 24 years old, but had already been through a World War. He soon got promoted and became a Corporal. His superiors found him a hard working non-commissioned officer who showed great technical skills with every task he was appointed to.

In 1952 he left the Army and started work as an ambulance driver. The same year he met his future wife Jean and they mar-

Edwin and Jean Ainsworth back in England

ried in 1953. Edwin was 30 years old by then. Jean was training to be a psychiatric nurse, but because of her marriage to Edwin she had to stop the training. At that time a married woman could not be a nurse. Edwin rejoined the Royal Signals and served between 1956 and 1967. Most of this was spent stationed in Salisbury. In 1960, when he was stationed at Chester, their elder daughter Jane was born. His younger daughter Susan was born in 1963 in the German town of Rinteln. One day, in the early Sixties, when Edwin was serving in the British Rhine Army (BAOR), he and his wife paid a visit to the German civilian, who, during Edwin's captivity, used to slip him food every now and then. They gave him a bottle of whisky as thanks. The man kindly but urgently asked them not to say anything about his help to the British prisoners during the war, because he still feared reprisals if his fellow villagers found out.

As a regular soldier Edwin was frequently transferred and he specialised as a motor mechanic. He had achieved the rank of Sergeant but declined the offer to become an officer, preferring to keep his own thoughts without having to live and work according to the regulations all the time. In 1968 he left the Army for the last time. Again with a glowing Certificate of Service:

> *"Sergeant Ainsworth has served as an Electrician-Driver and Vehicle Mechanic for the past twenty years, at home and abroad, and latterly had served as M.T.-Sergeant and Driving Instructor. His service was exemplary. He has carried out all his duties conscientiously and well and is a capable organizer and disciplinarian. He is honest and never requires to be supervised in his work. He has a great love for sailing and is a hard working forthright individual.*

That same year the family immigrated to Australia, where they lived in Brisbane, Rockhampton and Townsville respectively. Edwin and Jean ran petrol stations in these places. Edwin as a motor mechanic while Jean ran the restaurant that belonged to the station. They bought five acres of land in Townsville (Queensland) to build a bungalow. Things went well until 1972, around Christmas, fate struck and cyclone Althea ripped the roof off their house. The family had to live like refugees for a couple of weeks until they could return to their repaired home. However, in 1973 he and his family went back to England to settle in Blackburn, Edwin's place of birth. In the following years Edwin had different jobs. In September 1978, when he was an operator at a power station, he died suddenly of a heart attack at the age of 55.

His elder daughter Jane:

> *"I remember my father as a free-thinker. In his opinion, girls should also go to school and have an education and not be confined to house keeping and having children. He always encouraged me to study and set myself high aims. He was a heavy smoker and drinker, a loner with some very gloomy moods. At the same time he was brilliant with his pen in his fight for a just cause. He had a strong dislike for bureaucracy. I remember a case when the council decided, without informing neither us nor our neighbours, to introduce a parking prohibition right in front of our house, so no cars could be parked there any more. It must have been at the end of 1977 or the beginning of 1978. My father kept pressing the council so hard with strongly motivated and sharply formulated arguments against the parking prohibition that the civil servants eventually backed down and gave up their plan.*

My father enjoyed travelling through Great Britain, although the changes he saw in his country did not always make him feel happy. I knew he regretted his return from Australia to England. Although he did not like to talk about the past, it always seemed to be on his mind. I once asked him if he ever killed anybody during the war. He said he had, but added that if he had not then they would have killed him, he hated it."

Jane indeed finished her studies and today is a nurse manager running a very busy coronary care unit at an English hospital.

His younger daughter Susan wrote later:

"I was only 15 when my father passed away. My husband and I live in Bahrain now. We are about to be transferred to England with our family because of my husband's work. We have three children. One was born in England, the second in Thailand where we lived for six years and the third in Saudi Arabia, where we lived before coming to Bahrain. I suppose I have caught my father's travel bug. In the information you have sent me about my father I have read with disbelief how hard their training was. I only just now realise how courageous these boys were and I am proud of the fact that my father was one of them. For our children the lessons they get at school about the war are all of a sudden much more interesting now that they know their own grandfather was involved."

Norman Savage
When he was sent to Bergen in Norway with the First Border Battalion on 10 May 1945, a thrilling period started for Norman Savage. The German occupying forces there had surrendered unconditionally to the Allies at the same time as the remaining German armed forces in the rest of Occupied Europe. The rebuilt Border Battalion was to oversee the orderly disarming and screening of the German occupying forces, both military and civilian, after which the demobilised soldiers would be sent back to Germany. Together with others, Norman was instructed to ensure these Germans did not take anything back with them to Germany other than their personal belongings. Searching their luggage Norman found weapons, cameras and almost anything you could think of that was illegal. The Norwegian Resistance was also present and screened for Quislings (Norwegian Nazi-sympathiz-

ers) and Gestapo agents (German secret police). In September 1945 this period – which had been quite pleasant for the British – came to an end and Norman returned by boat to England. After Norway, the First Airborne Division was disbanded. Norman was transferred to Kassel, Germany, with The Border Battalion, as a unit of the 'Y' division. He remembered an inspection by Field-Marshal Montgomery. During this period, still in 1945, Savage was temporarily transferred to an American unit as part of an exchange program to improve the relations between British and American soldiers. Some friction had arisen because the Americans got higher pay, had smarter uniforms and therefore attracted a lot of attention from British women. The exchange program was meant to reduce the animosity. Every unit had three men of the other nationality billeted. Savage was sent to Landshut in Bavaria and remembered a notable incident. The first morning on the American base he went to the mess. Savage said:

> *"The bloke in charge of breakfast asked me how many eggs I would like to have. I was surprised because I had not had any eggs for weeks in the British army, so my counter question was if I could get more then one. Of course my friend, he answered. So I said, that is great and that I would like to have five. The American soldiers next to him all thought this was extremely funny."*

Then, after five and a half years of military service, in August 1946 he left the Army to his great relief. He was more than fed up with army life. At his parents' house, he threw his red beret in the burning hearth as if he was taking revenge on all that he had had to live through over the past few years. He told his parents who were watching him, worriedly, that he did not want to have anything to do with it ever again and that he would love to wipe out his memories of that period of time if he only could. Despite his outburst, he was able to leave his memories behind. Some 60 years later, he explained to me:

> *"I was quite easy-going at that age. Sicily, Arnhem, although very dramatic, were in themselves just isolated incidents. When they were over, I just kept on going. I did not have the perspective that life could be very different and that you could be permanently marked by what happens to you."*

Norman Savage with his wife Florrie and children Stella and Norman Jr. in Los Angeles, California, USA.

Initially he picked up his old job at the tannery. But Norman was not overly pleased with civilian life in after-war Britain. Due to the economic aftermath of the war, life remained sober, scanty and grey for a long time. Nevertheless, he met his future wife Florrie, which offered a sunny edge to all the dreary limitations of daily life. In January 1947, he and Florrie married and in 1947 their daughter, Stella, was born. The conditions in the United Kingdom depressed them more and more and they started to consider whether life elsewhere would offer more. In their opinion, life was about ambition and acquiring skills. In 1951 they took the big step and decided to immigrate to Toronto, Canada. Australia had also been considered for a short period, especially because the government paid for the passage, but Canada was more attractive to them. Norman proudly explained that they paid for the passage on the Queen Elizabeth to New York themselves. In Toronto, Canada, their son Norman was born. Initially they liked their start in the new world, but the long inclement Canadian winters with temperatures of minus

15° Celsius bothered them increasingly. The thought of moving again grew stronger with every harsh winter and in 1961 the family moved to Southern California in the Untied States. Immigration to the United States was easier in those days and, with pleasure, Norman changed his winter clothes for a T-shirt and a pair of jeans. In California the NASA space program was just about to develop and this resulted in an enormous need for staff. Norman found a job in the production of microchips. Training was offered on the job and his past as a radio operator at the Signal Section in 1 Border Battalion was probably of some advantage. The microchips he made were used for sonar purposes. These were very busy years for Norman and his family. A pre-requisite for working on the Space Program was that Norman had to accept the American nationality. He did not really mind and the new step turned out to be a good one. Everybody enjoyed the sunny climate. Their daughter Stella finished her study with a ten-week journey around the world. On her visit to England she liked it so much that she stayed there. She married the owner of a plastic factory in Liverpool. Today she has two children, both studying at university.

In the mid Seventies Norman lost his job because the space industry had to cut down drastically as a result of the conclusion of the Apollo program. Fortunately he managed to find another job and he became a bus driver for Rapid Transit in the area around Los Angeles. Life in the United States turned out to hold a risk, he realised, because social welfare facilities were limited. When his wife Florrie fell ill, he found out America is great for the strong, the young and the healthy, but whoever falls ill runs the risk of losing everything. "If you were not able to pay your health costs, they had no mercy and took your house away", he said. In 1983, when Norman was 60 years old, he returned to England with Florrie. They settled in Chorley, Lancashire. Their son Norman stayed in Los Angeles, California, working for NASA at Hughes Space & Communications.

In all these years after the war Norman had never met any of his old comrades again. Still, the memories kept coming back to him frequently. In 1994 on the occasion of the 50th Commemoration of the Battle he returned to Arnhem for the first time since 1944. To his great disappointment his organised bus trip for tourists did not come anywhere near the Drielse Veer or the Westerbouwing. Even the Airborne Museum Hartenstein was not in the programme. When the bus stopped near the Airborne War Cemetery for the Memorial Service and Norman and Florrie got off, they saw another British bus nearby. To Norman's surprise and excitement there were a lot of old comrades of B Company on it. Even though half a century had passed, one of them recognised Norman and shouted at the others: "Hey, Savage is here too!" However, they did not have much time to talk because the people of the organised bus trip were not allowed to visit the reserved seats for veterans. After the service, Norman and Florrie walked among the graves. Every now and then he recognised a name and he was flooded by memories and strong emotions which left him speechless and in tears. He didn't have the slightest idea of the presence of two other occupants of Horsa 166, Cyril Crickett of his platoon and Morley Williams, one of his pilots. Norman returned to England, a little disappointed about his lightweight tour, but full of strong impressions and revived memories. After a while he let his airborne memories settle down again.

Many years later in 2003, he was highly surprised when a friend from Bolton told him that there was a call in the *Bolton Evening News* from me, a Dutchman whom he had never met before and who was looking for him in connection with the Battle of Arnhem. He responded and appreciated the interest. He was pleasantly surprised when the Dutchman got him in touch with Cyril Crickett, Wilf Oldham and Johnny Peters. The last two were friends from sister platoons in B Company. He criticised the fact that school children were told about what happened in 1066 (William the Conqueror won the Battle of Hastings), yet they were not taught anything about modern history such as the Battle of Arnhem in 1944. In the Netherlands that was very different, he said. I agreed that school children near Arnhem and Oosterbeek indeed knew a lot about what had happened to their towns.

Norman said he looked back on an eventful life with a lot of ups and downs. However, his motto was that it did not matter how much you travel, home is where the heart is. It was the friends you meet on your way who make your path in life worthwhile, he believed.

Frank Evans
After Frank Evans returned home, life at first remained difficult. He struggled to find work for some time. The country was in ruins, the economy was down and there was strict food rationing. Hardly surprising then there was no work for a specialist and high class Silver

Service waiter. Frank, Jane and their daughter Beryl were forced to live with various relatives in Chester and made a bit of money by making brooches and rosettes from buttons and ribbon and selling them in pubs in the city center in the evening. Things slowly turned around though and eventually he was able to pick up where he left off before the war and could continue to be a waiter. His grandson Stephen Earlam recalls:

> *"I think he may have worked in the Far East for a while, possibly Singapore. Again having to leave his family. My Nan Jane had a small, elaborate china tea service that he brought back as a gift on his return. With 50 years he was relatively young when he died in 1964 from lung cancer. I was only 3 years old. My Nan was totally distraught. My mum, Beryl, said her mother got rid of everything that reminded her of him, even his war medals. I don't remember her ever speaking of him in any great depth. Consequently I only have one photo of him from a family wedding in about 1962. Foto 66 I always felt that my Grandfather had a story worth telling and feared that I was the only person left that had any knowledge at all of his contribution to our history. I'm amazed and grateful that his story has already been told in part."*

Frank and Jane Evans in 1962

Fred Terry

My call in the regional paper *Northern Echo* for more information on Platoon Sergeant Fred Terry was seen by his son Bob Terry. Unfortunately he had to tell me that his father had passed away in August 1997 at the age of 81. However, Bob was willing to tell me about his father's Arnhem stories.

He remembers that his father was rather thin when he returned home to the quiet rural town of Middleham from the PoW camp Fallingbostel in April 1945. To regain strength, he used to eat two boiled eggs with his tea in the first weeks after coming home. Bob was six years old at the time and he would have liked an egg every now and then as well, he confessed, more than sixty years later.

After his repatriation leave Fred Terry had to report again to the First Battalion, The Border Regiment. It was then stationed in Boston, Lincolnshire. To Bob's pleasure his father came home every weekend. The Battalion wanted to keep Fred Terry because of his experience and great military skills, but after six years Fred decided to say goodbye to his uniform and to build up a civil life. Due to the injury received during 'Arnhem', he couldn't go back to the stone masonry where he had worked before the war. He was no longer able to lift his left arm above his head and lifting heavy things had become difficult. In Middleham he took over a news agents and bookshop from an elderly lady, who had retired. One of his jobs was to organise the distribution of the newspapers in the neighbourhood, which he did quite well. Just after the war Fred had been back a couple of times to Arnhem, until he decided that he had to close that part of his past. Unfortunately, when I contacted the Dutch family Behr that he had stayed with, had no specific memories or pictures of Fred's visits anymore.

Fred Terry photographed for his work as a FA-official. (Photo FA).

Apart from Bob Terry, other acquaintances of his father reacted to my call in the *Northern Echo*. They, Audrey and Harry Waudby, also lived in Middleham. Harry had met Fred when the Borders were stationed in Bardney, probably just before the operation at Arnhem. Fred had not only taken care of their newspapers, he also was a good friend. They told me that Fred combined the newsagents with the job of Mayor of the village with 700 inhabitants at that time. "After coming back from the war he developed into an active advocate for the preservation of local history," they recalled. There is a lot of history in this medieval village that enjoys a reputation because of its racehorses and beautiful remains of a castle. The Waudby's sent me a cassette with a radio interview with Fred. After his retirement Fred moved to the village of Leyburn, on the other side of the valley. When he was 60 years old, he was chosen as district chairman in the North Riding County district of the British Football Association FA. He sat on the Leagues Sanction Commission and in the FA Vase Commission, which was the national competition for amateur teams. As an FA official he had been present several times at the famous FA Cup final in Wembley stadium. Until 1996 when his health started to decline, Fred had been active in the Football Association. In 1995 Fred Terry had some contact by letter with Cyril Crickett and Lieutenant Patrick Stott, but he never went to any of the reunions of the Border Battalion again.

John Wellbelove
In the period before John Wellbelove went to Great Britain, he was a parachute instructor in Esquimalt, British Columbia. He used to write home quite regularly, although he was not able to go into detail about where he was, because that had to remain secret. In his last letter to his parents he could only write that he was going to visit his aunts Emily and Jane, his father's sisters. His parents could deduce from this that he was to be transferred to England, because that was where his aunts lived. They did not hear about his service at the Battle of Arnhem until afterwards.

The last news on Lieutenant Wellbelove came from Corporal Wilson of the Border Battalion who had heard him shout on the Westerbouwing "Come on you Heini bastards". Since then nobody had ever seen him alive again. At the end of September 1944 his family found out through the local police office that a telegram had arrived reporting him as missing in action. John's family remained in painful uncertainty for months, but as time went by without any news, the likelihood that he was no longer alive grew. John's sister Mary remembered visiting Cliffy Aasen at an army hospital after he had returned to Canada. The only thing he knew was that John was officially still thought to be wounded and missing. Cliffy himself turned out to have lost both legs during the Battle of Arnhem and on coming home discovered that his wife had left him. "Where he went from the hospital I do not know", Mary said regretfully.

In August 1945 it was officially established that John Wellbelove had fallen during the fighting at the Westerbouwing and his family was officially informed. Several weeks later the family received John's dress uniform, cap, sambrown belt and swagger stick through the War Graves Commission in Ottawa, Ontario.

His sister Mary wrote:

> My brother was the relative I was most fond of. The few years I had with John as a brother, I knew he was very special with a strong character, and his war service seems to prove it. He was closer to me than my sisters, because I was a bit of a 'tomboy' growing up and considered the second son on the farm. As far as John's influence on my future life, it did change my choice of vocation. As his future was guaranteed with a promised job as a teacher in Agriculture at the University of Saskatchewan, he was going to give me his army service pay to establish my chosen career in dress designing. As that wasn't forthcoming I became a stenographer which was less expensive. As for the effect of John's demise on my parents, Daddy had just been nominated as a Provincial Parliament Delegate, so he then had to turn the running of the grain farming over to a neighbour to do the seeding and harvest. The settlement was done on a 50-50 basis of profit

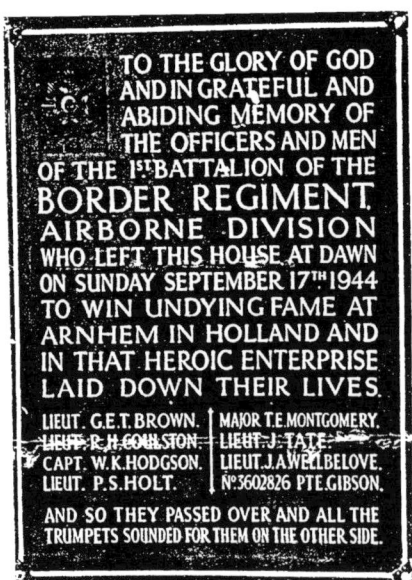

The plaque in the Burford Priory commemorating the officers and men that took off for Arnhem from the Priory.

as the wheat was harvested and sold.

How do I look back on Arnhem? We had no knowledge for some time after the war as to the fact that John was killed in Arnhem. When we did learn, it left a major hole in the body of our family as he was the only son and brother. Our only other connection to Arnhem was a book the War Graves Commission in Ottawa, sent to us years later showing pictures of the terrific care the school children and citizens in Oosterbeek take of the graves of the Canadian and other soldiers who fought to liberate your country. We were learned that this is an ongoing thing and we greatly appreciate the work and time that goes into it. So as a result of this I have nothing but a high regard for the area of Arnhem and the citizens of Holland.

With kindest regards

Mary

Bert Ilsley's wife Ruth added in October 2005:

"Afterwards, in May 1945, Bert was sent to Norway with 1 The Border Regiment to oversee that the Germans responded properly to their surrender. Later he went to Germany until he finally came home to Regina in 1946. In September/October 1979 Bert and I were on a European trip. From Amsterdam we took the train to Arnhem, and then got a ride to the Oosterbeek War Cemetery to take pictures of Johnny's grave. Before we went on the trip, Bert got the exact location from the Canadian War Graves Committee in Ottawa. Bert's friendship with Johnny was only for one and a half years, but it went very deep, I always felt.

There is a beautiful Saskatchewan War Memorial in Regina, our provincial capital. Furthermore. All Saskatchewan servicemen killed in action in World War Two are commemorated in a geo-memorial. This means that each and every one has had an island, lake or bay in the north of the province named for him. I believe Johnny is commemorated in Wellbelove Bay. It is located at 58°37' latitude and 102°58' longitude. A book has been printed about this. I know that had Bert's health been better he would have been very much interested to read about your research and no doubt it would have brought back many memories that might have contributed to the story of Johnny Wellbelove and his experiences in Britain. We hope you will get the translation published soon.

Very sincerely,
Ruth Ilsley

Back in Canada Bert found employment with a bank where he stayed his entire professional career.

Lines on a September Morning
To those who left this house at dawn, and died at Arnhem

Not as men doomed they went,
but as those who,
awaking to the September dawn,
left unseen the promise of the day,
the pollard willows
and the wolds in mist,
the dew still wet upon the rose.

Not as men dead
Are they remembered now,
all treachery spent,
and the killing done,
but as those who,
in these after days,
share with us the beauty of this hour,
the pollard willows
and the wolds in sun,
the warmth of life
still fresh upon the rose.

SrMB
(Plaque in the Lenthall Chapel)

In the year 2000 Garnet Keeler had organised an exhibition in Eston, John's place of birth, on the fortunes of the fellow villagers who fought the Germans in Europe. Mary visited the exhibition together with her husband Ray and discovered some new details about her brother's army life. The copy of a book about Arnhem, sent to them by acquaintances from the Netherlands, also brought some more clarity. The contact with these Dutch people arose from an initiative of other Canadians in 1999 to visit the graves of fallen countrymen, which in the end Mary and Ray did not join.

A more detailed idea of John's adventures came about when I combined the information I had gathered during my quest with the stories of his men. Mary Spokes explained that she did not know how her father would have reacted if he had known the strong language John had vented or his attitude regarding taking the lives of other people. Their father had quite a different outlook on life from Mary and John's generation, and religion played an important part in it, she said. Nevertheless, he would have been very proud of his son and it would have done him good to know that his son never gave up and had taken his obligations seriously. Mary still had John's sambrown belt and swagger stick, which she would pass on to her son Ron who lives in Saskatoon, Saskatchewan.

From the eight men of 13 platoon who were killed in action, Eric Melling, 'Click' Fidler and Frank Jarvis are still officially missing. 'Pip' Hulse was buried in Utrecht and John Glenn in Manchester. Only John Wellbelove, Bob Barnes and Tommy McDonald were buried at the Airborne War Cemetery.

Tommy McDonald
So there was absolutely no way Tommy McDonald could have sent me the e-mail that I found in my inbox on 8 October 2012, just before ten o'clock in the morning. As I said before, 28-year old Tommy, the sniper from Corporal Cyril Crickett's scout section, was killed south of the Westerbouwing on 21 September 1944.

Still, the e-mail was from a very much alive Thomas McDonald. This present-day Thomas explained that he was named after his uncle Tommy McDonald, from Leadgate near Newcastle, who was killed during the Second World War in North-western Europe in 1944-1945. This World War Two victim was a full cousin of present-day Thomas's father.

Sadly the latter hardly knew anything about what had happened to the man he was named after.

While researching, present day Thomas was surprised to find a similar call for information on a Tommy McDonald on the Manchester Evening News web site. One that I had made for my own 13 Platoon research years earlier. He contacted me to learn if his uncle might be the same person as the 'Arnhem' Tommy McDonald from 13 Platoon. Intrigued, I replied that all I knew was that his section commander, Corporal Cyril Crickett, vaguely remembered that 'Arnhem' Tommy might have come from Manchester. So, I couldn't tell if 'Leadgate Tommy' was indeed 'Arnhem Tommy'.

Thomas mentioned that on the War Memorial in Leadgate the name of a certain T. McDonald appeared. His family had strong roots in that village. If the name on the War Memorial could be linked to his uncle Tommy, then we might find a connection to Arnhem Tommy. So Thomas and his wife Margaret contacted the local Historical Society in Leadgate. They also told me what they knew about his uncle Tommy. That man was born on 14 August 1916 and was married on 9 September 1942 to Katherine Houghey in the Rotherham area (County Yorkshire), daughter of a Navy Officer. He was a lorry driver.

Then, after a few weeks, Thomas had news. Another relative had suddenly remembered a box with family pictures and letters. The box had belonged to the sister of his uncle Tommy. She had died young and therefore never passed on the life story of her brother. When Margaret went through the box, she found a clipping of the local newspaper which read: *"The bride wore a lace gown with a wreath of orange blossom and veil. She carried a bouquet of pink carnation."* They had spent their honeymoon in autumn 1942 in Derbyshire. That would fit in with the departure of Arnhem Tommy's battalion to North Africa in May 1943, I noticed. Then the marriage certificate of his uncle 'Tommy' and Katherine appeared from the box. On it was mentioned his Army number and I knew the Army number of Arnhem Tommy McDonald. They matched!

This linked Thomas's uncle Tommy from Leadgate conclusively to Arnhem Tommy. They were the same person. The family memories could now with certainty be connected to the story of Arnhem Tommy as a member of 13 Platoon and passenger of Morley Williams's Horsa 166. This exciting treasure chest also yielded Tommy's death certificate with 21st September 1944 as the date of his death. This further strengthened the link with Arnhem Tommy. Surviving letters showed that the family, understandably, had not been very happy when he so soon after having been married, went "off to war".

The historical society also confirmed that it was Arnhem Tommy McDonald who was mentioned at the Leadgate memorial. The Museum of The Border Regiment in Carlisle added that Tommy's regimental number indicates that he had joined The Border Regiment probably in 1940. They think that he served with the First Battalion through its training as a gliderborne Battalion in 1942-1943 and went with it to North Africa in 1943. He will also have served in Sicily and Italy. His service will have entitled him to the 1939-45, Italy and France and Germany Stars, 1939-45 War Medal and possibly the Defence Medal.

Still, the most baffling proof surfaced when Thomas and Margaret found a photograph of Tommy and Katherine's wedding. There stood Tommy McDonald, proudly in his uniform with his bride at his side. I suddenly noticed how strikingly similar it was to the picture on page 96 of No Return Flight. We knew that the seated person was Ted Clague but the standing person had remained unidentified. Now the wedding picture revealed we were looking at Tommy McDonald! He had already been in the book since it was published, but needed his namesake to tell us that he was Tommy McDonald.

> Thomas's wife Margaret concluded: *"We found a lot of 'new' material on 'Arnhem' Tommy. For example, photos showing him with shot guns. So we assume he was into country style life with shooting, etc. Maybe there is a link to having become a marksman in the Army? The Manchester clue from his Corporal might be a mix-up with Lanchester, which is a village nearby Leadgate. It seems as though Tommy had been lost all of these years but there he was in your book all along. As the 21st September this year is on a Sunday, it is our intention to have a mass of remembrance for Tommy in the church where he was christened, Our Lady and Saint Joseph Catholic Church Brooms in Leadgate. Furthermore, the family remembered that Katherine remarried in 1951 with*

Johann Klenai, whom they think was from Poland. They remember him as a 'very nice chap'. Katherine and Johann moved to Perth, Australia, in the early 70's and are believed to have passed away in 1997 and 2003 respectively." I was struck by the warm feelings from the family for Katherine and her new husband.

Major Armstrong
Company commander Tom Armstrong had been taken PoW on that disastrous 21st September 1944. After the war he returned to the police force, attaining the rank of Inspector in Motherwell before retirement in 1962. Then he joined the British Steel Corporation as Chief Security Officer for all security matters of the Corporation throughout Scotland, until final retirement in 1979. As a boy, he had run away from home before he joined the Merchant Navy. Sadly, he never spoke about his war time experiences and family members regarded him as a somewhat difficult man with a soft spot, a typical Army man. He had no desire to attend reunions. Not even those of The Border Regiment in the Regimental museum in Carlisle, which was less than 20 miles from where he lived. The war seemed to be a part of his life that he wanted to forget about. Although he did keep in touch with Captain Pat Stott and Lieutenant Arthur Royall of B Company and is said to have visited the Arnhem area and Airborne War Cemetery in 1969, possibly on his own. The obituary published in The Border Regiment magazine stated that ..."the spirit and comradeship for those privileged to serve under him still exists for some of us today." Unfortunately, Major Armstrong himself apparently did not take much part in that spirit and comradeship after the war, a close relative wrote.

Wilfred 'Gibbo' Gibson
Now that some light had been shed on their life after the war, it dawned on me that my quest into the fate of Morley's passengers was coming to completion. I once again looked at the names of those men I had not found out anything about.

Wilfred Gibson had remained elusive. In Norman Savage's stories he was referred to as 'Gibbo'. Taking the commemorative tablet in Burford Chapel as evidence I originally believed that Gibbo's nephew Joe was with 13 Platoon but this is not correct. Joe Gibson was the batman of Major Montgomery from A Company and it turned out that Joe was killed at Arnhem. Norman Savage told me that 'Gibbo' had come back with him across the river, but after that had dropped out of Norman's sight. He may have been with Z Reserve until 1948, lived in Gateshead and passed away in 1974. The Class Z Reserve was a Reserve contingent of the British Army consisting of previously enlisted soldiers, that could be mobilised quickly should military problems arise in Germany after their surrender.

'Click' Fidler

'Click' Fidler was mentioned with respect and friendship in the stories of Cyril Crickett, Ted Clague, Norman Savage and Johnny Peters; however, I had not been able to trace his family. When internet developed Facebook I at last did collect some stories on him, which I put together in "Box in the Attic' chapter. Then I looked at the last name on my list, Eric Melling.

Eric Melling

I had a picture of him, some stories and some information about his wife Annie Winstanley. It turned out that she remarried. On 20 August 1948, about four years after Eric went missing in action, she married Thomas Brown, a butcher. The wedding took place in the same church as Annie's wedding to Eric Melling. Forty years later, Annie Brown died on 3 September 1986 in Billinge Hospital in Wigan.

Next, I studied the sketches made by David Patterson and Norman Savage of the situation at the time when Eric was killed. They, and other former comrades, were surprised to find out that Melling was still missing. Then slowly a thought started forming in my mind. Could it be that the sketches offered an indication for a possible location of Eric Melling's field grave? Would this research lead to finding a missing soldier? With some hesitation I got in touch with Geert Maassen from the Provincial archives of Gelderland and put my thoughts to him. He reacted with

Despite that the spot where he was killed is known fairly exact, Lance Corporal Eric Melling is still missing.

calm realism and asked me for the sketches. He wanted to compare them with information in the files where locations of field graves were marked. It did not take long before he contacted me again. Running the coordinates through the computer did not result in the location of a former field grave on the spot indicated in the sketches. He explained that there were now two possibilities.

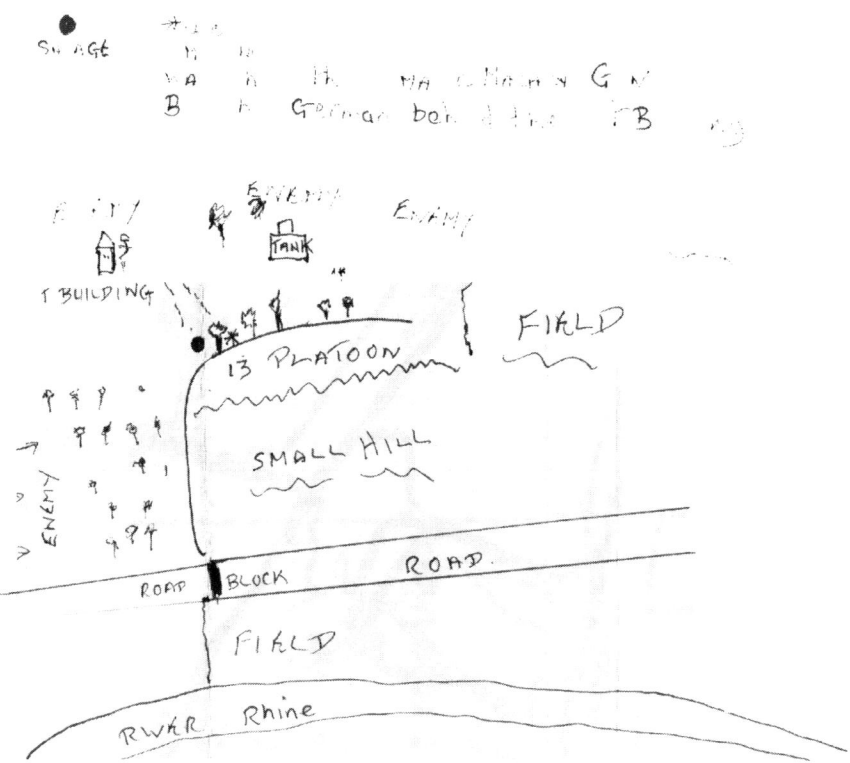

Sketch of the situation in which Eric Melling was killed, made by eye-witness Norman Savage.

The first was that Melling was buried immediately after the fight at another location nearby. Cyril Crickett suspected this could be in the grassland south of the Westerbouwing, because digging there was easier than on the Westerbouwing with all the tree roots. That could mean that he might have been found just after the war, without being identified. In that case he is buried at the Airborne Cemetery in Oosterbeek as an unknown soldier.

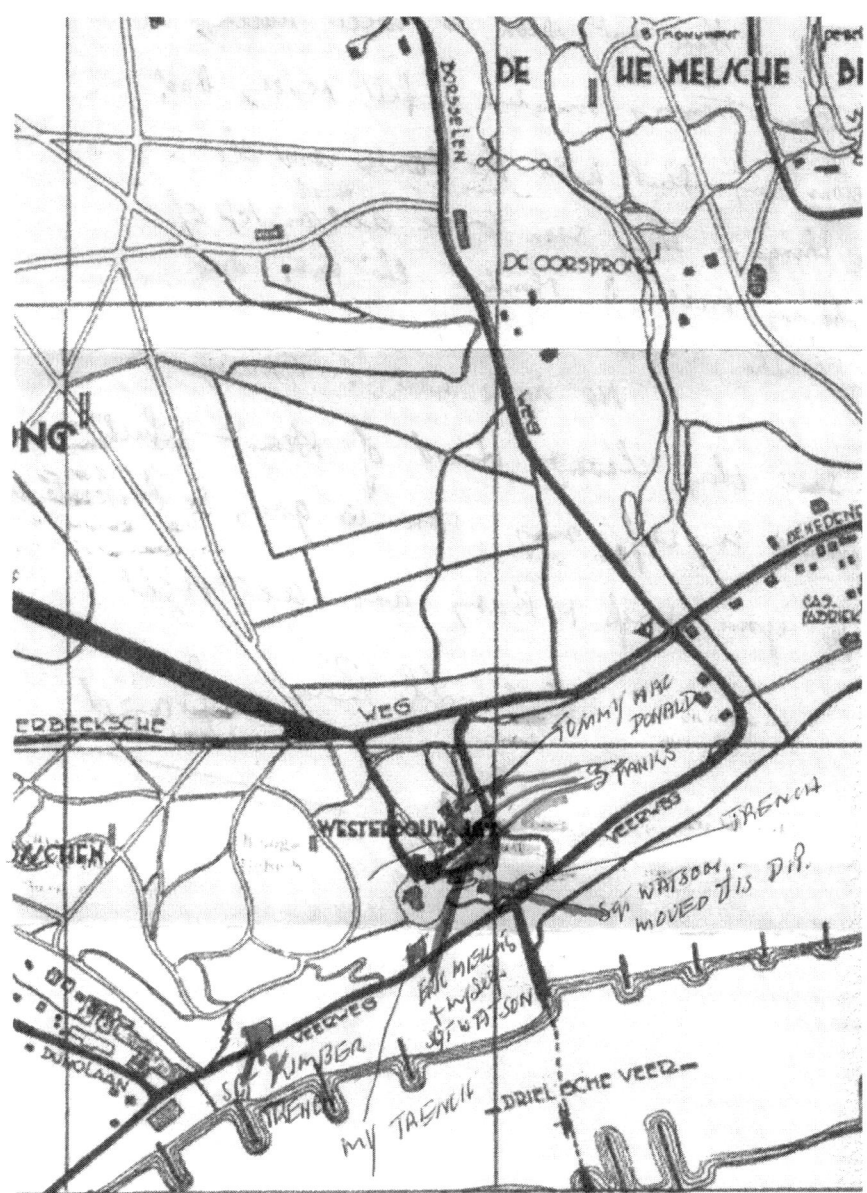

Memories from Corporal David Patterson of the spot where Eric Melling was hit.

The second possibility was that the Germans put Melling in a trench near the place where he was killed and buried him immediately. If the spot had not been damaged during the British artillery barrages from the south in the months after the battle, the field grave could still be intact. It was Maassen's suggestion to ask one of the 'friends of the Airborne Museum' to help conduct a search with a metal detector. It was March 2003 when I met Philip Reinders who had an official council permit for searching with a metal detector.

The fallen leaves of the past autumn were still on the woodland soil of the Westerbouwing when we started looking for the place where Eric Melling might have been buried. Reinders was wearing army clothing and turned out to be a security man for the Dutch Army. We crossed the car park under the bleak March sunlight and walked to the edge of the forest on the northern side of the Westerbouwing. Reinders moved the metal detector with swaying motions over the ground. Even before I had the opportunity to ask him how this search method actually works I heard a beep. Reinders moved some leaves and branches with his foot and uncovered a rusty beer can. False alarm. "Hmm yeah, I suppose there will be lots of those here with the restaurant within walking distance", he said half aloud. Half an hour later we had searched an area about the size of a tennis court. The yield was an iron pipe, several beer cans, sometimes from brands long out of production and a pigeon-ring. "What are the chances of actually finding something here?" I asked him. He told me that this place had already been officially searched in the past and probably illegally as well. The soil also contained a lot of rubbish and dirt that could interfere with the signal. It seemed that shell-splinters and cartridges were easier to find. However, there was still a chance that the field grave had not been found or damaged yet. It could be deeper if it was situated in a former trench. There were many of these, because the Germans had entrenched themselves here, after dislodging the British, until spring 1945. They did recover their own fallen, but had British PoW's bury the British casualties on the spot. The search at the southern edge of the Westerbouwing also remained without any result, apart from some shell splinters and the cast iron cover of a drain. The only possible place left would be underneath the parking place, but the signal of the metal detector did not reach under the tarmac pavement. Nothing had been found.

However, before I got the chance to abandon the idea, I came across a newspaper article on ground radar. This technique registers disturbances underneath asphalt or brick-paving. I started surfing the Internet and found the site of a Dutch company called T&A Survey, specialists in this field. I explained what I was doing and expressed my hope that maybe one day they could have a look at the car park. To my surprise the manager, Michiel van Oers, said that he was willing to do that and on 26 March 2004 that opportunity occurred.

For about two hours we walked up and down the parking place and its surroundings with some sort of measuring cart. Of course, we were armed with the necessary council permission. Michiel van Oers explained that the measurements did not yield direct conclusions but they would have to be analyzed at the office first.

Several weeks later I receive the following letter:

"Dear Haks,

I will start with the final conclusion. The measuring data did not show any specific location of a possible field grave. However, the underground underneath the centre of the parking place looks rather complicated. Particularly, measurements at the un-tarmacked centre part indicate digging and/or structures underneath. However, I lack information that would clearly explain the meaning of these structures. The possibility that these were caused by slit trenches can't be ruled out. It also has to be mentioned that these diggings/structures could mask smaller objects/field graves. In case you ever come into possession of information on the exact location of trenches I am always willing to have another look at the measuring information to see if I could match this with the sketches. If, at any time you have information on measurements with a metal detector that could detect metal objects at a depth of 1 to 2 meters you are more then welcome to send it to me again. I do feel instinctively that there is a distinct possibility that there are still traces from the Second World War underneath the tarmac. However the image is complicated to such a degree that no sound opinion can be offered based on the measuring information, without any type of indication about what is expected to be found there. In summary, although my conclusion is that there are no indications found for a field grave, this does not mean there is no such grave.

With kind regards,

Michiel van Oers"

This professional report marked the end of a remarkable search. It had brought no definite answer to the question where Eric Melling's field grave was situated, provided that it had ever existed. I knew already that this question would keep coming back every time I visited the Westerbouwing. Had this place been keeping a secret for 60 years or more?

Part 5

Epilogue

The Dutch version of the book hit the bookshops in late August 2004 and that was when I pushed back my chair and felt I had finished the book. However, I quickly found out that the book was far from finished with me. As proves this second English edition fifteen years later.

First came encouraging reviews, a radio-interview and the news that one hundred libraries in the Netherlands bought the book for their collection. Later in September, at the 60th Commemorations, came what felt like Morley's and my reward. He would meet some of his passengers again after 60 years and could finally put his anxiety to rest.

On the morning of Friday 17 September 2004, I stood outside the Airborne Museum amongst many hundreds of people visiting the commemorations and I waited for 13 Platoon member Norman Savage to appear. When he materialised from the crowd, I immediately recognised him, although I had never seen him before. We cheerfully shook hands, talked about the book and whether any other members of 13 Platoon would be there. I told him that Tim Rogers, TV journalist and Morley's godson, wanted to interview them for British Television on the Westerbouwing hill. I suggested that we should go there to see if the camera team and the others were already setting up. As we were walking towards my car, we learned that veterans of The Border Regiment had that same morning unveiled a memorial at Westerbouwing commemorating their battle. "Wait a sec", said Norman, "There's a Border man. I can tell by his cap badge, he might know more." Norman looked at a tall, grey haired, strongly built man with a maroon beret and many medals on his chest who was passing us by in the milling crowd. Norman looked again and the man looked back at him. A sparkle of recognition turned into a broad smile and much shoulder slapping. "Ted!! It is you!! Ted Clague! I can't believe my eyes!" exclaimed Norman baffled. Ted Clague, being somewhat less demonstrative, though equally surprised and glad to see his old 13 Platoon comrade, replied: "Well, imagine that! It is Savage, himself. How great to see you again!" He had overcome his doubts and had come to Oosterbeek with his son Doug. On the ferry they had met some present day British paratroopers. This had resulted in a very pleasant and rather late night.

Ted agreed to come to the Westerbouwing as well. Morley, Cyril Crickett, Tim Rogers and a camera team were all waiting there. Lots of handshakes and smiles ensued and after a while the fine gentlemen were ready for their interview which aired on British television that very same night. In the appendix of this book on page **303** a QR code and a link are printed that will guide you to the video clips on youtube showing the interview and the historic reunion of Morley and three of his passengers.

From left to right: Ted Clague, Morley Williams, Haks Walburgh Schmidt (author), Cyril Crickett and Norman Savage, at the reunion on 17 September 2004

The formal commemorations at the Airborne War Cemetery in Oosterbeek took place on Sunday 19 September 2004. It was a beautiful, sunny and peaceful autumn day fitting for such a moving ceremony. On the perfectly mown grass, between the gravestones of so many of their comrades in arms, stood these four elderly gentlemen. Silently they paid their respect to the men that had been with them in their glider to Arnhem, but who never had come back. Together they visited the graves of Lieutenant John Wellbelove, Private Tommy McDonald and Private Bob Barnes. They remembered Privates Pip Hulse buried in Utrecht and John Glenn buried in Manchester and thought of Lance Corporal Eric Melling and Privates Frank Jarvis and Telford Fiddler who are to this day still listed as missing in action. As the schoolchildren of Renkum laid their flowers on each individual grave, I watched the four veterans. It seemed they appreciated the chance to pass on their experiences, be together again after 60 years and see that still so many people cared. Cyril even shook hands with Prince Charles who attended the ceremony alongside the Dutch Queen Beatrix. He was almost boyishly proud of it.

After the commemorations we all went to Doedie Minderman's house where Morley was staying as usual. She had made sandwiches, and welcomed the small crowd into her home with great hospitality.

When all were seated I gave every one a copy of the book. All of them signed mine. They thoroughly enjoyed seeing the book and leafed through it eagerly. Their only regret was that it was all in Dutch. A lively conversation began and I explained as much about the book's content as I could and why it was in Dutch. I also promised to start the translation as soon as I could. In the following months I started to think about a plan to produce that translation.

Early 2005 there were worrying signs in Morley's health. I talked to him on the phone and he sounded tired but cheerful, still happy with the reunion and the book. I again promised him that I would start translating as quickly as possible.

The Long Wait
Back in England again, Cyril contacted me about Pte Frank Jarvis who was killed on the Westerbouwing and is still recorded as missing in action. While studying the book, Cyril suddenly remembered something that just might be a clue to finding Jarvis' field grave.

When Cyril had been taken prisoner, he was taken to a small wooden building that seemed like a small first aid station where he and Vinnie Swarbrick were given a drink of water. Could it be that the Germans had carried Jarvis to this make shift dressing station and buried him near that spot when he succumbed to his wounds? Cyril asked me if I could follow this possibility up, because no opportunity to retrace his comrade should be left unchecked. I agreed and asked him to describe the building.

He felt it looked like a sort of small sports pavilion for a large mansion or possibly a small sports club: "The hut itself was not in the woods. We did not go inside or see any German casualties there. Neither were there any ambulances or other vehicles nearby. There were two or three steps in the centre going on to the veranda. The steps were about two metres wide and the whole was about six metres wide. I didn't notice the length of the hut or pavilion. When we left it, we continued in the same general direction-westerly- along a narrow asphalt road for about 200 or 300 metres. There were lots of German soldiers in concealed positions alongside the road. Then we came upon a number of trucks. We got onto them, together with German wounded and waited until dark before we set off for Apeldoorn."

I wondered how to use this information. The best thing would be to try and get in touch with any of Frank Jarvis´ relatives again, even though earlier attempts had yielded no results. As he was from Sunderland I contacted the daily newspaper, the Sunderland Echo. They were very interested and ran a front page story early October 2004. Remarkably enough, this established contact with several relatives. The story ordered me back to my desk.

It was Colonel Arthur Charlton who started corresponding. He was married to a niece of Frank Jarvis. He happened to be the director of the Support British Reservists and Employers (SaBRE) campaign and was keen on military history. I explained my interest and told him what I knew so far. He in turn told me what his family knew about Frank Jarvis.

3 October 2004

Hello Haks,

Very many thanks for your very interesting e-mail regarding Frank Jarvis. Frank was one of five children born to Henry Charles Jarvis and Sarah Jane Jarvis. Henry Charles Jarvis was a Railway worker. The five children were Harold, Francis Edward, Florence Jane, Christine and Winifred. My wife's mother (Florence Jane Jarvis) went to Arnhem several times in the sixties and had a good friendship with an Arnhem resident, Mrs Behr.

She heard a story that he was hit by machine gun fire and possibly tried to crawl to safety in a nearby ditch in the Westerbouwing area. If that trench was subsequently run over and filled up by a tracked armoured vehicle as the family believes, that would account for him being killed, not being found and not receiving a proper burial.

I was intrigued by your mentioning that in 1995 the body of a British airborne soldier was found alongside the Benedendorpsweg-road that still hasn't been identified. You said there was no weapon found in this field grave, only personal kit and items carried on the person.

I imagine that might be in line with a badly wounded individual crawling away to find safe cover, leaving his rifle behind. Could it be that these remains and observations match with my uncle Frank Jarvis? Here are some photographs of Frank. One still as a young boy and the other in his The Border Regiment uniform and with his airborne badge on his arm.

I will be in touch again soon.
Best regards

Arthur Charlton

Frank Jarvis as a boy, with his sisters

In the family's story I recognised the presence of the Char B tanks but the rest of the story seemed to differ from my sources. With this in mind I advised Colonel Charlton to phone Cyril Crickett and hear his story. This he did and they had a very valuable talk on the matter.

The main question seemed to be why Frank Jarvis wasn't found and buried immediately after the battle, as were most other victims. All in all there seemed to be some circumstantial indications that the remains found in 1995, were those of Frank Jarvis. I felt that it would be best to contact the Recovery and Identification Unit of the Dutch

Army (BIDKL), tell them about our ideas and ask their professional opinion.

Keeping an open mind
Their reaction was swift and interested. They offered their services to further research the case. Early 2005 I met Sergeant-Major Instructor (WO2) Jonker and I shared my information and we discussed our ideas. They were delighted with the photographs of Frank Jarvis and also those of Lance Corporal Eric Melling who was also still missing in action. They welcomed my study into the fate of 13 Platoon as it brought them new information on the fate of these missing men.

I asked them if an identification of the 1995- discovery would be more likely now that relatives of Frank Jarvis had been contacted. They agreed that there were now two DNA-sources that could possibly be compared. But he warned me not to jump to any conclusions. He wanted to study the matter closely and would inform Colonel Charlton and me as soon as possible. In February 2005 Jonker reported that after having studied the data there was no match between the data of the Frank Jarvis case and that of the unknown British soldier found in 1995. Specialist research showed that this soldier must have been 35 years or older. And as Jarvis was 23 a match was not possible. He added that the pavilion Cyril Crickett mentioned might be a possibility, but that they had not been able to pinpoint that small wooden building on contemporary aerial photographs.

Some time later, the R&I Unit, asked our cooperation to evaluate a third indication. For this they needed information from the family on Frank Jarvis´ length, hair colour, hair style and length and any other physical features that they could remember. They asked me if I could additionally check with the veterans that I was in contact with what they remembered about Frank Jarvis. The R&I staff said they couldn't go into detail for privacy reasons, but that in their files they had a case that just might fit the description of Frank Jarvis. After the war in 1945, the field graves in the battle area were transferred to the Airborne War Cemetery in Oosterbeek. In one particular field grave a Private from The Border Regiment was found who couldn't be identified positively. Judging by the description it could have been Frank Jarvis. The hair colour auburn was mentioned. This man now only has a head stone that reads "A Soldier of the 1939-1945 War, The Border Regiment, known to God".

With the extra information that Arthur Charlton and I supplied a new attempt might be made to identify this unknown soldier. Should this be accomplished, a rededication of a specific grave on the Airborne War Cemetery to Frank Jarvis might become possible.

Wavy, not curly
Colonel Charlton agreed to ask in the family for more details about Frank Jarvis, but to avoid any mention of a possible match. Because for all we knew, these characteristics might apply to another unidentified individual. Keep an open mind was the message here. After some time in March 2005, Colonel Charlton came up with the following information:

Hello Haks,

It seems that Frank Jarvis's hair was best described as dark brown and wavy, not curly. His height can only be guessed at as between 5' 6" to 5' 8".

Best regards
Arthur

Private Frank 'Maggie' Jarvis, still missing after the battle at the Westerbouwing

Cyril and 14 Platoon member Johnny Peters came up with some other memories of their comrade Frank. The picture that Arthur Charlton had sent me was a great help in triggering their memories. Johnny Peters still had a vague recollection as they soldiered together in B Company on parades and manoeuvres. But as they were almost always wearing either berets or steel helmets, Johnny did not remember much about Frank's hair. Wilf Oldham, from 12 Platoon, remembered Frank more clearly and believed that he was about the same height as him, imperial height 5ft.7/8inches and slightly broader than he is. This would make him of average build. Wilf also came up with Frank's nickname "Maggie" which seemed to indicate that Frank was a fan of soccer team Newcastle United.

All the details that had come up seemed to be consistent with the information of the R&I Unit we learned. Or, at least none seemed to contradict the known facts. Still, there was one characteristic detail that needed to be cleared. That was the reason why in May 2005 I identified myself as journalist to an unsuspecting hair dresser's apprentice of not yet 18 years in a nearby shopping centre in my Dutch home town.

I asked her if the hair colour dark brown was close to the colour auburn. She took out a sort of display card with on it many small tufts of hair, used for hair colouring purposes. There, right next to each other and almost indistinguishable to the untrained eye, were displayed a tuft of dark brown and a tuft of auburn. "Almost identical", she said." But why do you want to know?" For a second I thought of explaining the reasons for my question, but when I looked for a good point to start my explanation, I abandoned the idea. "For a historical investigation "I replied cheerfully. She nodded slowly and stepped back a little.

I passed on my information to the R&I Unit and they looked into it. They concluded that it was useful. Their 'gut-feeling' was that the unidentified Border man could match the description of Frank Jarvis as there were no other candidates that fitted the description. On the other hand, all the evidence was indirect. The R&I Unit would send in the report on the case of Frank Jarvis to the Joint Casualty and Compassionate Centre (JCCC) in England to ask their opinion. This institute decides over matters like this. Hopes were that JCCC would also reach the conclusion that a rededication of this specific grave at the Airborne War Cemetery was appropriate.

But the people from the Dutch R&I Unit warned that this process usually takes a very long time and added that I should also realise that the area had probably been searched with metal detectors over a period of more than thirty years. Some of that 'souvenir hunting' will have taken place illegally and at night and so could mean that decisive items for the identification of Frank Jarvis and possibly others had fallen prey to modern day grave robbers. I passed this on to Arthur Charlton who received it cautiously. The R&I Unit advised: "Let's just hope for a positive reply, it may take years to come. You and Arthur Charlton have done all that possibly could be done."

Farewell too soon
In the summer of 2005 news of Morley's health became worrisome. I spoke to him a few times on the telephone and he asked me to replace the name "Taffy" in the book to Morley. This I promised to do. He said that he was now living in a home and spent most of his time resting.

Shortly afterwards Morley Williams passed away. Very unexpectedly and only a few weeks later, Cyril Cricket passed away as well. For weeks this sad loss made me doubt if I should stop with the English translation. I felt I had failed them both and all the work done after the Dutch book was published appeared futile.

After a while I slowly began to realise that these men had not only given me their time and stories for their own or for my sake, but first and foremost for younger generations to learn from.

I knew then that I couldn't give up and should deliver the English translation no matter what. To speed up matters, I asked relatives and friends to help me do the bulk of the translation. I was impressed by the readily offered assistance. Slowly my conviction to press on grew stronger as I realised I was the only one able to pass on their stories.

While the translating team and I were doggedly plodding along, in early 2006 I came across a little note that Morley had written to me, just months before the Dutch version was published in 2004. Should I ever need advice on an English version, I might contact a Mr. John D. Potts, an old friend who was a lecturer. The codeword 'Stinker' would identify me as friend of his, Morley had hinted. John Potts had met Morley in the Glider Pilot Regiment, they had flown together, both in the Hotspur and in the Horsa gliders and both had been prisoners of war. Mr. Potts had been captured during the D-Day operation in June 1944.

His reply to my letter 'Code word Stinker' gave a fascinating contemporary impression of Morley as a Glider Pilot that added perspective to Morley's own story.

23 April, 2006

Dear Mr. Walburgh Schmidt

You are absolutely correct, the letter is most unusual. That is under normal conditions, but with S/Sgt A. M. Williams nothing may be classified as 'normal'. All this has to be his parting shot from beyond the grave.

My association with Morley, or 'Stinker', stretches from early 1942, when we arrived as volunteers for the newly formed Airborne Division, went through Pilot Training together and then were reunited after the war as 'journeymen'. These were Pilots on several military aerodromes used for al kind of flying tasks until we were returned to civilian life in 1946. From thence, until his demise in 2005 we met up several times every year and corresponded by telephone and letter on a regular basis. We knew each other very well indeed!

In the very early days of the Regiment we realised we were something very special so the first activity to engage our attention was to expand the motto into, "The difficult is done immediately, the impossible takes a little longer but for a miracle we require 48 hours notice." What we are doing here is to take our real military requirements very seriously but at the same time injected it with a very British trait, 'turn it into fun'. A full and complete account of our wartime efforts vindicates our total attitude. The battles, the campaigns, the casualties, the gravestones, the medals, the decorations and the heroic accounts but above all this, and difficult to understand, was the SPIRIT we created for ourselves and the manner to which we adapted it. No Glider Pilot was ever charged or punished for dereliction of duty or cowardice.

So now I can produce my first hypothesis and one that could prove difficult to digest. Following the reading of your composition I reached a simple interpretation, and this is the integral difficulty, it's precisely what I would expect from the 'curricula vita' of any combat GP. I'm not certain of the number of Pilots who were actually engaged in combat, most definitely below 2000 but each and everyone would be able to deliver a similar account of their war experience. There were many who could produce most excellent accounts of 'derring do's'. S/Sgt Galpin in Sicily saw the problem at a bridge and landed his glider on the bridge; S/Sgt 'Buck' Turnbull was officially recommended for the Victoria Cross in the morning and Court-martialled for striking an Officer in the afternoon; on D-Day S/Sgt Shannon landed his glider in a minefield, he couldn't get out, the Germans couldn't get in but when they eventually captured him he shot his way off the Paris-Frankfurt train with a guard's rifle and waited with the Resistance for the Liberation in a brothel; S/Sgt Bone seeing the Merville attack in difficulty landed his glider on the gun battery; I helped seal S/Sgt Clenahan in the wall of a deserted brick factory during a blizzard in Silesia, he was eventually released by the Russians but didn't get back to the UK until Christmas 1945. The list goes on and on. The real statement should read, 'The extraordinary was the ordinary to the Glider Pilots. 'Taffy' was a great Pilot, a tremendous comrade and a fine gentleman.

I presume you are not quite familiar with the 'code-word Stinker' so let me attempt an explanation. The word is used mostly in male dominated groups and possesses no connection, whatsoever, with aroma. The vernacular stinker (often pronounced 'Stinkah') is used to describe a person who is 'irritating'. Let me explain.

Morley

The Glider Pilots, generally described as 'total soldiers', were a unique 'Band of Brothers'. The like of which were never seen before or likely to be seen in the future. One of the features of our Regiment was our smartness of dress, comparable to, or even superior to HM Brigade of Guards who are considered to be the best in the world. Within the ranks of several hundred Pilots 'Taffy' must have been the most untidy individual that ever wore the King's uniform. Therefore, in comparison with everyone else he was a 'Stinkah', a genuine, full-time non-conformist. And what is more, he knew it, deliberately maintained it and didn't give a damn. Nothing could move 'Taffy', not fire, sword, enemy action or the attitude of the general public or his comrades. For better or worse he was his own man, to all and sundry 'A right 'Stinker''.

I have included copies of two photographs probably never seen before. The date is around spring of 1946 and we are a group of 'general purpose' pilots just flying at the command of our superiors; we were judged to be very competent and reliable. Examine the photograph carefully and you will become aware that all the Pilots, with one exception, are wearing their correct uniforms. The one moustached gentleman in civilian clothes is S/Sgt A. M. Williams. He has decided that the conflict is well and truly over, so he is now almost a private person again. The photograph was taken outside a country Public House in the County of Worcestershire one Sunday lunchtime. In the top picture the two characters in working clothes situated on the right are two farmers joining in in the drinking with these 'Lords of the Air'.

In the lower picture the bemedalled Army Pilot on the right is me, 62 years ago. I've changed, I confess.

When Taffy was discharged, he joined forces with the most heroic Pilot of World War Two, Group Captain Leonard Cheshire, VC, DSO & Bars, DFC & Bars and several other Medals for bravery. He was in the B-29 bomber that dropped the Atomic Bomb upon Nagasaki in August 1945. Taffy and Cheshire had this dream; they created a Collective, rather like a Jewish Kibbutz, and sought to build a haven of peaceful existence wherein the members extracted only what they required and produced, according to their natural skills, everything for the commune. Although it was a vision of Utopian living, it couldn't exist in the environment of England. It was born, flourished for a while and then died. Taffy stayed with the Group Captain to the very end then departed to become a Civil Servant in the Government Mapping Department. As a matter of interest, the dream that 'Taffy' and Cheshire had all those years ago did not completely die. Through a series of strange events these eventually expanded into 'Cheshire Homes' which still exist today as Hospices for the terminally ill.

'Stinker' proceeded through life in the same semi-detached manner and in old age became more and more eccentric developing a dress style that reflected his renowned untidiness and, I believe, his apartment resembled an artist's garret in Paris. He still couldn't care less. He lived, as he died, his own man. I heard that whilst he was in the POW Camp in Germany, he would only speak Welsh to the Germans and as this particular language is completely unintelligible to any civilised person, you can imagine the chaos it caused the enemy. This, I think, is the clue to 'Taffy'. His life was chaos to himself and anyone with whom he came into contact but, at the same time, he was completely oblivious to his own state and the effect upon others.

The reason why he and I should have such strong ties over the years was that we were exact opposites but we understood each other and so became firm and lasting friends in an otherwise unfriendly world.

I can readily affirm that Taffy's wartime career had no effect upon his character or personality. He was exactly the same in the years after the conflict as he was in uniform, when he wore it. Why wasn't he punished or dismissed? Because he was one of us and we looked after our own.

In this indirect manner he has spoken from the grave I shall reply, "Good on yer 'Stinker'. Never change, I couldn't stand it!"

I hope my reply is satisfactory but you can always come back for any further questions, this I owe to a very old and trusted comrade.

Johnny Potts
The Glider Pilot Regiment

I smiled and my confidence grew that I could finish the task. Only one last lead had to be followed. It had to do with the missing Lance Corporal Melling.

Closer

Sergeant-Major, now Captain, Geert Jonker regretted that his unit did not have the means to mount a large scale search for Melling themselves at the present time. Therefore he introduced me to two Dutch researchers from the Arnhem area. David van Buggenum and Hans Timmerman had an official permit and support from the Renkum Council and the Police to search for missing airbornes and historic military material. They were planning to search the Westerbouwing area in the next few months. Would it not be a good idea to share my knowledge with them, so that they could keep a lookout for any new clues in the search for Melling? I agreed to the idea and he would establish contact with them for me.

I also asked if Melling might be matched to an unidentified Border man found in 1945 at the foot of the steep southern slope of the Westerbouwing. Geert Jonker was very clear. "No, that is very unlikely. Melling would have had a Lance Corporal stripe on his sleeve. And the unidentified man clearly did not have such sign of rank." Nor did his description fit any other unidentified airborne soldier in the area.

In the next few months David and Hans searched the Westerbouwing area several times. They found many small items, some British, but mostly of German origin. Usually empty cartridges, buttons and once a British military water bottle. Then came 1 April 2007. Finally, I had the opportunity to join them. That day David was accompanied by Ruud de Bie, a friend who assisted them sometimes. Also present was a man from the municipality of Renkum whom we had contacted to discuss specific search locations. We met in the parking lot at the Westerbouwing. It was deserted that early in the morning, apart from our three cars. At the foot of the hill the Rhine as always streamed past, grey and monotonously. There was no rain, but it was chilly.

The four of us discussed where to start. I proposed a small patch halfway down the staircase to the Veerweg. It was as good a start as anywhere, so we picked up the metal detector and two spades and proceeded down the stairs. The man from the municipality wished us luck, got in his car and left. He didn't expect any spectacular results. David put on his headphones and started swaying the detector. Within a matter of minutes he found a rod-shaped and very rusty piece of iron. With his hands he removed leaves and sand. "This is exceptional", he said surprised. "Do you know what this is? This is a rifle, look here, that is the bolt and there is the bayonet, still attached to it." He continued to examine the rifle remains and then saw that it was a German rifle. "A find like this is very rare indeed!", he said. What struck him was that it wasn't buried deeply in the soil, but only a few centimetres under the surface. He would report this find to the local Police. I congratulated David with this rather special find, but imagined that the chances of finding anything else would now statistically be very slim. Indeed, for the next hour nothing happened. We only found building debris. David got a reading from what turned out to be a slab of concrete covered with leaves and roots. It was about half the size of a table tennis table, but clearly a piece of a wall of sorts. Ruud and I worked hard to lift it with our spades. Then it gave way to more roots and leaves and soil. The detector reading continued and we wanted to know what caused it. After some digging a curved piece of metal came to light. We cleaned it and saw that it was a magazine for a Bren gun. In a flash I remembered the story of Norman Savage and John Glenn manning a Bren gun near the road block. This spot could have been their trench. This very magazine could very well have been used by them, I realised. At least it was fairly certain that it had belonged to 13 Platoon. I felt a circle being closed. Not only had I found stories of 13 Platoon, now I had also found physical evidence of their presence here. More than sixty years later.

David and I decided that after such a rich crop it was time to have a break. He had brought coffee in a thermos flask with him and I had brought along some snacks. These were still in the car. Ruud said that he still wanted to push the slab a little more to the side as the detector still gave a reading near the hole we had dug. David assumed that it would most likely be some more spent cartridges from the Bren gun and I joined him in preferring the coffee. We walked up the stairs. Five minutes later we sauntered down the steps again.

Ruud was holding something in his hands and called out to us. "I moved some roots aside and saw this. What do you think this is?" We joined him and saw a sandy brown coloured, more or less half round object. Ruud said: "It appears to be bark or a piece of coconut." I looked closer and said in shock: "That is a fragment of a human skull! Look on the inside. You can see thin lines that look like fontanels." We fell silent and my blood froze. What could this mean? In the back of my mind a thought started forming. The spot fitted the drawings from Norman Savage and David Patterson and the location of a field grave in a former trench matched the theory. I said to David and Ruud that we just might have found Lance Corporal Melling!

We looked again at the hole that Ruud had dug. It seemed there were more remains at the bottom. David used his metal detector and found a clip with British .303 cartridges for a Lee Enfield rifle in it. "This indicates that the person possibly was a British soldier," he theorised.

We decided that we should inform the Police and the Recovery & Identification Unit of the Royal Dutch Army. Sergeant Patric van Aalderen (R&IS) asked us to refrain from further digging and said that they would arrive within the hour, as did the Police. During that eerie hour we just sat and waited. It began to drizzle and sitting still, I felt the cold creeping up. It felt as if we time travelled back to the battle and that at any moment, someone from 13 Platoon would come to the stair case and yell down what the hell was keeping us there while the Germans were attacking.

Usually when remains were found, it happens by accident. Somebody starts digging in his garden or a new telephone cable was laid. This time it was a targeted search that had started at my desk which had led to this find. Bewildering, I felt.

Then at last, a small white van pulled up at the Veerweg. Sergeant Van Aalderen got out and I walked towards him to meet him. "What an excellent way of messing up our agenda's" he said cheerfully. "Now tell me, what have you got?"

We showed him the object and he confirmed our impression that it was the top of human skull. He got his gear ready and continued the dig. Although he was big man and he was digging at an amazing speed, it took him some time to find more artefacts. But then more and more elements of a skeleton emerged until it was practically complete. Other people started to arrive and it was clear that a buzz was developing. Later that afternoon the news would hit the national ANP-newswire.

"Wait, what is this?" he said suddenly, half way down the hole. He got up, removed the sand with a brush and identified the object as a button. To my utter disappointment he added: "It's a German Navy (Kriegsmarine) button." This was not very strange as the Germans had taken over this position from 13 Platoon.

Then other German objects appeared, more buttons, part of a wallet and a golden ring. It was a German identification disk that made it final. This was a German soldier that had been found. Not Lance Corporal Melling. Still remarkable, but not the news I was looking for. Sergeant Van Aalderen would inform Geert Jonker immediately and take the

German remains to their base for identification. A task not too difficult with the identification disk at hand.

I didn't know at the time but this search would for the time being, be the last one. A few weeks later Renkum Council forbade all searches until further notice. The possibility of finding still dangerous explosives was too great, they said. Renkum would study the matter to find a safe and sound approach to searching for missing British airbornes. They would consult the Dutch Army and Police on the matter. This meant that I wouldn't be able to get new information in the Melling case in time for the planned publication at the 65 year Commemoration. Why now? I thought to myself. Just as we are starting to get some results in the Melling case. After having been so close, I felt, this was difficult to accept. Only when I realised that the official way was the only way this search could be handled, and that my own book deadline was not very relevant, did I come to terms with the ban.

To symbolically conclude Morley's quest I donated 166 euro from the revenues of the book to the War Child organisation in 2009. I made the donation in the name of and in memory of all the occupants of Horsa 166. Somewhere in the world a war stricken child has benefited from the writing down and passing on of the Morley's memories, those of the men from 13 Platoon and of first pilot Ian Blackwood.

Spring 2015 brought an unexpected, but short-lived new search when the Gelderlander regional newspaper mentioned specially trained search dogs had found a car on the bottom of the Rhine near Arnhem with people in it that had been missing for 16 years. These remarkable dogs are trained to find human remains in war or disaster areas on land or even in the water. I asked the trainers from SIGNI if the dogs could help us find Melling on the Westerbouwing. They liked the idea and on 18 April 2015 two dogs did a search there. Remarkably they independently pointed to the same two locations, but further research with metal detectors sadly didn't confirm the lead. We did find an intact PIAT anti-tank grenade from the Westerbouwing battle in a spot that fitted exactly the sketches from Savage and Patterson. This was safely taken care of by the Dutch Army.

In the ten years between 2009 and 2019 new details and pictures on Tommy McDonald and Frank Evans were found. Even Telford 'Click' Fidler life's story was traced. These new initiatives were prompted by the news that the publisher asked for a second edition. Now all three men of 13 Platoon who are missing in action have a picture and their story in the book. Only of Wilfred 'Gibbo' Gibson's story little was not found.

Now, as it seems all trails have been followed it is time to put the search to rest. There was nothing more to add or to follow up on. Apart from Telford Fidler's account, Morley's quest has been fulfilled and the story has been told.

Box in the attic
There is an attic somewhere in the UK and I believe it is in or not far from Workington in Cumbria. The attic holds a box that contains letters and pictures of a life long forgotten. For more than ten years I have tried to reach that box so I can give Telford 'Click' Fidler back his life's story. He is the third man of 13 Platoon who went missing in the Battle of Arnhem. And to give his relatives an impression of what happened in those brutal September days in 1944.

Telford was described by Cyril Crickett as having black curly hair and a very good sense of humour. With 28 years 'Click' was older than most airbornes. His favourite saying was: *"My name is Fidler by name, but not by nature."* His army comrades used to call him 'Click' because of his full denture that made a clicking sound when he talked. They also recall that when he was in a pub with them, he would put his false teeth in the breast pocket of his army uniform jacket. Just to make sure he wouldn't lose them if more than two pints came his way. By September 1944 he was a seasoned soldier. He had been to North Africa with the First Airborne Battalion, The Border Regiment and landed in the Mediterranean with a glider during the invasion of Sicily in 1943. Here is what Cyril Crickett, who was in the same glider remembered: "After several hours in the water and clinging to the floating wooden glider wreck three lads decided to swim to shore, despite the risk of exhaustion. I recall that 'Click' was amongst them. We agreed that the ones who stayed behind at the plane would regularly shout and whistle, so they would be able to come back to the wreck if they wanted to. One of them actually returned. The other two, as we found out later, were picked up after a while by a Greek destroyer. The lad who was with Fidler was admitted into sickbay as he showed signs of exhaustion. We were shocked to learn that he was later killed on that ship, when it took a direct hit in the sickbay."

Cyril Crickett also recalled that Telford was the 2inch mortar man of their platoon. During the Arnhem operation, on the Westerbouwing, he fired a parachute flare from behind the roadblock on the Veerweg to illuminate an enemy patrol that they felt was approaching. He fired it in a westerly direction as ordered. However, the wind got hold of the flare and it drifted to the east, illuminating the British positions most unwelcome, as if in daylight. After the battle at the Westerbouwing on the 21st September, Fidler managed to get off unharmed and reunited with the main group survivors at the Hemelsche Berg estate. Johnny Peters and Ted Clague, army friends of Telford, saw him on 23 September in a trench in an open field with two other soldiers near the Border Battalion Headquarters on the Van Lennep Lane in Oosterbeek.

That was the last anyone would ever see of Telford, because after that he went missing. Johnny Peters recalled: "*When I passed by their slit trench I saw Telford and two other men. They had not been visibly wounded, but their airborne Dennison smocks had been blown up from their waists to partially cover their heads. This suggested to me that their lungs had collapsed due to the blast of a nearby shell explosion.*" Norman Savage and Gibson were nearby in a trench close to `Click` Fidler's. When the heavy shelling was over, they too saw that Fidler and the other two had died. All three are still listed as missing in action to this very day and are commemorated on the Groesbeek Memorial for those with no known grave.

Who was this airborne soldier who nowadays is mainly remembered because he was lost and forgotten? Would we ever find get an impression of him from that imaginary box in the attic?

Numerous attempts in previous years had remained fruitless, but it would take Facebook to contact a distant cousin and a young mother who would have been his granddaughter if he had survived Arnhem.

Both of them are from the area of Workington. This happened in 2018. They confirmed Telford was borne as the only son of Telford and Diane Fidler on 28 June 1916. Among his family and friends, he was called 'Telf'. They lived in a house in the Extensive View part of Broughton Moor, near Workington. It seems his father was killed in a mining accident in the thirties. The residents of these modest houses in this so-called pit village were miners and their family. They had to get their water from a well as they had no piped water. They had two bedrooms upstairs and two downstairs living rooms. These houses are gone now, demolished many years ago, leaving only open countryside. Like the man, his childhood home is no longer there.

Telford enlisted into The Border Regiment on 15 March 1940, for the "Duration of War" and volunteered for the 1 Airborne Battalion. In 1943, Telford was 27 then, he married Edith Roach from 46 Bolton Street, Workington. It seems they lived at 31 Cliff Road in Whitehaven. He was baptised at Christ Church on 22nd October 1924 and educated at Holy Trinity School. They didn't have any children together. In May 1943, Telford and 1 Battalion were engaged in North Africa and in the airborne landings at Sicily. When the Battalion returned from the Mediterranean in December 1943, Edith and Telford will have spent Christmas together. Before the Arnhem landings in September that year, they will have been together several times, when Telford was on leave. But then their future together was brutally cut short when Telford perished, without anyone knowing where his grave is.

After the war, it appears the sole survivor of the Fidler family, Telford's mother Dianne left Broughton Moor. I would imagine to the village or town where she was borne. Telford's wife Edith waited two long years for him until after the war. Then she must have accepted that there was no reasonable chance any more that Telford would miraculously return from the war torn Continent. In 1946, she became Edith Blacklock when she married James Blacklock in 1946.

Years passed by and it would take the computer technology of the 21st century to establish contact with Edith's granddaughter. Sadly, Edith had passed away in 1999, but granddaughter Lyndsey was interested in the Telford story herself: *My nana always told us he got shot down.* She is fascinated to learn that the actual story is a little different and his life a few days longer.

Then Facebook helped me to contact Dave, a member of the Fidler family. Telford was the uncle of his grandfather. A strange thought hit me. If Telford would have survived, then Lyndsey and Dave would have been relatives. Now they are total strangers to each other. I gave them both Telford's story at Arnhem and they agreed to search for old letters, photographs or stories on Telford.

Then a third contact was established when Trevor Cummings mailed that Telford was mentioned in a World War Two memorial in St James Church in Whitehaven. He also was a member of the Workington Past and Present group on Facebook. It said that there should be a newspaper item from the Whitehaven News of 9 November 1944 which reports his death in the Arnhem operation. The article was found at the Cumbria Archive and Local Studies Centre in Whitehaven and is printed in this book.

Killed at Arnhem

Pte. Telford Fidler, a native of Whitehaven and a former pupil of Trinity School, was reported killed during the fighting at Arnhem. Aged 27 years, he had been in the Army 4½ years and served with The Border Regiment (Airborne Division). His widowed mother lives at Broughton and he was well known in the Frizington and Cleator Moor district.

So now the story of his Army life and that of his personal life have been retrieved. No longer is he just a name of an airborne missing in action. The wait is on for him to be found on the Oosterbeek battle field. Perhaps even the box in the attic will one day open up his life's history.

Appendix

Individual overview

Name	Rank	Battle of Arnhem 17-26 September 1944	Profession after 1945
John Wellbelove	Lieutenant	21-9 killed in action, 25 years	-
Fred Terry	Platoon Sergeant	21-9 wounded and prisoner of war	Newspaper Agency/Mayor of Middleham. Passed away at 81 years (1996)
John Kimber	Lance Sergeant	21-9 wounded and prisoner of war	Head of Transport Dept of brewery. Passed away at 79 years (1992)
Cyril Crickett	Corporal	21-9 wounded and prisoner of war	Ministry of War Pensions, Head of WWI- dept. Passed away 2005, 84 years
David Patterson	Corporal	21-9 prisoner of war	Joiner. Passed away at 83 years (2002)
Ted Clague	Lance Corporal	26-9 Returned across Rhine	Contractor in the building trade, Passed away 2014. 90 years
Eric Melling	Lance Corporal	21-9 Killed in action and missing, 21 years	-
Eddie Flinn	Private	21-9 wounded and prisoner of war	Joiner. Passed away at 82 years (2007)
'Pip' Hulse	Private	21-9 wounded, prisoner of war. 3-10-1944 died of wounds in Utrecht hospital, 21 years	-
Tommy McDonald	Private	21-9 killed in action, 28 years	-
Jim Isles	Private	21-9 wounded and prisoner of war	Operator ICI Chemicals Passed away at 63 years (1987)

Name	Rank	Fate	Post-war
Bob Barnes	Private	21-9 killed in action, 20 years	-
'Gerry' Greasley	Private	21-9 wounded and prisoner of war	Building trade Passed away at 70 years(1983)
Wilf Gibson	Private	26-9 Returned across Rhine	?
'Click' Fidler	Private	23-9 killed in action and missing, 28 years	-
Joe Winstanley	Private	21-9 wounded and prisoner of war	Train driver. Passed away at 52 years (1972)
Edwin Ainsworth	Private	23-9 prisoner of war	Regular army/ garage owner Passed away at 55 years(1978)
John Glenn	Private	21-9 wounded and prisoner of war	Died of Arnhem wounds, 24 October 1945 in Manchester, 23 years
Vinnie Swarbrick	Private	21-9 wounded and prisoner of war	Shop owner, bin lorry driver, passed away at 71 years, April 1995.
William 'Johnnie' Walker	Private	26-9 Returned across Rhine	Bus conductor, Technical salesman, passed away, 12 May 1982, 59 years
Norman Savage	Private	26-9 Returned across Rhine	Assembling microchips for NASA, Bus driver, passed away 2011, 86 years
Frank Evans	Private	Prisoner of war	Silver Service Waiter, passed away 1964, at 51 years
Frank Jarvis	Private	21-9 killed in action and missing, 23 years	-

	Pilots Horsa 166		
Ian 'Blackie' Blackwood	Squadron Sergeant-Major	24-9 wounded and prisoner of war	Bank employee, Passed away at 79 years(1996)
Morley 'Taffy' Williams	Sergeant	20-9 prisoner of war	Map Maker, Ordnance Survey, Tax Officer. Passed away at 88 years (2005)

Early 1945 many PoW Camps in the East were evacuated for the advancing Soviet Russian Red Army. As there was no transport available the POWs simply had to walk vast distances to the west without protection from the weather and without sufficient supplies. Below is one march. It is assumed that several men of 13 Platoon were on this march.

Evacuation march from Stalag VIIC Sagan in Silesia.

Date	Distance in km	Accommodation	Destination	Weather
8 February	22 km	Glass Factory	Mariadorf	Fair
9 February	23 km	Wood	Friebau	Rain
10 February	15 km	Stalag	Muskau	Rain
11 February	24 km	Football Ground	Spremberg	Snow
12 February	24 km	Football Ground	Bedlitz	Snow
13 February	22 km	Football Ground	Ruhland	Snow
14 February	21 km	Stalag	Weizig	Sleet
15 February	20 km	Barn	Weifz	Sleet
16 February	25 km	Barrack Riding School	Oschatz	Mild
17 February	18 km	Barn	Gotwitz	Mild
18 February	18 km	Barrack Riding School	Gumma	Cold
19 February	16 km	Barn	Colpecker	Fair
20 February	20 km	Brickyard	Cudigiest	Fair
21 February	22 km	Barn	Runthal	Fair
22 February	26 km	Barn	Grossjena	Fair
23 February	21 km	Barn	Bad Saltz	Fair
24 February	21 km	Old Castle Barn	Kapellendorf	Mild
25 February	34 km	Barn	Feudenbach	Rain
26 February	25 km	Barn (Air Raid)	Gotha	Wet
27 February	14 km	Barn	Mechlenstadt	Wet
28 February	25 km	Barn	Stedfelt	Wet
	======			
	459 km			

Date	Distance	Shelter	Location	Weather
1 March	25 km	Barn	Ginverge	Cold
2 March		First Rest Day	Ginverge	Very Cold
3 March	14 km	Barn	Nulbodtshausen	Very Cold
4 March	32 km	Barn	Crefenberg	Very Cold
5 March	7 km	Barn	Ruchers	Very Cold
6 March	Rest Day			Very Cold
7 March	Rest Day			Very Cold
8 March	25 km	Barn	Menef	Cold
9 March	23 km	Barn	Stainau	Mild
10 March	Rest Day			Mild
11 March	Rest Day			Mild
12 March	Rest Day			Mild
13 March	16 km	Barn	Bad Orb	Fair

14 March: The survivors are deloused and housed in the Stalag at Bad Orb after having walked 605 km in 31 days. The march started with approximately 2000 PoW's. 53 people didn't survive the ordeal, 173 men were hospitalised. The others were dazed and exhausted and covered in filth and lice Many of them don't have proper shoes anymore or lack sufficient clothing. There were many other marches away from the Russian Red Army, several others ended up in Bad Orb as well.

Daily ration:
Bread   200   Gram (approx)
Sugar   6   Gram
Potatoes 275   Gram unpeeled
Flour   75   Gram
Coffee   2,5   Gram
Meat   22   Gram
Jam   50   Gram for 11 days
Cheese   525   Gram for 15 days

(Source: notes by Corporal Bob Ivison, formerly 13 Platoon who was in this march)

What manner of men

The Devil at table prepared to dine,
said where is Death? He is past his time;
He knows our rule that we dine at ten ,
And he merely went out to make cowards of men.

Then a stir was heard outside his gate,
Soon, Death limped into his hall of state,
With broken scythe, his beard awry,
and a terror that shone from fear lined eye

And the Devil, he roared with all his might
What happened that thou art in such plight?
Hast felt the weight of some heavy hand,
that thou in such mortal terror stand?

Thy orders, said Death, were but show my face
And they'd blanch , these men of inferior race,
But they hurled me forth, with my neck nigh out
to the Devil with Death, I heard them shout

What manner of mortal can these be,
said the devil, to make such sport of thee?
As the old man tenderly smoothed his hide,
They're the men of Arnhem, sire, he cried.

But you'll make them fear us, the Devil roared
Ere again you sit and sup at board
Then I sup no more, old Death replied
For, as I left them, they laughed and died.

By Harvey Heywood, published in the Daily Dispatch in September 1944

While progressing with the English translation of the book, I found that an Airborne Officer's view on the battle would be a welcome addition to the story. It might put the events in a wider perspective and it might help to filter out mistakes I might have made. Sadly, Major Armstrong had already passed away in the Nineties of the last century.

In April 2008 I joined a battle field tour given by Colonel John Waddy. As a Major he had also commanded a B Company in the Battle of Arnhem. But his was B Company of the 156th Parachute Battalion. In 2008 he was a leading member of the Arnhem Airborne community and several times Leader of the annual Pilgrimage. Even though John Waddy was a Paratrooper and not an Air Landing soldier, his views and comments would be a contemporary and expert addition to the story. I was very proud when he replied that he agreed to check my findings and to give some thoughts on the battle that was fought at the Westerbouwing. This he has done in a lucid way and I welcomed his interesting comments.

Some thoughts
By Colonel John Waddy, former CO B Company, 156th Parachute Battalion at Arnhem 1944

Operation Market Garden, that most ambitious and adventurous plan presented such high hopes of success, which had they been achieved, might have altered drastically the course of the war and perhaps the future of Europe, but it failed in its ultimate aim.

The reasons for this failure, particularly that of the 1st (British) Airborne Division at Arnhem, have been endlessly discussed over the years, mostly by the military fraternity, in order to learn the lessons in the hope that they will not be repeated in future conflicts.

An acknowledged author, misquoting one of Shakespeare's plays, titled his book "A Tragedy of Errors". The operation, from the start, was bedevilled by errors in the initial planning by the higher HQ's- the restriction to one lift per day, and in daylight; the restrictions on operations by the Tactical Air Force in support; the decision not to make the capture of the Nijmegen bridge a priority target; the refusal to allow landings by parachute or by glider coup-de-main parties close to the Arnhem bridge; the denial of vital intelligence information to the 1st Airborne Division, coupled with the absence of action to deal with this threat.

In addition, HQ 1st Airborne Division made some inexcusable errors in its' tactical and landing plans, which contributed strongly to the Division's inability to take and hold the bridge in strength. To take but one aspect of the tactical plan, was the failure to appreciate the importance of the Driel ferry and the Westerbouwing heights. All emphasis in the plan was to capture the two bridges at Arnhem. The railway bridge at Oosterbeek was to be crossed, but the fourth crossing, the Driel ferry, was ignored.

The plan, after the capture of the bridge was for the division to hold a wide defensive perimeter of which the 1st Air Landing Brigade would hold the western edge. In that line of defense, the 1st Borders were allotted a long stretch from the Sonnenberg down to the river at the Driel ferry, a length which even with this numerical strong battalion would not allow a connected defensive line.

It would seem that into the atmosphere of almost euphoric enthusiasm by the higher HQ's, insufficient thought was given to the small but dominating feature of the Westerbouwing and the value of the ferry. This failure seems to have been repeated at other levels; for example HQ Air Landing Brigade and HQ 1st Borders.

Did the CO 1st Borders, while still in the UK, allow B Company's plan to defend Westerbouwing with only one platoon? Initially, it would seem that only one platoon, the under strength 13 Platoon, was detailed to defend this vital feature, while the remainder of the Company dug in at the base of the hill.

It was not until the 20th September that OC B Company posted two of his other platoons, with support detachments on to the hill in order to bolster its defence. It is not known whether this was done on his own initiative or on orders from his battalion or brigade HQ's, or even from Division HQ; for it was on this day that General Urquhart had realised that he could no longer take the bridge with his remaining forces in Oosterbeek and that all that he could do was to hold a tight perimeter at Oosterbeek, based on the river and the ferry, and to await the arrival of XXX Corps. Perhaps, he might have appreciated the importance of the Westerbouwing and wanted to reinforce its defence, but at that time he did not have sufficient strength for after the virtual destruction of 1st and 4th Parachute Brigades and the KOSB and South Staffordshire Battalions, only some 3600 soldiers were available to hold the perimeter, against the expected counter attacks from all sides.

Now, some 65 years after the events, it is difficult to ascertain with any accuracy the details of these decisions and of the defensive layout of the perimeter; and of the actions to defend the hill. However, from this long distance view point, and it is my personal view, it would seem that B Company did not have sufficient time to prepare their defences and that they may seem to have been surprised by the suddenness and strength of the almost fanatical attack which drove them off the hill; or did they withdraw too soon?

Some patrols had been sent forward, but to what depth and in what strength is not known. An accepted practise in such circumstances would be to establish a forward defence, probably platoon strength, with fire control detachments, some 1000-1500 metres forward of the main defence with the aim to patrol forward to gain information on the enemy advance and to take action to delay and disrupt it as the platoon withdrew in stages to the main position. It would have taken the sting out of the enemy attack.

With the enemy on the hill and thus dominating the ferry, it would have taken a strong counter attack to retake the position across the open ground; but at that time there were no reserve forces to take on that task. In the midst of the battle, was 13 Platoon of B Company. They were under command of Lieutenant Wellbelove, a Canadian Officer on loan to the British Army. At a range of over half a century, Dutch journalist Haks Walburgh Schmidt has obtained through diligent research over many years as much of their story as he could discover, from the time they set off from southern England, to their landings, their subsequent actions in battle at the Westerbouwing feature; followed by eight hard months that some of its surviving members had to endure in German captivity. His research started with the desire of a Glider Pilot to discover what had happened to the soldiers that he flew to Holland in his glider and it culminated into this most interesting account.

While researching and writing I received a lot of help from Edward 'Johnny' Peters, who during the Arnhem battle was a Private in 14 Platoon, B Company. My questions of course focused on 13 Platoon, but he also told me about his personal impressions. As they are probably quite typical for all men of B Company and 13 Platoon, I felt it important that they were included in the book as well.

Hello Haks,

You have asked me about my personal experience on the Westerbouwing. Here are a few of my memories. I hope they give you an idea of what we went through.

There was no visual contact with the enemy, until early on the morning of 19 September, when the Germans started to mortar and, later, shell us. It is my belief, that Lieutenant Colonel Haddon, CO of 1 Border, did not plan for only one platoon, namely 13, to be the sole defenders on the Westerbouwing. If it was, as suggested, that 13 Platoon were in position on the heights of the Westerbouwing, why should we be surprised at the suddenness of the attack by the enemy if 13 Platoon had engaged the enemy? The two platoons that were in fact near the Restaurant were 11 Platoon and 14 Platoon with 12 Platoon dug in on the lower eastern slopes. There was no one positioned along the road adjacent to the Driel Ferry, as we had this in constant observation. The trench that I was in faced the Rhine. I had my back to anyone else. My job was to observe the lower road. This was a bit of an impossibility, as I could not see it. I could hear the Dutch civilians, who were making their way towards Renkum or to the ferry.

As regarding patrols, I believe that 14 Platoon were the only ones who went on a fighting patrol, which was when we encountered a German tank and troops. A previous patrol, which I went on as a three man patrol, was to ascertain the strength of the Germans at a nearby crossroad, where I do not remember. There may well have been other patrols, but I was not made aware of them.

I had a high opinion of Major Armstrong, having served under him in North Africa, Italy and England. I regarded him as a good officer, a disciplinarian, sometimes rather hard on his men and fellow officers. Yes you are quite right, we took our orders from Platoon Sergeants, Corporals and Lieutenant Stott. There was no wireless communication between platoons, but there may have been 'runners', I don't really know, and towards the end the order was given "Every man for himself "by Major Armstrong.

Let me say that this was one of the most frightening time of my life as a soldier, three to four days of pure and sheer hell, with only food for the first morning, coupled with anxious times in a slit trench, on my own, hearing the continuous explosions of shell and mortar fire, too close for comfort, and the screaming noise of the Moaning Minnies, the cries of the wounded calling for stretcher bearers and lack of sleep. The only comfort was shouting to our comrades in adjacent trenches. Daytime was much worse than at night, because there was the added fear of being overrun by an unseen enemy. To have been there, and to see and hear it, is indescribable.

I can only add that the other scene from hell was on the night at the dyke near the church, whilst waiting to escape across the river. These occasions will live in my memory for ever.

I am afraid, Haks, that the general feeling, during the remaining days after evacuating the Westerbouwing was that one was leaderless and had to fight one's own battle. This was no big deal, as this was what we were to expect in our training and we had been taught to handle any weapon.

I admire your interest in Market Garden, and it is the likes of you, in your research, which will keep it remembered.

Yours aye,
Johnny Peters

14 Platoon

PUBLISHED SOURCES:

S. Eastwood, C. Gray, A. Green. *When Dragons flew, an illustrated history of the 1 Battalion The Border Regiment 1939-1945*. The Border Regimental Museum in association with Silver Link Publishing, Ltd 1994.

M. Middlebrook. Arnhem 1944, *The Airborne Battle, 17-26 September 1944*, Penguin Books, 1994.

R. J. Kershaw, *It never snows in September*, Ian Allan Ltd, Shepperton, Surrey.

A.J. van Hees, *Tugs and Gliders*. A.J. van Hees Eijsden, 2000.

J.G. Raatgever, *Van Dollen Dinsdag tot de Bevrijding*, Publisher "De Telg" Amsterdam.

J.A. Hey, *Roll of Honour, Battle of Arnhem, September 1944*. Published by the Friends of the Airborne Museum Hartenstein Association, Oosterbeek 1999.

A. Junier, B. Smulders and J. Korsloot, *By Land, Sea and Air, an illustrated history of the 2nd Battalion The South Staffordshire Regiment 1940-1945*. R.N. Sigmond Publishing, 2003.

P. Pronk, Airborne Engineers, *an illustrated history of the 9th (Airborne) Field Company Royal Engineers 1939-1945*. R.N. Sigmond Publishing, 2001.

P. Wilkinson MC, *The Gunners at Arnhem*, Spurwing Publishing, 1999.

Glider Pilot Regimental Magazine *The Eagle*, December 1991, Portrait of a Pilot.

Glider Pilot Regimental Magazine *The Eagle*, August 1990, Padre Pare's Arnhem Story.

L. van Aggelen, *Airborne Forever, The Life of an Arnhem Veteran*, White Elephant Publishing, Arnhem, 2013.

David Pasley, *Arnhem on the Horizon, The Story of WW2 Glider Pilot Sgt Johnny Wetherall*. 2014.

Mike Peters & Luuk Buist, *Glider Pilots at Arnhem*, Pen & Sword Military, 2009.

UNPUBLISHED SOURCES

1st Bn The Border Regiment War Diary for period 17-26 September 1944.

General H. von Tettau, *,Gefechtsbericht über die Schlacht bei Arnheim 17-*

26.9-1944' through the Municipal Archives from Renkum Council. Oberstleutnant F. Fullriede. Hermann Göring Regiment, Diary 31-8-1944 tot 2-10-1944 through the Municipal Archives from Renkum Council.

Words of gratitude
The memories from and of the people in Horsa 166 could only be recorded and forged into a story through the kind and selfless co-operation of so many people in England, Wales, Canada and the Netherlands. I am very grateful for the support, patience and help from my wife Marleen and sons Jesper and Stefan who gave me the opportunity to do the time consuming research and writing.

I would also like to express my gratitude to Arthur Morley ('Taffy') Williams for his inspiration and *Stalag Days* notes and to Cyril and Beryl Crickett for their countless letters and stimulating help. I am sad to say that Morley and Cyril passed away in 2005, but their friendship to me and sacrifices for a free Europe are recorded in this book. Much information, encouragement and interest were received from Susan Smith, Jane Cannon, Keith Ainsworth (family of Edwin Ainsworth), Frances Barnes, Lily Watson, Teresa Penrice, (family of Bob Barnes), Doug and Ted Clague, Eddie and Eileen Flinn, E.A Flinn (family of Eddie Flinn), Mary Edmundson and Jas Duffin (family of John Glenn), Ken Greasley (family of Gerry Greasley), Bernard and Michael Hulse (family of Pip Hulse), John Isles (family of Jim Isles), Arthur Evans (formerly Able Seaman HMS Beaufort), Rose Ball, Joyce Marryfield, John Kimber (family of Jack Kimber), John Reed (former colleague of Jack Kimber), Eric Hollerton (Central Library North Shields), John Kelly (family of Eric Melling), David and Kerry Patterson, Norman Savage, Bob Terry and Sergeant Denis Soulsby (family of Fred Terry), Audrey and Harry Waudby (friends of Fred Terry), Mary and Ray Spokes (family of John Wellbelove), Garnett Keeler (Also from the town of Eston), Lorette Crowder (family of Joe Winstanley), John Blackwood and Anne Suter (family of Ian Blackwood), Colonel Arthur Charlton (family of Frank Jarvis), Christine Ashcroft, David Fidler and Lyndsey Dobinson (in the search for Telford Fidler), David O'Neill, Pamela Wilson, Elaine Kelly, Len Gittins (family of Vincent Swarbrick),Thomas and Margaret

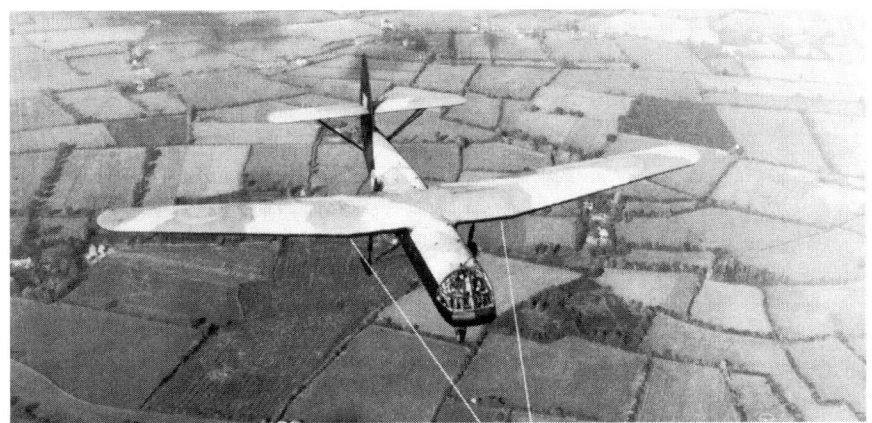

McDonald(relatives of Tommy McDonald), Anthony and Susan Walker (relatives of William 'Johnny' Walker) and Steve Earlam (relative of Frank Evans). Also thanks to Doedie Minderman, Tim Rogers, Jan Cooper and John D. Potts for their stories on our mutual friend Morley.

Furthermore I would like to express my gratitude to Drs Aad Groenweg OBE, Robert Sigmond, Robert Voskuil, (Vereniging Vrienden Airborne museum), Philip Reinders (idem), Martijn Cornelissen (idem), Eugene Wijnhoud (idem), Stuart Eastwood, (Curator Border Museum Carlisle), Johnny Peters, Wilf Oldham, Patrick Stott, Arnhem veterans from 1st Battalion, The Border Regiment, War Experience Center (Leeds), Arie-Jan van Hees, The Royal British Legion and Colonel John Waddy, former B Company Commander in 156 Parachute and Leader of the Pilgrimage to Arnhem. Their expert knowledge, support and advice have greatly contributed to the book.

A rather special word of thanks goes to Captain Geert Jonker and Lieutenant Patrick van Aalderen of the Dutch Army (Grave and Identification Unit), David van Buggenum and Hans Timmermans for their invaluable and still continuing help in the search for Lance Corporal Eric Melling, (missing in action since 21 September 1944), the identification work on Frank Jarvis and in the search for Telford Fidler.

Furthermore I like to express my appreciation for the help of the Manchester Evening News, Lancaster Evening Telegraph, Wrexham Evening Leader (Robert Bellis), Family History Monthly, Northern Echo, Winsford and Middlewich Chronicle, Evening Chronicle Newcastle, St. Helens Star, Grantham Today, Bolton News, Whitehaven Times and Star and many, many other newspapers in England.

Special thanks to Michiel van Oers (T&A Survey) for his expert help in the search for Lance-Corporal Eric Melling and to Renkum Council for their quick supply of the necessary license.

Also I would like to apologise all the families that have the same name as one of the 13 Platoon members for the letters I sent them while searching. Frans Kuijf (picture and lay-out advise), Marleen Kuijf (design and production of maps), Paula Kenyon (English addresses) and the Canloan Army Officer's Association. A special word of thanks to Geert Maassen (Gelders Archief) for the valuable information and constructive criticism he supplied.

For the English translation I am indebted to Karin Wintels, Jet Bloemers and Dorien Walburgh Schmidt and Harko Walburgh Schmidt. Their tremendous help in translating the text into English provided the first major step in this exciting project. Also Thomas van Slooten and Bart Bijl deserve my thanks for their help in recomputerising substantial parts of the text after serious digital problems. English teacher and herself daughter of a Para Grace Reukers spent much time in editing the complete text and removing various non native constructions. The time and effort she put into this task are greatly appreciated.

For the second edition I was helped by Dave Fidler, Trevor Cummings and the Cumbria Archive and Local Studies Centre in Whitehaven in the search for the story of Telford Fidler. In the story of William 'Johnny' Walker his son Tony and granddaughter Sue supplied me with an unexpected wealth of material. Steve Earlam told me about his grandad Frank Evans. And the story of Tommy McDonald was passed on to me by his namesake Thomas McDonald and his wife Margaret. My writing for the second edition was watched over by Karin Wintels and Ellen Bakker and the cover was masterfully designed by Frans Kuijf. The search for Eric Melling got a new edition with the help of SIGNI search dogs. Sadly though, no one of the three missing men has been found. But we will not ever forget them.

See Morley Williams on video

In 2004 Glider Pilot Morley Williams was accompanied by his godson Tim Rogers on his annual visit to Arnhem/Oosterbeek. Tim, an award winning TV-journalist, interviewed Morley on video. A few clips of these interviews have been digitalised, especially for the second edition of No Return Flight. Enjoy this remarkable opportunity to see Morley in person, after having read his story in this book. To see him talk about his experiences and watch the reunion with some of his passengers, you can

Video 1:

Morley Williams remembers the Battle of Arnhem and meets three of his passengers again after 60 years.

   Visit: www.youtube.com and type in *Morley Williams* and the video will appear.

   Or type in the link in the google search bar: https://youtu.be/2852X3Eicjs

   Or use this QR code on your cell phone

Video 2:

Glider Pilot Morley 'Taffy' Williams remembered

   Visit: www.youtube.com and type in *Morley Williams* and the video will appear

   Or type in the link in the google search bar: https://youtu.be/zfmJTf1lNwk

   Or use this QR code on your cell phone

Shields Sergeant Liberated

Arnhem Men Queued For Potato Peelings

QUEUEING for potato peelings was one of the features of life in the German prison camp, Stalag 9B, at Banorb, where the majority of the prisoners were men who had taken part in the Arnhem operations. This story was given to The Evening News today by Sergt. John Kimber, of the Airborne Division, son of Mrs. and the late Mr Richard Kimber, of 2 Henry Street, North Shields.

The men were given the peelings from the German cook-house, and scrubbed them and boiled them in a butter tin.

"We peppered and salted them when we had any condiments and, as we thought, had a good meal," said Sergt. Kimber. "We used to be supplied with soup in which there were potatoes, but you were lucky if you got one. The first 24 men in the barrel got the potatoes."

The camp was released by the 9th American Armoured Division on April 2. Sergt. Kimber only returned to North Shields on Tuesday. He has

SERGEANT KIMBER

been staying with friends in the South of England.

BEATEN WITH BUTTS

Sergt. Kimber was a prisoner in Stalag 8C at Sagen, but the camp was marched 400 miles to Banorb. There was very little food on the journey and some of the British prisoners, while passing fields, attempted to steal mangolds. They were beaten with rifle butts by the German guards.

The men were given one loaf between four to last 24 hours, and sometimes a little margarine. They also received a tin of meat between six of them.

"A few dropped out on the roadside," said Sergt. Kimber, "and later we learnt quite a few of them had died on the march."

The men stumbled through snow and blizzards and for five nights slept in football fields. Although weary, they had to keep marching at night in order to keep warm. The rest of the time they slept in old buildings and barns.

"By the time we reached Banorb, it took 31 days, we were covered with lice," said Sergt. Kimber.

While in Banorb, the men slept two in a bunk. There were 500 men in barrack rooms, which were intended to hold only a hundred.

The men could hear the Americans approaching, and later the German guards left the camp. After being given food and cigarettes by the Americans, the prisoners were told to take any extra food they wanted from the German civilians.

"Two of our men died the day after we were released," stated Sergt. Kimber. "They went out and got two chickens. They died from over-eating. They could not digest the food."

Sergt. Kimber was flown from an aerodrome near Banorb to Oakley, England, in three and a half hours. He arrived in this country on April 19.

SECRET WIRELESS

The men had a secret wireless in Sagen. The Germans tried to find it with a radio detector, but the wireless was dismantled and each man carried a small part. The valves and other articles needed for the wireless had first been acquired by bribing the Germans with cigarettes.

Wounded by a sniper during the Arnhem operations, Sergt. Kimber was taken prisoner on September 22, 1944. He was taken to hospital in Utrecht, where he was well treated, and then transferred to Stalag 11B near Hanover, and later moved to Stalag 8C.

Sergt. Kimber was also injured in the invasion of Sicily. His glider crashed into the sea and he was 8½ hours in the water before being picked up by a destroyer and taken to Malta. Sergt. Kimber fought in Sicily and later in Italy. He then returned to Britain and last September took part in the Arnhem landings, when he was captured.

Before joining the Army nearly five years ago he was a barman at the Royal Arms, Nile Street, North Shields.

His father was killed in the last war. Sergt. Kimber has two brothers serving in the Forces, one in the R.A.F. and the other in the Defence Equipment Merchant Service attached to the Royal Artillery.

Mrs J. Saint, of 74 Norfolk Street, North Shields, has received a telegram from her husband, Fusilier Joseph Saint, aged 27, saying that he is now in England, having been a prisoner of war in Germany for nearly five years.

Fusilier Saint was taken prisoner at Arras in May, 1940 and while a prisoner he has been engaged on farm and forestry work.

WAR ORGANISATION of the BRITISH RED CROSS SOCIETY and
ORDER OF ST. JOHN OF JERUSALEM PRISONERS OF WAR DEPARTMENT

P 1/B. Revised
June, 1944

ARTICLES WHICH MAY BE SENT IN NEXT-OF-KIN PARCELS

The following is subject to change without notice but alterations to these instructions will be published in the Journal as they occur. A line in the margin indicates a change or addition since the last issue of this leaflet.

IMPORTANT.

To allow for the ¼ lb. of Red Cross gift chocolate the parcels must not weigh more than 9½ lb. when posted by the next-of-kin, and if additional chocolate or soap is required the corresponding weight must also be allowed for.

Attaché cases or small bags (not exceeding in measurement 12 inches by 18 inches by 6 inches).
Badges of pre-war Regiments, ranks, trades, etc., but see Badges overleaf.
Belts and Braces.
Blankets.
Boots.
Boot and shoe laces.
Brilliantine in tins.
Brushes of all kinds.
Button cleaning outfits (solid **not** liquid polish).
Chewing gum.
Chocolate in solid slabs (no filling). For details see General Instruction leaflet issued with first label. NOTE.—The maximum amount of chocolate which can be supplied by the Red Cross has now been increased to 2 lbs. (price 3/-).
Cigarette filter tips and cigarette rolling machine but **not** cigarettes or cigarette papers.
Clothing :—
  Uniform i.e., battle dress, service dress, overcoat. (Coupons may not be used for the purchase of army uniform, including battle dress, except for officers).
  Knitted comforts in service or plain neutral colours (*i.e.*, grey or fawn).
  Dressing Gowns (patterned materials recommended).
  Pyjamas (of striped material).
  Shorts. (Service colours only will be forwarded unless the sender attaches a note to the garment saying it is to go at sender's risk.)
  Shirts (not navy blue or any dark colours).
  Underclothing of all kinds.

Coloured silks and cottons, plain linen or canvas for embroidering, without any printed pattern or design.
Dentifrice (powder or solid, in flat tins, but **not** in tubes).
Frames with talc or unbreakable glass, **not** photos or snap photos.
Housewife containing usual items and mending materials.
Insecticides (powders only).
Kit bags (any size without locks, or printed marking).
Knitting needles and wool (in skeins if possible).
Medal Ribbons.
Metal mirrors.
Metal polish in blocks, or powder in tins, **not** wool or paste because these are inflammable.
Overalls. Only if asked for by prisoner. Must be one-piece type (not separate blouse and trousers) in khaki, brown or navy blue.
Pencils.
Pipes and tobacco pouch. Pipe cleaners but **not** feathers.
Safety razors and blades.
Screw tin openers. **Not** the cutter type with handle.
Shaving soap **not** in tubes.
Shoes, plimsolls, indoor slippers.
Shoe polish (solid, **not** liquid or in tubes).
Sleeping bags—**not** padded.
Small musical instruments.
Soap. The total amount of soap now allowed in any one parcel is 11 oz. For details see instruction leaflet issued with the first label.
Towels, face cloths and sponges.

FOR CIVILIANS

MEN.—Complete suits, coloured trousers, including grey flannels, sports coats or blazers, mackintoshes or any kind of overcoat.

WOMEN AND CHILDREN.—All types of clothing.

Note.—Parcels may **not** include clothing other than that intended for the personal use of the person to whom they are addressed.

[Please turn over

ARTICLES WHICH MAY NOT BE SENT IN NEXT-OF-KIN PARCELS

The following is subject to change without notice but alterations to these instructions will be published in the Journal as they occur.

Food—except solid chocolate.

Written communications (all letters to Prisoners of War must be sent by letter post).

Books, note books, music or any printed matter.

Pictorial illustrations and photographs.

Money, stamps, stationery and playing cards.

Articles in glass containers, tubes, tins and other receptacles which are breakable or cannot easily be opened for inspection.

Badges of Regiments formed since September 3rd, 1939, and all formations. These include Commandos, Paratroops and Airborne Units, R.E.M.E., etc.

Candles, spirits or solidified spirit for cooking stoves, matches or any other inflammable material.

Complete suits, coloured or grey flannel trousers, black and dark coloured shirts, civilian ties, sports coats or blazers, mackintoshes, windcheaters, leather waistcoats or any kind of civilian overcoat. (These, excepting black shirts, may, however, be sent to civilian internees.)

Fountain pens and pen nibs.

Glass mirrors.

Gum boots, Wellingtons and goloshes.

Haversacks.

Medical comforts. This includes medicines of all kinds, drugs, pills, pastilles and bandages.

Nail files.

Photographic apparatus, field glasses, sextants, compasses, electric torches and other instruments that could be used for Naval and Military purposes.

Rubber soles and heels.

Sleeping bags (padded), cushions or pillows.

Sleeping suits other than pyjamas.

Soap flakes and soap powders.

Tobacco, cigarettes.

Toilet paper.

Watches, scissors (except small nail scissors), knives and tools.

Special Note.—(1) Please allow for the weight of chocolate and soap which you wish to have added at the Packing Centre. The parcel including these additions must not weigh more than 10 lbs.

(2) Please note that the limit of 11 oz. of soap must not be exceeded whether it is sent by the Next-of-Kin or purchased from the Red Cross (soap sent in excess of this limit has to be removed at the Packing Centre but cannot be returned to the sender).

(3) A great quantity of sweets and chocolate is wasted because the Next-of-Kin do not pay attention to the rules regarding chocolate. Please note that <u>only solid chocolate is allowed</u>. No chocolate with any sort of filling can go and no sweets must be sent at all.

[Please turn over